Crabtown, USA
Essays & Observations

Rafael Alvarez

PMMP

Perpetual Motion Machine Publishing
Cibolo, Texas

Crabtown, USA
Copyright © Rafael Alvarez 2015

ISBN: 978-1-943720-03-3

www.PerpetualPublishing.com

Cover picture by
Macon Street Books

Other Books by Rafael Alvarez

Fiction

The Fountain of Highlandtown
Orlo and Leini
Tales from the Holy Land

Non-fiction

Hometown Boy
Storyteller
A People's History of the Archdiocese of Baltimore
The Wire: Truth Be Told
The Tuerk House

Praise for Crabtown, USA

"In Crabtown USA, Rafael Alvarez recalls his long love affair with a vanished Baltimore—the world of the hot dog king Polock Johnny, the irascible news vendor Abe Sherman, the erratic chef Morris Martick and the ghosts of Seymour Attman and his father Harry on Corned Beef Row—along with countless other zanies who gave the Jewel of the Patapsco such singular character. Crabtown USA is a lively and bittersweet meditation on what once was."

—Christopher Corbett,
author of *Orphans Preferred: The Twisted Truth, Lasting Legend of the Pony Express* and *The Poker Bride: The First Chinese in the Wild West.*

"The work of Rafael Alvarez is a celebration of the place where Frank Zappa got his promising start and Edgar Allan Poe found his unhappy ending by a writer exquisitely steeped in Baltimore lore."

—Scott Shane, reporter and author,
Dismantling Utopia and *Objective Troy*

In memory of
Gilbert L. Watson III
[1944 to 2015]
Newspaperman

Introduction
by Mark Kram, Jr.

Wink your eye at a homely girl. That's what H.L. Mencken told us in his epitaph that we should do if we remembered him and wished to please his ghost. My late father, Mark Kram, did just that when he wrote about Baltimore for *Sports Illustrated* before the 1966 World Series. But the wink Dad gave his old hometown stopped far short of what Rafael Alvarez has given it during his journalistic romance with the city. Rafael not only winked, he laid his Orioles jacket over a puddle for her as they crossed Eastern Avenue and eloped with her to Dundalk. Baltimore is nothing less than a beauty queen to him. Chances are she also works a day shift down on The Block, but hey, nobody's perfect.

Baltimore has been the inspiration for a great many storytellers. Some you know—John Waters, that impresario of bad taste who hatched *Hairspray*; Barry Levinson, who charmed us with a quartet of Baltimore films that included *Diner*; and David Simon, who excavated the underside of the city in *The Wire* in a way that had never been seen before. It says something about our times that the wider public has come to know each of them not through print but from their work in film. But there are storytellers you do not know that you should—

and perhaps would if we lived in a less trivial culture. They worked on newspapers. They were big deal columnists and energetic reporters who gave voice to the neediest among us and who held power accountable. For those who gravitated to the profession with a sense of purpose beyond the swindling paycheck it offered, it would not be an exaggeration to say that it was almost a sacramental calling.

It seems a quaint notion now that evisceration of newspapers is in its final stages, but it was once a fascinating way of life that was full of interesting, colorful encounters. No one loved it more than Rafael—AKA "Mr. Baltimore."

In his many years wandering the city in search of narrative for just about any publication willing to take his work, Rafael immersed himself in the tales of the unknown, ordinary lives that would have been otherwise overlooked were it not for the value he assigned them. In doing so in these pieces, which vary in length from full blown articles to one paragraph vignettes, he performed an act of cultural preservation. "It is said that as long as there is someone alive to remember us, we never die," he writes, dropping a hint to his animating sense of purpose. "And if we are remembered with love, we are immortal."

One whiff of the writing life and Rafael was hooked. Though his father worked in the engine room of a tugboat, Rafael became enamored at an early age with the beauty and power of words. It was not long before he began his apprenticeship as a clerk at *The Sun*, where he remembers that he had a "front row seat to everything that moved." There, he worked side by side with a city room crew full of characters, including an editor by the name of Norm Wilson who used to tear a sheet of paper from his typewriter, hand it to a copyboy and bark, "This page has a train and a plane to catch, so move it." Off the lad would scoot to the composing room. Reading this reminded me of the world I found as a young man at the *Baltimore News American.* I would be laboring on a sports piece when my dear colleague, David McQuay, would poke his head into the secluded room I had found to work, remind me with a twinkle in his eye that the cocktail hour was at hand and say, "Give it a sleigh ride."

Though Rafael and I would not become acquainted until years later, the Baltimore that he sprang from is the same Baltimore I knew as a boy. My father grew up on Hudson Street in the Canton section of East Baltimore. I have walked the same streets. So when Rafael alludes to kielbasa and sauerkraut cooking on a stovetop, or of butting the ends of hard-boiled eggs at Easter, or eating rice pudding at the Sip & Bite, or of attending Catholic Mass on Sundays at St. Casmir Church, these are experiences that I shared in, too, and think back on with ineffable fondness. And only in Baltimore is "Hon" such a colloquial endearment, or are of newspaper articles called "write-ups," or anyone who cannot hold his liquor is denigrated as a "rum pot."

But the Baltimore that Rafael remembers from his boyhood is not the Baltimore that exists today. Urban developers long ago razed the decaying waterfront along Pratt Street. Harbor Place and its crowds of tourists are there instead. The avaricious "rum pot" Robert Irsay spirited the Colts to Indianapolis in a cowardly escape on a snowy night. Baltimore now has the Ravens. Cozy old Memorial Stadium has been vanquished by the wrecking ball and with it the hallowed ground that Brooks Robinson patrolled at third base. The Orioles now play at Orioles Park at Camden Yards. And yet Rafael holds dear not just what the city once was but what it has become. "Do I love

Lombard Street? Yes, even though it no longer exists in a way I care about," writes Rafael, who remembers how as a 5-year-old he joined his Italian grandmother there and watched a butcher chop the head off a chicken. Poultry is no longer slaughtered down on what is known as Corned Beef Row, yet as Rafael observes with the eternal optimism that is his calling card: it is still the place to go for lean corned beef.

What remains of *The Sun* is the sagging husk of what had once been a great newspaper. Once, as Rafael remembers, "the Sunday paper was as thick as Aunt Myrtle's ankles," full of dispatches from reporters stationed around the globe. Now, it has become so thin that it seems as if you could slide it under the door with the mail. With only a few talented holdovers from better days, it has become a mere ghost of its former self, done in by the same lunk headed management that has undermined newspapers across America. City rooms are no longer a place where copy has "a train and a plane to catch." And the only "sleigh ride" that is taking place is out the door in the form of buyouts. Thus, Rafael and the paper parted ways in 2001. In the years that have passed since he left, he worked on a cable laying ship, wrote for *The Wire* at the invitation of his ex-*Sun* colleague Simon, and has published collections of his various writings.

To borrow a phrase from the legendary Scatman Crothers, Crabtown: USA brims over with "nine-kinds-of-what-have-you." It is full of characters who could have only come from Baltimore, including: David Franks, the Fells Point poet and prankster who once had Jorge Luis Borges autograph his chest; Jean Honus, the stripper from the 2 O'Clock Club who became peeved when Rafael did not return some photographs to use with a story (and suspected he held onto them for his own, ahem, entertainment); and even legendary Orioles manager Earl Weaver, who as his underperforming team was on the verge of losing the 1979 World Series to the Pirates, told a cop sitting with him in the dugout that his team had no heart. Along the way, Rafael acquaints us with a savory deviled egg recipe, explains that Baltimore women who employ the word "Hon" always keeps a clean house "because you never know who's going to drop by," and reports that you have not been served authentic crab soup unless there is a half-a-crab in the bowl.

So turn the page. And do yourself a favor: Whip up a batch of those deviled eggs.

Mark Kram, Jr. is the author of Like Any Normal Day: A Story of Devotion, *which was recipient of the 2013 PEN/ESPN Award for Literary Sports Writing. He has also edited a collection of his father's magazine work under the title,* Great Men Die Twice: The Selected Works of Mark Kram.

Oh, Baltimore

MY BELOVED

There was always a buzz.

If you're lucky, you know what I'm talking about: a carbonation of the blood that bubbles with intrigue, recklessness, and lust.

Insane, clandestine.

Irresistible.

My affair with the City of Baltimore went public—out-in-the-open, I don't care who knows: LOVE—in the autumn of 1977, when at 19, my head filled with drums and guitars and literary dreams, I began writing about my hometown for publication.

In the decades since, "I've been around the world . . . I've seen a million girls."

Yet to this day, a half-step slower and some thirty years wiser, my obsession with and devotion to the Jewel of the Patapsco remains the longest intimate relationship of my life. My beloved—Crabtown in all its shame and glory—is the hard-headed, kind-hearted lover with whom I am in a constant state of reconciliation.

'Til death, my sad and gorgeous baby, do us part.

~~~

It began in the Belair-Edison parlor of a loud-mouthed longshoreman named Gilbert Lukowski.

Around Labor Day of 1977, I signed off the *Mayaguez*,

a World War II-era container ship captured by the Khmer Rouge two years earlier after the fall of Saigon.

I had just finished my second summer working as a wiper in the engine room, sailing from Dundalk to Puerto Rico to New Orleans and back, making enough money to pay for my sophomore year at what was then Loyola College, North Charles and Cold Spring Lane.

At sea, I vowed to make good on a dream I'd carried since the third grade: I was going to be a writer, wanted it fiercely and reckoned that it was mixed-up with chasing something extraordinary and writing about it until your knuckles ached.

Down the gangway and back to school.

At Loyola, I spied a skinny tabloid that called itself the *City Squeeze*, called up the editors, and said I was a writer. It wasn't a lie (I scribbled furiously at sea) but it was not quite the truth (I was unpublished).

They told me to come down to the *Hopkins News-Letter* office, where the fledgling rag was produced under the university's nose. I was eager to write anything. Anything was what they wanted and they wanted it right away.

Enter Gilbert Lukowski, older brother of Jerome, my father's best friend from the Baker-Whitely tugboats.

Baltimore seafarers like "Romey"—who went crabbing in wooden boats with one oar between two men, drank National beer before noon when it was still brewed on Dillon Street and told stories I never heard at the dinner table—were the matchmakers for the city and me before I learned to write my name.

Gilbert was an official in the stevedores' union. In the fall of 1977, as I was looking for something to write about, the International Longshoreman's Association went on strike and shut out all media.

Crabtown, USA

"Call up Gilbert," said Pop. "He'll give you a story, Ralphie."

And he did.

I banged out the story on a secretary's IBM Selectric after working the night shift in *The Sun* circulation department, scooped the city's three dailies and took the published *City Squeeze* story to Dick Basoco, then head of the *Sunpapers's* personnel department.

I said that if I was going to be a clerk on Calvert Street, I ought to be a clerk in the newsroom. Basoco agreed and soon I was compiling horse race results from tracks around Delmarva in the sports department.

[And becoming telephone friends with every hardcore gambler in Baltimore who wanted results the minute they landed, including Joe Challmes, a rewrite man and autodidact I hardly knew at the time and the late Orioles' trainer, Ralph Salvon.]

Soon it was on to the City Desk, where I remained for the next 23 years, covering everything you can imagine (library closings, fatal car wrecks, water main breaks in February) and some things even I couldn't conjure, like the quadruple execution and subsequent funeral for a pair of pot-dealing sisters and their husbands, four open caskets in a single room.

I always felt like a ghoul on those assignments and have not missed the experience. But I remember every funeral home parking lot I once haunted with a notebook and a pen. I spent a lot of time at the March establishment near Green Mount Cemetery on North Avenue.

The slow, ugly and unnecessary death of newspapers and their place in American life was part of the reason I quit the *Sun* in early 2001. The Tribune Company had just swallowed the Times Mirror Company, which fifteen years before had bought the *Baltimore Sun* from its founders, the A.S. Abell Company. People were being paid to leave.

Every now and then, you know beyond thought which way to go.

[Less than a decade after I left, in April of 2009, some 60 employees—including some of the best journalists of their generation, such as former Jerusalem correspondent, Ann LoLordo—were shown the door without so much as a nickel. This was what I'd seen written on the newsroom wall a decade earlier.]

By my early 40s, I had spent more than half my life going to work at 501 North Calvert Street. For some time, I'd wanted to tell stories outside the narrow margins of newsprint and the geographic boundaries of my personal Holy Land.

I took the buy-out money, paid off bills and went back to sea, working as an Ordinary Seaman on Seafarers International Union-crewed ships. The pay was low, but I had great health coverage, and time to write.

Just before quitting the paper, I wrote Gilbert Lukowski's obituary.

"Nobody gives a damn about the past," he'd said once, staring at his dead mother's shuttered saloon on Thames Street, tears in his eyes. "But I think about it every day."

<hr>

Does absence make the heart grow fonder or the eye stray farther?

In 2005, for the first time in my life, Baltimore became the taken-for-granted spouse.

After a couple of years on ships and a couple more writing for *The Wire*, I landed in Los Angeles to script network television. It didn't seem like my life, but apparently it was. Outside of the writers' rooms on networks like NBC and FX, whenever I stumbled upon a story worth telling, I resisted, blocked by geography that didn't speak to me.

I had business cards printed up near the Cosmopolitan Book Shop on Melrose Avenue that read, "Mister Baltimore in Exile."

I wound up living in Los Angeles for about four years—April 2005 through July 2009—and made frequent trips back on through 2012 to look for work.

During that time I met Sheldon Schwartz, who created *Gilligan's Island*, on a Writers Guild of America picket line in 2007, shared breakfast with Frances Kroll Ring, who as a young woman was Fitzgerald's secretary at the time of his death in 1940, taking dictation for *The Love of the Last Tycoon*, and experienced something so ugly, petty and disingenuous that my yearning for the simple social contracts of Baltimore jumped up to 11.

Around the Fourth of July in 2012, I drove from Baltimore to Los Angeles, returning out of financial fear, taking meetings to write for shows I didn't want (and didn't get) while writing a romantic comedy about the music business and alcoholism with my oldest daughter, Amelia.

In the late afternoon I would visit a book store off the corner of Argyle and West Franklin Avenue in Hollywood (I bought "The Shawl" by Ozick for a buck) and take a drink at the juice bar next store. There, I ordered a "Blood Transfusion" "cleanser" shake of Thai coconut blended with spirulina and coconut water, sipping it at an outside table while watching the hipsters line up outside of the Upright Citizens Brigade theater.

A hail of pennies flew past my head.

The coins landed in the gutter outside of Real Raw Live at 5913 West Franklin Avenue, where I had purchased the drink for $5.

Like a fool—Muckle John, Singer's Gimpel, the one on the Hill—I looked up to see if the pennies had come from an upstairs window or the roof. Perhaps they'd fallen from sky, the clouds of Los Angeles encouraging me, as they had for der Bingle, to carry my umbrella upside down.

Calmly, I pocketed the change—one penny short of a dime—and sat back down to drink and read.

Later, I walked back to where I was staying in the shadow of the Castle Argyle. On the way, I stopped in the Bourgeois Pig for a double espresso (the dual nature of my Gemini birth—caffeine versus coconut—in near constant battle) and dropped the pennies in the coffee house tip jar without incident.

The next day I was back at Real Raw Live for a $5 "cleanser" of lemon juice, clove and maple syrup.

———

I was waited on by the same guy who'd made me the coconut drink the day before: an aloof somewhat surly manager in his late 30s or early 40s given to salt and pepper stubble and zippered hoodie sweatshirts.

After paying for the drink, I dropped a couple of quarters in the tip jar. The manager turned to me and in front of two employees and at least one customer said: "We don't want your pennies."

"Those were quarters."

"Yesterday," he said. "Pennies."

"Are you the guy who threw them into the street?"

Smug and righteous, he said, "Yes."

"Why?"

"They're an insult to my employees."

Crabtown, USA

The allegedly offended employees, two young women manning juicers behind the manager, turned and caught my eye in sympathy.

There was so much I wanted to say to this guy.

That my mother and grandmother rolled coins when I was a kid to help pay for a family trip to Spain, whether he'd asked the help if they believed a penny saved is a penny earned, if a dime was only nine cents away from being offensive.

How a penny is still a penny where I come from.

But I was angry (it is especially unsettling to be treated rudely at a place in business to promote wellness) and I feared my thoughts might spill out in three words or less.

Mystery solved—the pennies were mine and they'd come back according to the proverb—I took my drink and left. I tried to remember how many pennies I had dropped in the juice bar's tip jar the day before. It seemed I had made a few cents on the deal.

As I continued the campaign to eat a healthier diet, I had lunch later in the week at Leonor's "100 percent vegetarian" Mexican restaurant on Moorpark in Studio City. Leonor's is a family-owned business and when I paid for my wheat-crust pizza with soy "cheese," I asked the young woman at the register if they minded pennies in the tip jar.

Not at all, she said, giving the impression that it was a silly question.

I asked what they did with their pennies.

They are counted out, rolled and put back in the register, which saved the owners trips to the bank to get pennies for change.

———∿∿∿———

I love pennies.

I like finding them, collecting them, rolling them into 50 cent tubes to trade for coffee and turning over a facedown penny in the street so the next person who comes along finds it heads up, believing themselves lucky.

Heads up pennies—Honest Abe facing east—are often left on the Booth family monuments at Green Mount cemetery in Baltimore. The actor and assassin John Wilkes Booth lies with his kin somewhere below the sod, exact location unmarked.

When I wrote for the FX show *Thief* in 2005, I had the good-hearted moll of one of the safe-cracker's sport earrings made of pennies. The lowly pence made her more compelling in contrast to her boyfriend's lust for millions.

In an unproduced 2010 pilot I wrote for the Sundance Channel, the lieutenant in charge of the homicide squad sits at his desk sorting through water jugs full of pennies as a way of calming his thoughts as he puzzles through cold cases.

And in 2012, with the help of the Farantos family at G&A Coney Island Hot Dogs on Eastern Avenue, I collected $700—the bulk of it in pennies—to help keep the doors open at the Edgar Allan Poe House on Amity Street.

The "Pennies for Poe" idea was inspired by a similar collection by Baltimore schoolchildren after the Civil War to purchase a marker for Poe's grave in the Westminster Churchyard downtown.

Every day, tourists and others enamored of the poet leave pennies on the handsome monument bearing a disc—not unlike a giant penny—of Poe's face. The Westminster staff dutifully collects them—"see that my grave is kept clean," as Blind Lemon Jefferson sang—and the next day a handful more have taken their place.

Crabtown, USA

On a whim in 1979, I walked the streets of Manhattan until I had polled one hundred people with the same question: What do you think of when you think of Baltimore?

Most answered "the Orioles," who would go to the World Series that year, losing to Pittsburgh in seven games. The next most common answer was steamed crabs, followed by William Donald Schaefer and a football team forever known as the *Baltimore* Colts.

I wonder how Gotham pedestrians would answer the question today.

I bet most of them would say *Hairspray*—the Broadway and Hollywood versions furthest removed from the John Waters's original.

[When people in L.A. say, "What's Baltimore really like?" I tell them that Waters's movies are really documentaries.]

Instead of being known for products—steel and blue crabs and factories manufacturing Noxzema, bottle-caps and raincoats—Baltimore is now a product unto itself, a place that seems to try harder than it used to just to be what it already is.

When I yearn for the Baltimore that exists perfectly in my imagination [thousands of good jobs at Sparrows Point, my grandparents alive, peeling potatoes for dinner over yesterday's paper], I remember that the ever-widening herd of thugs is balanced by just enough do-gooders to keep the city from expiring.

Brendan Walsh and Willa Bickham of the Viva House Catholic Worker soup kitchen come to mind, among a small army of lesser-known heroes like Father Dick Lawrence of St. Vincent de Paul Parish on Front Street.

As a young reporter, I wrote the weepy sidebar to nearly every front-page homicide in town, back in the days when the slaughter of a 14-year-old for his jacket or his shoes—and sometimes just because—was still news in Baltimore.

I'll never forget the autumn of 1986 tragedy of Trudy Ann Levin, the Friends School student from Cedarcroft Road lured to the 25th Street railroad tracks by a monster named Featherstone. I became friendly with Trudy's mother during the trial and conviction and she came to trust me.

I called Mrs. Levin about 20 years later to see if she wanted to talk, but couldn't think of a good reason to persuade her that we should.

From bodies in alleys to the evening tide at Fort Smallwood, the current of narrative reminds me of a line sung by Muddy Waters, whom I interviewed in the basement of the Congress Hotel in 1978, back when used car dealer Scott Cunningham ran the Marble Bar as a juke joint:

"Brooks run into the ocean, you know, [the] ocean run into the sea . . ."

In the Spring of 1983, *Sun* features editor Steve Parks sent me to Chicago to cover Muddy's funeral, a coup that would be unthinkable in the decimated newsrooms of today.

That summer, the late and legendary *Sun* metropolitan editor Gilbert L. Watson III sent me to cover the summer season in Ocean City, which becomes Crabtown-by-the-Sea each year between Memorial Day and Labor Day. There was even a restaurant back then called "Pinti's Highlandtown Inn," where Eleanor Pinti Frazier made homemade meatballs and tomato sauce like her grandmother used to do back in the neighborhood.

Crabtown, USA

At the beach, over the summers of 1983 and 1984, I wrote about a semi-recluse named Watterson "Mack" Miller, a hotel janitor, heroic ocean swimmer, and one-time heir to the *Louisville Courier* newspaper fortune who drank his way to sobriety and sanctuary in a derelict ice-cream truck on the fishing docks.

Leo Ryan was a kid then with a summer job at the Castle in the Sand hotel where Miller did anything the bosses asked.

"I remember his deeply weathered skin and tattered pants with a rope belt," remembered Ryan, who became a Maryland district court judge. "I'd offer to give him a ride home and he always declined with a simple, 'No thank you.'

"To a kid from Northeast Baltimore entranced by the ocean, Mr. Mack was a mythic figure. Tales of his swims a mile out to sea and across the inlet, with its treacherous tides made him a character only Hemingway could have invented."

I felt the same way. I still have an old saloon chair from Mr. Mack's shack, and when I sit in it, I feel like a character in a story bigger than one I am capable of writing.

When the more brutal truths of life in Baltimore broke my heart, I'd follow elephants down Pratt Street when Ringling Brothers came to town—once a man with a bowl of white bread and "neck bones" ran out to watch in his stocking feet—and hid from my editors with a few of the more seductive trapeze girls over coffee and rice pudding at the Sip & Bite.

[For seduction under the Big Top, no chariot swings closer to yearning than Solveig Dommartin in Wenders's *Wings of Desire*.]

I followed a New Orleans funeral march through Fells

Point when blues communicant Larry Benicewicz flew in musicians from the Crescent City to honor longtime Cat's Eye Pub bartender and Abe Lincoln look-alike H. Jefferson Knapp.

"I seen it on TV," said an elderly Polish woman, peeking out her storm door at the second line. "But I never seen it on Wolfe Street."

The most fantastic spectacle I had the privilege to document in Baltimore—God help me, it was cooler than John Paul II saying Mass at Camden Yards—was the funeral of Willie "Pistol" Brown.

Pistol was an a-rabber and the son of an a-rabber, the men who have sold fruit and vegetables on the streets since the founding of Baltimore Town. When he died in July of 2000, his flag-draped coffin was pulled by pony from alley stables on Lemmon Street to a funeral home on Wabash Avenue, a grand workingman's parade followed by compatriots leading their own carts, family members in limousines, and photographers on foot.

One drop at a time—a spot of blood on the apron of a butcher at Victor's Meats in Roland Park, tears in the eyes of grown men as Mayflower vans rolled off to Indianapolis—I amassed an ocean of "write-ups."

That's what my Polish grandmother, Anna Potter Jones of Dillon Street, called newspaper stories: write-ups.

Like the one I did on her in 1992, documenting her life as a waterfront cannery worker.

Anna Jones spoke Polish growing up in Canton during the First World War and dropped out of grade school to help raise her siblings when her mother died. She had a way with the local *patois* that I inevitably conjure for characters in my fiction and screenplays, not cartoons like the beehive pretenders at that shit-hole restaurant in

Hampden but real people who live with the water of Bodkin Creek in their veins.

We called her "Booshie," a mangled pronunciation of "Babcia," which is Polish for grandmother.

Her favorite expressions included: "Don't let 'em cheat ya," when she'd give us money for snowballs; "I'll be goddamned," when something surprised or angered her; and—when us kids were getting on her nerves—"Stop *agitatin'*."

And she was root-beer-coming-out-of-your-nose funny, telling stories about neighborhood "rum pots," and how you could tell if local punks were using heroin. If one of the neighborhood morons—or "hoodles" as the old ladies called them—was sweating profusely, it was proof that he was "on that goddamn dope."

Over raisin bread and coffee, she'd remember long days making slipcovers as a member of the International Ladies' Garment Workers' Union. Different colored thread affected the respiratory systems of the workers. "If you were working with red," she'd say, "it would come out red in your hanky when you blew your nose."

You don't forget that kind of stuff when you're 6-years-old. And if you have any sense of drama at all, you use it to wrestle a blank page into submission.

In 2007, I dedicated "First and Forever," my neighborhood history of the Archdiocese of Baltimore, to my Catholic grandmothers.

My father's mother, Frances Prato Alvarez, died when I was at sea in 1976, just a year or two before I realized that while good stories can be found all over the map, the best ones are stirring something on the stove with a wooden spoon.

It is said that as long as there is someone alive to remember us, we never die. And if we are remembered with love, we are immortal. No one keeps this fiction alive better than writers betrothed to a specific dot on the map.

In my time on the obit desk, I packed off a boneyard's worth of Baltimore luminaries, beginning with Dr. Leo Kanner of Johns Hopkins, an early autism researcher known as the father of child psychiatry.

[Alas, it ran on the Sunday front page without my byline, which would have been a coup for a 21-year-old if not for the lingering stodginess of the old *Sunpapers,* which did not put bylines on obits.]

More frequent were obits on my elderly neighbors when I was a newlywed living at North Ellwood Avenue and Monument Street. Some of them remembered when Monument Street was a dirt road. One of them was named Clare—the last name escapes me, it was either German or Polish—and she would bake a cake for any occasion: births, deaths, new neighbors and anniversaries.

The short headline below her name in the deaths column simply said: Baker of Cakes.

The love of which I speak is nourishment; timeless in a way that the *scandal du jour* cannot be; the verity of eggs, butter, and flour whipped up in a wallpapered kitchen to make someone feel better about a friend who has died.

A while back, I wrote dialogue for an audio exhibit about old Lombard Street, once the *shtetl* of Baltimore, for the Jewish Museum of Maryland.

As a 5-year-old in 1963, holding my Italian grandmother's hand, I watched one of the last kosher butchers on Lombard Street cut the head off a chicken. It was still warm in the white paper when we brought it home to Macon Street.

Years later, I filed a story—anger rippling beneath the surface of a story not intended to be an editorial—on the razing of the buildings where tens of thousands of chickens were dispatched to *Olam Habah*.

Do I love Lombard Street?

Yes, even though it no longer exists in a way I care about.

Do I love it because I can still get a lean corned beef sandwich amidst the ghosts of Seymour Attman and his father Harry?

Of course. Seymour was the greatest.

But mostly I love it, and the city that endures around it, because my grandparents took me there when I was a kid. When those chicken houses fell to the wrecking ball, I was close to tears.

Those tears were not shed for brick and mortar.

And I will be writing my way home for the rest of my life.

Thames & Broadway

SOUTH BROADWAY

One could easily sail from the foot of Broadway in Fells Point to the Prospect Bay country club near Grasonville on Kent Island.

It would be a short voyage: shove off from the Broadway Recreation Pier on Thames Street out to the Patapsco River shipping channel. Beyond the Key Bridge, push down the Chesapeake Bay. Just past the Bay Bridge, set course for Kent Island.

At Kent, put in at the quiet of Prospect Bay where Tony Jutchess spends long afternoons mediating on the clamor and chaos—the smell of canvas and cabbage—of a childhood along narrow streets and alleys where the journey began.

Once a Baltimore kid—even at age 65 with poor health and most of his adventures in the past—always a Baltimore kid.

"Growing up, we'd stick our heads in the door of the Acropolis bar for a peek at the belly dancers," said Jutchess, remembering the Greek nightclub at the corner of South Broadway and Lancaster. "If you stood in the right spot on Broadway you could see them changing clothes on the second floor."

The seafaring spirit is Tony's birthright. He was conceived on a merchant ship sailing to New York City from Poland in the first months after World War II. It followed a chance meeting between his seafaring father and a local woman as the old salt strolled down a Gdansk street with half-a-load-on singing a Lithuanian love song.

Or so the story goes.

Alfred "Whitey" Jutchess fell for Barbara Malewska, who pitched woo by crooning the second verse to the song. They were married in a Polish Catholic church and sailed for America.

In Crabtown, Whitey shipped out of the old Seafarers International Union Hall on Gay Street, sailed deckhand on the Baker-Whiteley tugboats and raised his family at 910 Fell Street. The backyard where Tony's mother hung wash was once the early 19th century shipyard of William Price, who circa 1805 built a schooner called the *U.S.S. Hornet*.

Tony got married on a boat in Baltimore and as a kid, he stole fruit off of banana boats, hopped waterfront freight trains and each summer leapt into the brackish basin with the other Huckleberry Finn-kowskis.

But old family wounds and resentments—having to chase down Dad at gin mills like Zeppie's or Miss Effie's (with the talking mynah bird) for what was left of his pay—got the best of Tony. He decided to go another way, the bigger paydays of the business world, an ultimately lucrative decision he now laments.

"I fought tooth and nail so I'd never go hungry," said Jutchess, who knew that ache as a child. "The thing that hurts now is I know it could have been better."

After a long business career and an operation for lung cancer, Tony arrived on the Eastern Shore after leaping off a sinking clothing chain called Merry-Go-Round. Two decades ago, he was a senior construction manager when the Baltimore-based clothing firm had 1,500 stores.

Merry-Go-Round—the rock and roll baby of Leonard

Crabtown, USA

"Boogie" Weinglass—crashed as spectacularly as it sailed, filing for bankruptcy in 1994, kaput by '96.

But yellow bell bottoms and blue platform shoes are not what Tony wants to talk about when he crosses the Bay Bridge to have lunch at Roman's Place in East Baltimore with men who knew his father.

"I should have been a tugboat man or a Bay pilot," he said over crab cakes. "It was all laid-out for me. But I didn't want it."

Evelyn Butterhoff

PATAPSCO PIANO

"Sometimes I'm tired as anything, but I'm swinging anyway . . ."

Evelyn Butterhoff, 1924-2011

T he woman behind the piano was wild, gifted and fearless.

Music was in Evelyn Butterhoff and it had to come out, whether in gin mills, Holy Roller churches (doesn't a piano sound better with a tambourine?) or events at which someone had already been hired to play the piano.

"At my 40th birthday party on a boat in the harbor, Mom asks if she can play a song or two. She's the mother of the birthday girl, so what's the guy going to say?" laughed her daughter, Mary Carol Ambrose of Parkville.

"She sits down at this electric pi-*annah* and RIPPED it up! The band didn't know she could play. Everybody's screaming for more and the regular keyboard player didn't want to follow her."

Evelyn Butterhoff—who gave virtually all of her 86 years to music—died at the Hamilton Center nursing home on Harford Road on April 11, 2011 from complications of dementia and a stroke suffered in 2005.

Her last performance was more an act of bravery than entertainment.

"Mom's sister [Dorothy] was visiting not long before she died and took her downstairs to see if she could play the piano," said Ambrose. "My mother played 'Auld Lang Syne' and 'Goodnight Sweetheart' with her one good hand."

Evelyn could do more with one hand on a set of 88s than most folks can do with two.

"That girl can *play* . . . she plays for a few lousy dollars [in saloons]," said the pianist's mother—Agnes Beck—not long before her own death in 1990.

"It breaks my heart to see these other people with no talent who have two or three homes and cars."

The former Evelyn Anna Beck was born at the height of the Jazz Age to a Baltimore factory worker named John Charles Beck and his wife, Agnes Smrha.

The couple belonged to St. Wenceslaus Roman Catholic Church at Ashland and North Collington avenues in the days when the parish was strictly Bohemian and Czech. It is where Eveyln and her three siblings were baptized.

The Beck family lived at 443 North Curley Street near Orleans Street, just around the corner from Butterhoff's Grocery on North Rose Street where Evelyn's future husband was born.

"Mom's father was a natural musician," said Ambrose. "He played piano, violin, drums and mandolin. Never took lessons."

Evelyn attended St. Elizabeth of Hungary parochial school near Patterson Park and began 50 cents an hour piano lessons with a neighborhood woman her mother described as an "old maid."

At age 12, Evelyn began studying with Jack Rohr at the Hammann Music Company in the 200 block of North Liberty Street downtown. Those lessons cost $2 each.

"Jack really socked it to me," said Evelyn in a 1986 interview, recalling Rohr as the biggest influence on her playing, particularly in regard to keeping time. "He taught me sonatas, Beethoven, how to change keys, improvise and fake it."

In 1940, Evelyn graduated from St. Elizabeth's business school. Her first professional job came when she was 17, a gig with Frank Skalski and his Silver Eagle Orchestra at the Polish Home Club on South Broadway in Fells Point.

In those pre-Elvis days—when pianos were as common in bars as shuffleboard tables—Evelyn played a wide range of Baltimore taverns, restaurants and social clubs, most of them long-gone. And kept at it through the dark epochs of disco, grunge and gangster rap.

A quick sampling of the houses rocked by Evelyn Butterhoff includes Meushaw's Restaurant on Frederick Road, the old Finnish Hall in what is now Greektown; various Democratic clubs and Odd Fellows halls; the fabled Emerson Hotel at Baltimore and Calvert streets; dance halls at Moose and Elks clubs and nightclubs from Essex to Pasadena.

"Mom had to deal with crappy pianos in bars and hated it," said Ambrose. "She played many a crappy piano."

Toward the end of her career, Evelyn's regular gigs were at Rickter's on Belair Road near Herring Run Park, a job behind the organ at Winston Avenue Baptist Church on East 39th Street and the Glenmore Tavern on Harford Road.

"I never hired her," said Cal Bitner, who owned the Glenmore at the time. "She'd just come in and play the piano."

A pass of the hat might be enough for Evelyn to get a sandwich and cab fare home with a few nickels leftover.

In 1950, Evelyn joined the Queens of Rhythm, an all-female band that played in the mid-Atlantic area. A surviving band member—Viola Stelmack of Essex, still playing music—was one of the mourners at her old band mate's funeral, a Mass of Christian burial held at St. Pius X Church in Towson.

A year or so before joining the Queens, Evelyn married John Frederick Butterhoff, Jr. Family legend holds that John—a drummer who graduated from Mt. St. Joseph High School—was smitten by Evelyn's talent as well as her beauty.

The attraction set in motion a conflict—the life of a musician versus the more mundane obligations of a wife and mother—that dogged the couple to the end of their days.

"Mom had no interest in domestic things," said Ambrose, noting that her mother was a loving parent whose interests lay outside the home. "She absolutely did *not* want to be a homemaker. She wanted to play music."

Ambrose said that when she turned 18 in 1968 her mother "ran away from home," leaving Mr. Butterhoff on Sagra Road off of Loch Raven Boulevard with her and her brothers.

"We didn't even know where she was at first," she said.

John F. Butterhoff died at age 78 in 2004. A Navy veteran of World War II and Korea, he was stationed in Yorktown, Virginia in 1944 as a stenographer and typist assigned to a lieutenant commander and was discharged as a Yeoman Second Class.

The old Navy man was buried at the Garrison Forest Veterans Cemetery in Owings Mills. And although he hadn't lived with his wife for the last 40 years of his life, Ambrose put Evelyn right next to him.

"In life they were too hard-headed to sit down and

have a sane conversation, so now that they can't talk anymore I put them in the ground together," laughed Ambrose.

"I fixed the situation."

I met Evelyn Butterhoff in the mid-1980s when I was living on Kentucky Avenue in Mayfield and she regularly played Rickter's (now Slim's Ace of Club) on the Belair Road side of Herring Run Park.

I was thrilled by her Keith Moon approach to the piano—she would whoop and holler and smack a hanging plant while playing. Legend holds that Rickter's installed a steel plate under the piano because she had stomped a hole in the floor.

And we shared an almost illogical affection for our hometown.

"My mother loved Baltimore, are you kidding?" said Ambrose, who is determined to document what is left of the legion of women who once "squirted down the pavement." Evelyn, she pointed out, didn't have time for simple chores but she did like to treat herself to a nice afternoon now and then.

"She thought going to Phillips at Harborplace to eat dinner was like being on vacation."

Evelyn got to these places on foot or by bus. Once in a while, if it was late after a gig, a friend or tavern owner would force her into a cab after last call.

"Mommy was absolutely fearless," said Ambrose. "She wasn't afraid of the city, of walking the streets. She was mugged once, but it didn't stop her."

In addition to the Inner Harbor, Evelyn was fond of the old Baltimore haunts—Marconi's on Saratoga Street and a long gone gem from Foster Avenue in Highlandtown called Winterling's and, naturally, Haussner's.

"Who didn't like Haussner's?" said Ambrose. "She loved their Tyrolean dumplings."

A lifelong Roman Catholic and always a woman of faith—sanctity and the rollicking fun of a good-timer living side-by-side in the same heart—Evelyn attended services with a brand of Catholicism known as the "charismatics."

Her faith was tested—and faltered, according to her daughter—when she began encountering health problems.

"Mom had breast cancer and a mastectomy in 1994 and she was never the same after that," said Ambrose. "It shook her faith. And after the chemo she was less lively. Never the same."

Evelyn Butterhoff is survived by sons, John J. Butterhoff of North Charles Street and Robert W. Butterhoff—a drummer in a 1970s local band called Fresh—who lives in Manchester.

Other survivors include her sisters, Dorothy Beck Hutchins, wife of the retired *Sunpapers* photographer Paul Hutchins and a sister Marie Kohl of Ellicott City as well as three grandsons.

Evelyn also leaves behind her piano, an upright made by Meissner of Milwaukee. She bought it used on Joppa Road in 1975 for $250 and paid it off by installments.

The piano—faithfully tuned over the years by Evelyn's cousin, Bernard Hauser—is "safe and sound," according to Ambrose, in the home of good friends in Fork, Maryland.

Not the newsroom

CLOWN CORRESPONDENT

In *The Sun* newsroom—landing at age 20, departing almost a quarter-century later—I often felt like McCandlish Phillips, even though I'd just about taken leave of the City Desk before I knew who he was.

A *New York Times* reporter from 1955 to 1973, Phillips was a poetic writer and respected reporter whose prose, remembered Pete Hamill, had a "texture that was sensual."

But when it came to the things he believed in most—the stories he really wanted to tell, like the life of a circus clown named Otto Griebling—no one seemed to care.

In his 2013 obituary, it said that after a few small potatoes editing jobs in New England, Phillips served with the Army from 1950 to 1952 and was stationed at Fort Holabird in Baltimore's Dundalk neighborhood.

It was there, Phillips later said, that he attended a church service at which he was "born again."

Years later, Philips walked away from his byline without fanfare, disappearing into the obscurity of passionate Christianity. When I walked away from Calvert Street for the last time, it was not for Catholicism but family's earlier faith: the sea.

The last packing house in the city

CHARLES RIEMER

Charles "Don't call me Charlie" Riemer grew up doing odd jobs around the neighborhood like a lot of kids, shoveling snow and running errands for small change.

"I'm so used to working all my life—it's all I know," he said.

The East Baltimorean left grade school to help bring money into a house of seven boys and a widowed mother. His first real job was in 1960. Reimer was about 17 years old and worked for a long-gone supermarket in Highlandtown called Brill's.

Riemer remembers the pay more than the work: less than a dollar an hour in the first years of the New Frontier.

"Screw that," said Riemer.

Adios Brills, hello H&S Bakery in Fells Point, where the Greeks were getting rich selling bread.

"I was feeding the number one oven down there on the day JFK was assassinated," he said.

From H&S, Riemer jumped over to hominy packing house at 2425 Foster Avenue, not far from where young Charles grew up near the corner of Fait and Kenwood. It was back in 1904 that Mike Manning's grandmother started a food-canning business in the backyard of her Foster Avenue rowhouse.

"She was working in canning and got the idea of

packing hominy," said Mr. Manning. "She was the boss and my grandfather was an engineer who worked the boiler."

When waterfront old-timers talk about Baltimore's canning industry they say things like: "The last packing house I know was Lord-Mott's down Broadway on Fell Street."

But every morning that Mike Manning shows up for work at 803 S. Clinton St., he puts the lie to an old tale that says all the packing houses shut down long ago, producing 10,000 cans of pearl-white hominy each working day.

The drafty brick building, built in 1933, is the last packing house in a city that once led the nation in the canning of fruits and vegetables. It was back in those days that German immigrants Margaret Manning and her husband, Michael, first put a cup of steamed corn into a tin can.

"It's a family responsibility," said Mike Manning, 68, president and chief floor sweeper of Mrs. M. Manning Inc. "I was practically raised here when my father was living. Sometimes I don't know why I'm still here."

He is here—with 19 mostly minimum-wage employees, two engineers to work the boilers, his brother John on the production line and his sister Lena running the office—almost two decades after the other packing houses vanished from Southeast Baltimore.

When Mr. Manning says, ". . . you don't make a lot of money. The last couple of years have been pretty close," you sense that he has hung on because once he walks away from Clinton Street the family business will go the way of the once ritual scrubbing of white marble steps.

His children, he said, aren't interested in taking over the business. Even one that gets fan letters.

Crabtown, USA

To satisfy the public's appetite for hominy—steamed kernels of white corn larger than those used for the more common grits—Mike Manning cranks up an operation right out of the Industrial Revolution.

Off to the side of a huge open space holding 20 pressure cookers, anywhere from eight to 10 women in hairnets sit on low stools at individual conveyor belts as millions of kernels of corn roll past. It is their job to pick out the odd, derelict kernels shipped to Baltimore from mills out West. The women search for pieces of cob, a yellow kernel or one with a spot, anything that isn't pristine and white.

"The main thing is the picking," said Mr. Manning, who says the job is crucial to maintaining his product's reputation for gleaming pearl hominy. It is not a chore he trusts to machines.

"The electric eyes miss a lot, they only see the surface of the kernel," he said. "My workers have a certain loyalty, they know the quality I'm after and they respect that."

The kernels that pass inspection fall off of a conveyor that moves down toward the pickers' laps and into large metal containers, the thin and constant ping-ping-ping of corn sounding like tiny hailstones hitting a tin roof.

"You have to have good eyes to pick the hominy," said Viola Skahill, who celebrated 50 years with the company in July of 1992. "It's tiresome sometimes."

The corn is steamed and canned the day after it's picked, and when Mr. Manning calls for a shift in production, the women in the picking room put on their sweaters and walk down into the concrete-and-cinder-block chill of the labeling room. They follow cans that travel there in round crates of 252 cans each that move along the ceiling.

The cans are dumped into 6,000 gallons of water that

cool the hominy. After that, a wooden conveyor moves cans past women who straighten them for a noisy ride through the chutes of the labeler; women who check the cans for dents; women who fold the boxes that contain the product on its journey to markets, and women who make sure a label is securely glued to each can.

One thing the women at Manning's don't do is label the cans by hand, as the packinghouse women of years ago did.

"We're not that antiquated," said Mr. Manning. "We have a machine that labels."

The machine was made in 1939.

Charlie Riemer wasn't long for Manning's, either. The money wasn't good enough. He moved to Koester's Bakery near Lexington Market (where he was on duty when Martin Luther King was shot) and then Schmidt's Bakery at Carey and Lawrence Streets.

"Still getting paid under a dollar!" said Riemer of the jobs. "They all sucked."

In March of 1975, Charles hit the big-time: good wages, benefits and job security with the City of Baltimore.

His wife at the time had a cleaning job with the city school board. An eastside Italian-American, she also had connections to legendary southeast Baltimore councilman Dominic "Mimi" DiPietro [1905-1994], a native of Abruzzi for whom an ice skating rink in Patterson Park is named.

Mimi took good care of his Highlandtown taxpayers, keeping rats at bay long before it was cool to have the image of a rodent on your bumper as a symbol of home; fixing potholes and finding jobs for friends, neighbors and relatives who were sure to vote the Democrat ticket come November.

Mimi made a call, Riemer was in and all of a sudden the eastside hustler was shampooing carpets. Lots and lots of carpets. And not for nickels either, up to $18.50 an hour after several decades of service.

"I've [shampooed] all nine police districts, City Hall, the temporary City Hall on Redwood Street when [councilman Dominic] Leone was shot, the courthouse—east and west—the housing department and Transit and Traffic across from the *Sunpapers* on Calvert Street."

"I worked alone, never had any help," he said, and he liked it that way. "Four offices every morning, four offices every evening."

He's the skinny guy with the hard-earned image hipsters strive to emulate: well-worn navy blue pants and navy work shirt with his name on a patch over the breast pocket and a sleigh ride's worth of keys jangling from his belt.

Riemer laughs: "I call 'em city hall jewelry."

Sometimes, said Riemer, he'd overhear a boss exchanging some kind of favor with another ranking bureaucrat with the words: "I'll send my man out to shampoo your carpets."

Riemer was that man through the mayoral administrations of William Donald Schaefer, Clarence "Du" Burns, Kurt L. Schmoke, Martin O'Malley, Sheila Dixon and now, Stephanie Rawlings-Blake.

Asked to name his favorite, Reimer's eyes twinkle. Ever the streetwise diplomat, he says, "All of 'em."

He's also the ceiling tile fixer, light-bulb changer, officer furniture mover and the flag guy.

Riemer makes sure the Stars & Stripes, along with the Lord Baltimore-themed flag of the Old Line State and the yellow and black of the City of Baltimore are up when they're supposed to be up, half-mast after prominent deaths and replaced when needed.

"I changed the flag on the Shot Tower a couple of weeks ago," he said. "No elevator—303 steps."

Rafael Alvarez

[Today's flags are made of durable fabric, "storm" worthy pennants that stay on the pole until they begin to tatter. "You put'em up and leave'em up," said Reimer. "Used to be they'd go up in the morning and come down at night.]

"I put up the War of 1812 flag at City Hall earlier this year," he said of commemorations honoring the 200th anniversary of struggle in which the patriots of North Point were essential in vanquishing the British.

Now, formally retired from the city since 2007 and doing his old chores part-time, Reimer has had enough, confident that after this December 31st he won't be taking the No. 20 bus from the corner of Gusryan and Boston streets to Holliday street downtown anymore. At least not to change light bulbs.

"I never missed a day," he said with pride. "You know how you last on any job? You don't go around saying, 'he said, she said.' You don't go into a [gossip] huddle and run your mouth. You do your damn job and go home."

Now what?

"Nothing," said Riemer.

A man has got to do something.

"I love doing things for people, I mean that," he said. "I just don't want to be stepped on or used. If you go to work every day and save your money, you can have some nice things in this world. But once I'm retired I hope I'm doing nothing.

"No more 99 bosses telling me to clean 99 buildings. I'm 70. I'm winding down."

Charles Riemer died in May of 2013 without enjoying a single day of retirement.

Rafael Alvarez and Frances Prato
Baltimore, 1929

ALVAREZ AFFIANCED

My grandparents were married at Our Lady of Pompei on Conkling Street more than 80 years ago, at the beginning of the last economic collapse.

The folks who knew where they went afterward to celebrate—Uncle Ernest and Mr. Sanchez, Miss Jenna Rose and my grandmother's good friend, Lucinda "Sonny" Ares—are not around to tell the story.

"I remember that generation entertaining in their homes, enjoying each other's company and having feasts," said Joseph Ares III, grandson of Joe and Sonny Ares, as close a friend to me as our grandparents were to one another.

"People would stop in my grandmother's house on Savage Street and she'd pour a few cordials, probably Spanish cognac or brandy and put out some cookies. They'd sit around and talk. That's how it was.

"My grandmother's lady friends came by during the day and sat with her talking in the kitchen but at night, the Spaniards sat in the parlor and my grandfather smoked a cigar. Mr. Garcia would walk down the street and knock on the door and he and my grandfather would drink and talk in Spanish."

On November 14, 1953, my mother and father said "I do," on the altar of St. Casimir in Canton. The reception was held in the rowhouse where my father grew up—627

South Macon Street. Joe Garcia and Joe Ares (my grandfather's best man in the 1920s) and their wives and all the others were there and my mother's Aunt Hilda turned the Alvarez home into a Polish wedding hall.

Hilda, who died in 1997, and her husband, Albert Lockwood, who died in 2001 at age 91, made big pots of homemade kielbasa and sauerkraut, chicken and potatoes and bowls of carrots and peas, not typical fare in a basement kitchen accustomed to *bacalao* and fried eggplant.

My namesake grandfather stood aside and turned the house over to his son's new in-laws: The tough Spaniard from Galicia was accepting a Polish daughter-in-law from Dillon Street.

The iconic photo from that day—taken by East Baltimore wedding photographer Paul Jordan, who kept a studio at 3121 Eastern Avenue—is a black and white shot of the bride and groom toasting one another in the front window with stars in their eyes. When my parents celebrated their 40th anniversary, we had the party at that same house on Macon Street and recreated the image.

On December 6, 1980, I was married at the Loyola College chapel on North Charles Street to Deborah Rudacille of Dundalk, two days before Beatle John was murdered in New York City. The reception was held in Fells Point at the Polish National Alliance, just off of Broadway on Eastern Avenue.

It was a spectacular Deer Hunter affair with a rocking combo called the Romanos playing everything from polkas to DEVO's "Whip It" to "New York, New York," during which everyone made a huge circle and kicked their legs in the air.

What no one knew was that Deborah was a couple of weeks pregnant when we walked down the aisle and we would be parents before we figured out how to be husband and wife.

[We never did puzzle out that one. It's a story—with a genuine happy ending— for another day.]

In early September 2009 in Montauk—"the end" of Long Island—I walked the child born eight months after my wedding day down a carpet made of pink and orange rose petals as John sang "All You Need Is Love."

Amelia Jean Alvarez was married to Mark Griffin Champion in a weekend that would have been unfathomable to my immigrant grandparents and was a bit exotic for my own hometown boy sensibilities as well.

Friends and family arrived from across the country— Roland Park to Nashville to San Antonio to Los Angeles; stayed for three days at a resort called Sole East; ate grilled steak and sautéed fish with bok choy and asparagus spears; and danced to Dr. Dre and Notorious B.I.G. under a Great Gatsby party tent.

It was a vacation weekend shared with the people we love the most in this world and when it began to wind down on Sunday morning, the young people lay poolside sipping Bloody Marys and reading all about it in the wedding pages of the *New York Times*.

Before I hopped in the truck to drive home to Macon Street, I took Amelia aside and asked: "Was it what you wanted?"

"It was," she said.

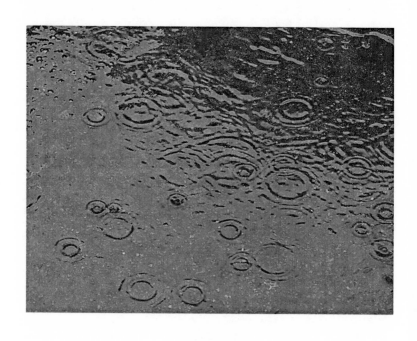

Go Away!

GUILFORD AVENUE

"This is the equation: supply + demand + magic . . ."
                                                            —Roberto Bolano

W hen things come in pairs—in they went, two and two, reads Genesis—the existing order tends to hold. When the material world is divided by three and spliced back together like a coil of hawser, something new is born.

I have experienced this many times while casting about for the best way to coax a story from the other side of the veil.

A short item in the newspaper—the death of Matel Dawson, the Detroit forklift operator who gave $1.3 million to charity—is mere fact, and though fascinating, not enough.

Add an anonymous snapshot found in a puddle or the wisp of lyric from Tin Pan Alley—*"one half so wondrous . . ."*— and the unknown sits upright.

Mix all of it with the scent and mystery of a troubled young woman pushing through the revolving door of a downtown department store that will be demolished before her next birthday and . . .

Eureka!

In my years as a reporter at the *Baltimore Sun*, I was

fascinated by the block-long expanse of Guilford Avenue that runs behind the newspaper building.

Newsprint was once delivered there by rail car, the Jones Falls Expressway overhead is busy with traffic either escaping or pouring into the city and from the old fifth floor newsroom you could see the Dog House weiner joint at 617 Fallsway and the nickel-gray pyramid atop the Maryland Penitentiary.

When I walked out the back door of the paper for the last time in January of 2001, I took a knapsack of reporter's notebooks for future use—I'd long archived the ones used for obits and *pierogi* recipes—a severance check, and doubts about what I would do with stories yet to come.

A reporter without a newspaper, I found myself on Guilford Avenue where, over some 25 years at the paper, I did all kinds of things under the stretch of the JFX encompassing the 500 block.

[The most expensive was accumulating enough parking tickets to buy a good used car and the least interesting were late afternoon naps before the first edition deadline.]

Guilford Avenue was where the boys from the composing room drank beer after the final edition went to bed; where viewers of *The Wire* met a fictional city editor named Gus Haynes sitting on the newspaper's loading dock.

"Gus Haynes, the patron saint of journalism," said Clark Johnson, the veteran actor and director who played the role. "The perfect editor."

Perfect as Haynes may have been, it's unlikely that he could have gotten away with running (at least more than once) the stories that began to haunt me toward the end of my peculiar run at 501 North Calvert Street.

Crabtown, USA

In 1993, I persuaded Bill Salganik, a staunch union leader and then editor of the "Perspective" section to publish an essay I had written about All Souls' Day. The piece cataloged prayers offered for the soul of Richard Manuel (pianist and founding member of The Band and a 1986 suicide) at various shrines and sanctuaries across the United States.

It was called "The Richard Manuel Indulgence Tour" and at least one carpet-bagger editor on Calvert Street thought it a waste of newsprint. That man, however, is long gone while the story—like Manuel's ethereal, fragile voice—endures.

Four years later, I had less success persuading feature editor Jan Winburn to get behind a similar story with one significant difference: this tale was not about prayers for the dead but a visit from them.

I wanted to write about two weeks in August of 1997 when—oppressed by heat and humidity, a high fever from a stomach flu and a diet of grape Popsicles—I saw the specter of Anne Frank hovering along the ceiling of my East Baltimore rowhouse.

Sick in bed, I'd been reading about the last person to see Anne alive, a fellow prisoner who'd reported that the young writer was dying of typhus, naked beneath a filthy blanket had "no tears left to cry."

Not only did I see Anne's ghost beneath a blanket—hovering in a corner of my tin-ceiling—but for the rest of that year, by diminishing degrees, it felt as though she and I were the same person, that I had somehow become Anne Frank while remaining myself.

Relating the story to an Orthodox rabbi friend I bumped into downtown, the man said, without guile: "You were Anne Frank for two weeks and you didn't tell me?"

That same day, to Winburn: "That's what I'd like to write about."

Jan looked at me sympathetically (at least I think she did) paid for our lunch at the long-defunct Calvert House next-door to the paper and never again asked if I had any ideas up my sleeve.

Roberto Bolano, who chose work as a night watchman at a Spanish campground over any job that might bleed his pen, would have run that story.

※

In a little more than two decades as an agate clerk and daily reporter, I filed millions of words of copy.

I wrote about the weather—too hot, too cold, deluge and drought; all manner of violence both depraved and stupid; tedious, late-night meetings about sewer systems, school subsidies and Social Security and recaps of boring speeches, once sitting through the blowhards Farrakhan and Sharpton in the same week, sealing my decision to leave the paper.

Though these pieces afforded the rare, winning quote—"It's so hot the chickens are standing in line to be plucked!"—my interests increasingly wandered toward the mysticism I believed to be in concert with Baltimore's surplus of suffering.

And Guilford Avenue, less than a Hooverville since the days of the Reagan Administration, was always fertile ground.

At the end of the summer of 1994, after returning to Baltimore from a month-long road trip with my youngest child Sofia, now a New York playwright, I made a late-night bee-line to the newspaper to bang out the tale of our adventures.

I'd just driven 2,000 miles—Baltimore to Pittsburgh to Chicago to Nashville to Atlanta for a night at the Open Door prison and homeless outreach community and a stroll through the Jimmy Carter Presidential Library to Disneyworld and back to Crabtown.

Yet the defining moment of the trip waited for me in Baltimore, occurring late at night on the day I returned.

The summer of 1994 was not an easy one. Sofia's mother and I, divorced for five years, had been going on occasional dates to see if the family might live together again.

The kids weren't aware of these outings: a movie, coffee and pie, going to see The Band sans Manuel and a gig by Chrissie's Pretenders, a band important in our courtship some 15 years earlier. But the outings were more like opportunities to re-break bones that had not set properly than nights on the town.

In time, there would be reconciliation but not reunion. None of this was clear the night I drove to *The Sun* after four weeks on the road.

It was raining hard as I drove past the corner of Madison Street and Guilford Avenue, a little before midnight.

Noah and his old lady Nahmah hard. Morton Salt girl without her umbrella hard. Little Bobby Zimmerman a-hard-rain-is-gonna-fall *hard*.

At times I couldn't see through the windshield, as though mercury were cascading across it instead of water, the highway above Guilford Avenue providing temporary relief as I idled at a red light a block from the paper.

I had Johnny Winter on the tape player—*". . . it's my own fault, baby, treat me the way you wanna do . . ."*— and an ex-wife on my mind when I glimpsed a particularly Baltimorean version of the American Gothic.

To my left, perhaps trying to flag a cab in a town where taxis are hard to come by in good weather, stood this line-up in the downpour: a tall transvestite; a teenager dressed in the uncompromising uniform of the corner; and a young woman holding a baby that looked like it had been born that morning.

The baby clinched it.

Fuck.

What's a Catholic boy to do?

I rolled down the window and asked where they were going. The guy in drag said that some of them were headed one way, some the other.

Forcefully: "Where do you *want* to go?"

The mother handed the infant to the transvestite, who began walking in the direction of the penitentiary with the corner boy; hopped in and told me to take her to Cherry Hill, a public housing neighborhood in far south Baltimore.

THE TRANSVESTITE WALKS INTO THE TEETH OF A MONSOON WITH A NEWBORN WHILE THE KID'S MOTHER GETS A RIDE HOME!

Quantum narrative—supply and demand and magic—had somehow held sway with enough stagecraft on a dark and Biblically thunderous night for me to tell my ex-wife that our year of exploratory surgery was over.

I didn't even try to interest the newspaper in this one.

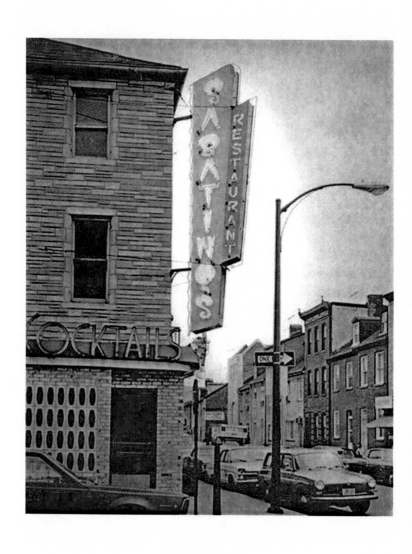

Sabatino's

PEACHY DiPIETRO

A long with recipes for "pasta fagiole" and gnocchi (my Aunt Amelia Kouneski Adornato makes the best "fa-zool" in the family) you will find a whole lotta Crabtown in "A Peachy Life," by Leonora "Peachy" DiPietro of Highlandtown.

In it, she recounts her years working at some of Baltimore's most fabled eateries: Johnny Unitas' Golden Arm; the Circle One revolving rooftop restaurant at the downtown Holiday Inn (where the Beatles stayed in September, 1964; the incomparable Haussner's; and her four decades at Sabatino's.

The joy is mixed with bushel baskets of pain but there's Peachy on the book jacket, smiling, not regretting a thing.

Restaurants—the funny part of the book.

Family—the loving parts.

Men?

Don't ask.

NARROW ALLEY

Near the Safeway in Canton and the 1000 block of Binney Street—where Roberts Packing House once stood and my mother played with bushel baskets as her mother skinned tomatoes and snipped beans during the last Depression—stands a most narrow alley in all of Baltimore.

When I was in grade school, it was just wide enough for a skinny kid to walk down with a modest Easter basket, but somehow the heavy-set Polish women who lived there were able to drag a garden hose out to the street to squirt down the gutters and the drunks didn't have to reach out very far to find something to hold for balance.

Years later, during middle-of-the-workday dates with women unfamiliar with the warrens of Crabtown, I would treat to snowballs and lead them through the alley, thrilled to peek over the cinderblock wall behind 2729 Dillon Street and say, "That's where my mother used to take a summer bath in a washtub back when FDR was Jesus Christ in a wheelchair . . ."

. . . in a 1955 Plymouth.

RAFAEL / MANUEL / RAFAEL

My father Manuel sits under a dogwood tree in the suburbs of Linthicum, reminiscing about his childhood on Macon Street in East Baltimore, where they sat around a table in a basement kitchen drinking wine and eating cod fish, reminiscing about the Old Country.

"When I was a little boy, my father and his friends used to hear stories about Spain—everyone was hard-working and honest except for the southerners, who had some Gypsy blood," said Dad, not endorsing, simply recounting.

"When I met your mother in high school, I entered a world I didn't even know existed and all I had to do was walk a mile or so from Macon Street to Dillon Street. And when I had a son, he would be Ralph and that was it.

"I didn't sit down at 18 and decide my first son would be named for my father. I knew it."

The ladder of years: Manuel Alvarez, who ran a hauling business with an ox and cart, was born in the mid-to-late 19th century in a small village in Galicia, an area of Spain that might as well have been the Middle Ages well into the 20th century.

His son was Rafael, born in the same Galician village near Chapela in 1904. He came to Baltimore on a merchant ship about the age of 20. His son—my father—was Manuel, born in "the Hill" neighborhood of

Rafael Alvarez

Highlandtown—now known as Greektown—in 1934. My father was not given a middle name. When he joined the Coast Guard during the Korean War, they insisted he acquire one. He chose Rafael.

Your correspondent—me, Ralph/Rafael/Ralphie—came along in the spring of 1958—May 24, Bob Dylan's 17th birthday.

In 1983, I had a son, Manuel Jacob Alvarez, an artist.

"I was working on the tugboats when you were born, about 3 a.m. in late May," said my father, sitting under that dogwood tree with a beer.

"Your mother and I were living out of the city by that time but the night you were born I spent the night with my parents on Macon Street," said Dad, Italian on his mother's side.

That night, he said, "Aunt Mary [Adornato] made *pasta fagiole* in red sauce with the prosciutto bone. She knew I liked it and had me over. The next day, my father and I drove to [St. Agnes] hospital in a two-tone, blue and white '55 Plymouth.

"There was a strange sort of modesty from my father when I told him on the ride over that I'd named the baby for him . . . it was a happy time . . ."

David Franks at the corner of Bank and
Regester Streets.

FOOTLONG FRANKS

David Franks—as the late David Franks often said—"tells stories and some of them are true."

Not true was his age, about which, like the temperamental matinee idol that he was, Franks lied; secretly shaving five years from the date on his birth certificate.

True this: David's ideas floated through the empyrean while his feet trudged the streets of Baltimore.

His work—archived in the clouds at the top of the Bromo Selzter Arts Tower—will be studied for generations to come.

And his mind worked like no other (the sacred and profane side-by-side in a heart above which Borges once autographed) and surely, all who knew and mourn him concur, will not see the likes of him again.

—∽∾—

My father knew David Franks long before I did. It was back around 1971 and he and Franks were on opposite sides in a changing of the guard along the southeast Baltimore waterfront that is all but complete today.

Dad was a tugboat man in the engine rooms of the Baker-Whiteley Towing Co. and Franks was a dashing young poet, visionary and Lothario who'd moved into a

Fell Street apartment across from the pier where the boats tied up.

I was in the 7th grade, too young to run with the freaks turning the old seamen's village into the Greenwich Village of Baltimore; convinced there was something beyond the middle-class suburb my father's labor had earned us and unaware that much of what I aspired to existed alongside the tugboats in the person of David Franks.

The son of a Washington, D.C. physician, Franks was a boy wonder instructor at the Maryland Institute, College of Art, where he led students in assignments that sometimes caused disciplinary action and protests of censorship.

[Franks relished all of it, throwing himself under the Magic Bus just to see who would come to his flattened aid only to pop up like a circus clown to do it all over again.]

Along the cobblestones of Thames Street, he suffered the taunts of the old salts and stevedores eager to conclude that the long-haired "professor" was a queer except for the plenitude to the contrary.

When his cat got loose, they'd claim to have drowned it in the Patapsco.

"But not your father," recalled Franks. "Your father was never cruel."

My old man respected Franks for his education and perhaps wanted something similar, but less eccentric, for me: the turning of pages over the turning of wrenches.

But common sense told him that artistic monkeyshines and the shot-and-a-beer world of gin mills like Zeppie's and Miss Effie's were irreconcilable.

"He's lucky one of those guys didn't throw him overboard," said Dad.

Franks once used a shotgun to blow holes in letters his

own father had written to him, using the leftover words to fabricate new epistles.

Took up collections as a "crippled sex symbol" from a wheelchair onstage at Root Boy Slim concerts.

And, as mentioned, prevailed upon Jorge Luis Borges to autograph the spot on his chest above his beating heart.

But the magic trick that tickled me most was the time Franks conducted a "tugboat symphony" requiring the cooperation of the same men who'd given him a hard time.

Though he had a dissertation's worth of theory behind this "non-futile exercise in futility," David's greater achievement is having persuaded a half-dozen tug captains to repeatedly toot their whistles in a certain cadence until he was satisfied.

David Franks represented the confluence and divide of what I wanted for myself and what Dad hoped for me as the first generation to get away from the waterfront through college.

I would grow up and take both, dipping a quill in the Patapsco to write stories of dreamers and sea dogs with equal affection; laboring for the emotional beauty of Franks's best work in concert with images of waterfront ruins.

Complete and dazzling.

More than 20 years after Franks recorded his "Whistling in the Dark" symphony of tugboats, I hosted a reading in my Macon Street rowhouse, the house where my father had grown up before going to sea as a teenager. Franks and I were friends by then, having met at the Orpheum Cinema above what used to be Mooney's Rope Shop on Thames Street.

Franks arrived with a tray of *kiszka*—a Polish delicacy made of buckwheat groats, pork and beef blood.

Across the kitchen, my father saw David Franks for the

first time in two decades at, of all places, his boyhood home. And they shook hands in acknowledgement of tales saved for another day.

The poetic stuntman David "Footlong" Franks was found dead in his Fells Point apartment the second week of January, 2010, not long before his 67th birthday. He was honored in an especially poignant obituary by Arthur Hirsch in the *Baltimore Sun* on January 17th, 2010.

In late November of 2005, as Franks recovered from lung cancer brought on by heavy smoking, I visited his apartment in an old barbershop at the corner of Bank and Regester streets in Fells Point. I brought Thanksgiving leftovers from my mother.

On November 29, I received this note from David.

I sent your mother a thank-you—it was the best Thanksgiving food I've had since my mother cooked for family & guests & she was a great cook.

Thank you for being so thoughtful & bringing it over—I had enough for another delicious meal yesterday which is a GREAT treat for me.

What do you do about eating?

You're one of my only friends that also lives alone. That's not really important—what is important is if we can get together again soon & do some more reading (ourselves & others), talking . . . let me know what your time is like . . .

When you were here, I read poems and you read from your journals. They were personal [entries] & I happen to love personal essays & journals & letters—always have.

Sometimes it's a matter of finding out how other writers felt, but really the lowly "journal" is

Crabtown, USA

*also where I find so much THAT I can relate to
about being alive, even though it is not my life.*

*Sometimes it shows me other ways of seeing
things that are part of my life (in their presence
or absence) that I haven't seen until then . . .*

Love, David

How would it sound underwater?

I met David Franks when he worked the popcorn machine at the Thames Street River of Light known as the Orpheum.

I tell stories, he said, and some of them are true.

I write poems that can no longer suffer the poet.

He put his forehead where his mouth was: smash your head against the wall.

Once I told him that I had strolled side-by-side with as many beautiful women as he.

And the fabled Footlong just chuckled—like Ty Cobb dismissing some punk named Pete Rose—and asked if I could run him up Broadway to the dry cleaners.

He signed his missives: "Kill you later . . ."

Kill you later, kill you later . . .

Borges autographed his chest, right above the heart.

PAY ATTENTION: Jorge Luis Borges autographed the chest of David Franks RIGHT ABOVE THE HEART.

"It is magic!" exclaimed the Argentinean maestro.

I introduced Franks to the Angel of Christ, a beauty whose mother put hard-boiled eggs in spaghetti sauce. The daughter of a bookseller, also dead, she promised to go with me to the memorial. And then changed her mind.

"He gave ME a golden wishbone too. And now that he's gone I read about other recipients."

But, I asked, "Aren't they cool?"

"Yes," said Angela, "all glittery and gold and full of hope that only a dead fowl (the turkey/wishbone) can offer."

My father knew David first. In the wheelhouse of a tugboat, he taught me that when the whistle is ready, the conductor will appear. But I knew David better.

And believed him when he said: "Motherfucker, if you had one tit I'd marry you . . ."

<hr/>

I first met David Morley when he was a student in Barbara Simon's English class at North County High School (originally known, without irony, as Andover) in the Linthicum neighborhood of Anne Arundel County.

I was a reporter for the *Sunpapers* of Baltimore, Barbara—president of the Maryland State Poetry & Literary Society until her death in 2007—was still with us, and Morley was a kid who wanted in on the writing game.

I'm not sure what I told the students that day, probably something about telling stories because they need to be told.

Several years later I bumped into Morley at the Daily Grind on Thames Street in Fells Point. He reminded me of my visit to his class, and I soon commissioned him to write a chapter about Holy Trinity parish in Glen Burnie for a history of the Archdiocese of Baltimore I was writing.

Titled *First and Forever,* the book was released the year Barbara Simon succumbed to pancreatic cancer.

By then, Morley had made a "documentary" worthy of *This is Spinal Tap* in which he plays a Crabtown street poet named Butchie—complete with ridiculous fake mustache—called *Southside Survivor*.

The parts about a niece gone wrong, Butchie scaring

away a flock of pigeons, and the local delicacy known as "pit beef" are especially memorable.

The movie poster is a send-up of the cover of Springsteen's *Born in the USA* album. But instead of a red baseball cap stuck in the back pocket of Butchie's jeans, it's a soiled, old-school Orioles cartoon bird hat.

One summer I took *Southside Survivor* down the ocean to watch with the kids and their mother. My then-teenaged son and I laughed like idiots. The girls and Mom thought it was the stupidest thing they'd ever seen. That's how good it is.

Then came Morley with new work, a video documentary of the January 31, 2010, memorial service for the poet at the Patterson Theater on Eastern Avenue in Highlandtown.

"I didn't know David Franks very well," said Morley. "I met him a few times when I was slinging coffee at the old Daily Grind, where the maritime museum used to be. I remember hearing his name—*that's David Franks*, someone told me—and hearing about his work. Our relationship was peripheral at best."

Franks, found dead January 2010 in his Fells Point apartment just before his 67th birthday, had an epic notoriety that led folks to whisper: *"that's David Franks."*

It might be followed by a welcome embrace or a quick exit, stage left before Footlong recognized them.

David Morley learned more about poet David Franks by filming his memorial than serving him coffee, back when the Daily Grind was a real coffee house (with the Orpheum Cinema above it) and Franks banged out tales on a Hermes 3000 typewriter beneath photos of him with in New Orleans.

"Given the number of people speaking at the event, I

opted to keep video activity to a minimum—using two cameras and shooting the entire memorial without interruption," said Morley.

"For me, the most rewarding part was being able to hear the speakers and readers over and over while I edited . . . people speaking of their love for David, his work, his antics. It's sad to sit with the knowledge that David will never touch our lives in the same way, but will now only reach us across time . . ."

Of the tributes to Franks captured by Morley, one of the most poignant was David's friend and South Broadway neighbor Glenn Moomau, author of the rock-and-roll road trip memoir, *Ted Nugent Condominium*, released in 2001 by Tom DiVenti's Apathy Press.

Here follows Moomau's remarks to the crowd of about 150 friends and admirers among the curious.

"What you just watched and heard was proof that David's art always led him in brilliant directions, in this case working with a hand bell choir and a videographer in presenting one of his compositions.

"Throughout his life he sought collaborators of all kinds for their knowledge, technical advice, and inspiration. It helped, too, if that partner had the emotional fortitude, and the patience of Job, to follow his vision.

"He worked with an oceanographer, dead poets such as John Keats, and those unfortunate people in New Orleans who called his phone by mistake. He sought the expertise of sound engineers, other poets, lovers, visual artists, at least one tug boat company, and even the drunken bar patrons who David enjoyed recording as they fought in the alley outside his apartment.

"David loved the word 'collaboration' and his work with others could be roughly categorized either as 'voluntary' or 'involuntary.' The collaborations with Keats, who is dead, and the wrong-number callers, were most definitely involuntary arrangements.

"I know that some of you aren't sure into which category your collaboration with David fell; for some, it started out voluntary, and then things, well, it went . . . ahhh . . . yeah. 'Kill you later, motherfucker,' as David often said in lieu of goodbye.

"David and I had nearly two decades of unbroken friendship precisely because I refused ALL of his offers—and they were many and constant. David's first known involuntary collaboration happened when he was a boy.

"With a tape recorder he'd gotten as a birthday present, he recorded the arguments between his parents that began after his mother discovered that his father had a girlfriend.

"He did this by holding a microphone to his bedroom wall's heating vent and capturing an echoing, distorted version of his parents' voices. Late night after late night he made these recordings—this went on for weeks!

"Screaming, crying, cursing; murmuring, beseeching, and plain cold logic. The fights got ugly. On at least one night, it got violent.

"How terrible that must have been for David, who loved and admired his parents, especially his father. But in those recordings, he would later discover one of his methods, which was the transfiguration of human voices, turning suffering into beauty, using all manner of conceptual brilliance to do so.

"All of you know that when you called him and he wasn't answering the phone, even then he was inviting your collaboration. It didn't matter if you were a friend, a bill collector, or an exasperated landlord. For at least 19 years, David's voicemail message never changed:

"'You have reached a recording of David Franks. If you would like, please leave a recording of your own.'

"When I saw David for the last time, a week before his death, he told me that he was worried about becoming isolated, having just moved to a new apartment back in Fells Point.

"This was nothing new for David: isolation was one of his recurring fears, and so it makes sense that for all of his productive life he didn't want to be that lonely boy hiding out with a tape recorder full of terrible voices, but wanted to work with others to make beautiful things.

"And what beautiful things he did make with the help, advice, love and—sometimes, lack of consent—of others!

"Some of these collaborations are still in progress. Over a decade ago, David was bemoaning to me how difficult it would be to realize his most ambitious collaboration, one that he wanted to make, essentially, with The Entire City of Baltimore.

"It doesn't matter that this project has yet to be finished: In this case, as in many others, David's reach exceeded his grasp. He didn't have enough time; he didn't enough money, and he didn't have a helicopter . . .

"Yet he still figured out a way to leave us with the project's simple and lovely 'David Franks brilliance,' captured at its moment of conception:

"Note how many actual and potential collaborations exist in these few words:

Last summer in the car on the way back from recording the magi-cicadas this happened:
  . . . suddenly .
I'm composing a piece in my head . . . of Carillons. & .
church bells . connecting one to the other.   Over tones.

Crabtown, USA

    Touching to carry a song in a ring ringing around
the entire city at dawn.
     steeple to steeple
    One song . of unity . praise . & joy—transparent &
I tell . Becky Bafford
my simple transcendent vision
      Fearfully . as such simple beauty . mostly seems
madness
     Until it's heard . but she says . "oh that's beautiful!
     I know you will do it" . & . I'm thinking . yes .
probably
    I will . . ."'

Home is where the pizzelle iron is . . .

KITCHEN OBSCURA

Cocina. Kouzina. Cuisine.
Kitchen.

Absent the bedroom —a source of much comedy and tragedy—what room in the house conjures more emotion than the kitchen?

[In bad times, or merely chaotic ones, the rooms can be one in the same. David Schearl, the child narrator of Henry Roth's monumental novel *Call It Sleep,* often slept on a cot in the kitchen of his tenement apartment.]

The kitchen can be a difficult place, particularly for picky-eater kids who must clean their plates before being excused.

AW, MOM—SHRIMP CREOLE AGAIN?

Profound conversations take place in the kitchen—scenes of break-ups and bankruptcy—and silent glances between parents over dried-out meatloaf echo across the decades to rattle the couches of shrinks.

I have often wondered which of the following scenarios would be preferable: lousy food regularly eaten by a happy family or especially good food eaten under a sad roof.

There's a fabulous scene in Stanley Tucci's 1996 movie *Big Night* in which a woman—having eaten herself to the periphery of a coma at an Italian feast—lies across the table and cries: "My mother was such a terrible cook . . ."

Mine is not—in fact she is world class—and perhaps that grounds my notions of the kitchen as a magical place.

Mom (or Grandma or Uncle Charley in a multi-generational family) stirs something at the stove and the house is perfumed with onions and cooking oil; a kid does his homework at the table (or pretends to while writing a note to a girl in his class) with a ballgame on the radio and the dishwasher running; curtains over the sink billow when a breeze wafts in.

Too romantic?

Beginning on Mother's Day 2011, I began commissioning pictures of kitchens from people across Maryland and posting them on a website called welcometobaltimorehon.com. It was called the Baltimore Kitchen: a different photo of a different kitchen from a different person every day all the way to Mother's Day 2012.

There was no method to it. I simply asked anyone who came along if they wanted in and received kitchen pics from family, friends, friends of friends and strangers along with worth-a-thousand-words-superstars like Jennifer Bishop.

Add the kids from the St. Francis of Assisi school photo club in Northeast Baltimore to the mix and you have a nine-course meal worthy of Terrence Malick.

The images confirmed my belief that the kitchen is a place where memories are forged more indelibly than a mere living room or a ridiculous man cave.

July 14: Vicki Contie's vintage B&O railroad china in Ellicott City.

July 4: An old farm house sink—deep and porcelain, the kind for canning peaches—at Cecilia Stackna's house in Lansdowne, Baltimore County.

On the days when a photographer cannot be found

Crabtown, USA

before midnight, I take shots of my grandparents' basement kitchen in the East Baltimore rowhouse where I ate Sunday dinner just about every week of my life while Grandmom and Grandpop were alive.

I love the beauty of it, the simplicity of it and the W. Eugene Smith obsessiveness of it.

Want a peek at the bounty?

Call me from the rotary on the wall across from the fridge.

NANTUCKET ISLAND

Stevens Bunker as a ship's boy.

JOSEPH CONRAD

"There was the strong bond of the sea, and also the fellowship of the craft, which no amount of enthusiasm for yachting and cruising and so on can give . . . One is only the amusement of life . . . the other is life itself."
—"Youth," Joseph Conrad, 1902

These words have stayed with Stephens Bunker for half-a-century.

Bunker, the son of a chief engineer whose career reached back to the last days of the square-riggers, first read Conrad as a scrawny wiper, not more than a ship's boy.

Though Bunker's life as a mariner is now but a memory, the idea that going to sea is a vocation in the religious sense remains with him to this day.

"Conrad's saying that the sea means something different to men in the merchant service," said Bunker, 61, proprietor of the China Sea Marine Trading Company in Portland, Maine, a business that operated on Baltimore's Thames Street waterfront for two decades. "You immediately know that he knows what he's talking about."

Born Jozef Konrad Korzeniowski in 1857—the son of Polish aristocrats living in a part of the Ukraine controlled by Russia—Conrad was orphaned as a boy.

At 16, he fled to Marseilles to avoid conscription in the Russian army. There, his shipboard apprenticeship began in the French merchant fleet. Conrad would rise to master in the British merchant service (though he only commanded one vessel), and sailed for some 20 years before coming ashore for good in 1894. He then settled in England to write full time.

Conrad died in 1924 at age 67. His life at sea—recounted in a 1906 autobiography *The Mirror of the Sea*—inspired the bulk of his literary work.

"He assumes you into that world," said Bunker, again using the language as a theologian might: taking someone from one place and transporting him to another.

No small trick for any writer, much less an expatriate writing in a language he didn't handle especially well until his early 20s.

Through *The Heart of Darkness*—said to be the most widely read short novel in English—*Lord Jim, The Nigger of the Narcissus, The Secret Sharer* and *Nostromo*, as well as scores of short stories, Conrad became a patriarch of modern fiction.

He emboldened many giants who came after him—pens as disparate as V.S. Naipaul, William Faulkner and Jorge Luis Borges—and has been enshrined as the sire of the psychological novel, the political novel and the intellectual mystery tale.

[As he filmed *Apocalypse Now* in the Philippines in 1979, Francis Ford Coppola was rarely without his battered copy of *Heart of Darkness* upon which the movie was based.]

In Conrad, said H.L. Mencken, is "something of the vastness of a natural phenomenon."

The sea itself.

Yet the sea is never still for long and the question the 21st century tide brings is this.

Crabtown, USA

Is Conrad relevant to the modern sailor?

Mariners familiar with him and devoted academics say yes. The relevance depends on who still reads Conrad in an age of short attention spans and the moving image. Finding anyone in the general population who reads Conrad—exempting ninth graders assigned *Heart of Darkness*—is no easy thing.

Though reading habits have devolved, the sea does not. Nor the challenges of loneliness, monotony and occasional danger which the sea presents to those who dare cohabitate with it.

When Captain Paul Caubo first went to sea after his graduation from the U.S. Merchant Marine Academy at Kings Point, he was not only reminded of "Youth" by Conrad, but felt like a character in the story.

"What hooked me was it was about a young man star struck by the industry, and a hundred years later it could have been my story," said Caubo, now a Chesapeake Bay pilot.

"To Bangkok! Magic name, blessed name . . . remember I was twenty and it was my first second-mate's billet," says Conrad's favorite narrator, Marlow. "The East was waiting for me."

As it awaited the rookie Caubo aboard the military sealift *USNS Harkness*, embarking on oceanographic research in the Indian Ocean.

"I sailed as third mate on the most atrocious vessel with the most atrocious contract and a crew of punks and borderline criminals," said Caubo of the trip. "But there is something powerful and romantic about this profession, and when you're young and first at sea you overlook a lot.

"I stood my watch and thought, 'Here I am! A third officer at sea! I thought it was all wonderful.'"

[Though I was reading Dickens and not Conrad, I felt

the same when I first sailed out of Baltimore right out of high school in 1976, standing a 4 to 8 morning watch, seeing the sun rise everyday over the bow of an old freighter converted to carry containers.]

Such improbable joy connected Caubo to Conrad's equally green Marlow attempting to save his own wretched vessel—this one in flames off the coast of Australia.

"The whole crew ends up in lifeboats, and he winds up commanding one of the lifeboats, thinking to himself, happily, 'Here I am, the master of my own lifeboat!'

"A hundred years later," said Caubo, "it could have been my story."

The closest Joel Hawtof gets to a seaman's life these days is kayaking past ships in Baltimore Harbor. An electrical engineer who spent a year working as a deckhand on the tug Athena along the Delaware River, Hawtof said Conrad speaks to him not as a sailor or even a man.

The author, whose masterpiece *Nostromo* is imbued with an insecurity so profound it has come to stand for the wounded spirit of the modern age, addresses the reader as simply human.

"There have been moments when reading Conrad has helped calm my anxiety, has made me feel more connected to everything," said Hawtof, explaining why Conrad endures in a way that other writers do not.

Perhaps, said Hawtof, Conrad resonates so strongly with him "because of not being proud of everything one has done in life, even when you try to do the right thing."

"Reading about Conrad's flawed protagonists in all these backwater 19th century ports," he said, "affirms that we are not alone."

None more flawed perhaps, than the central character of the Far East tale *Lord Jim*.

Crabtown, USA

This is the story of a young sailor whose momentary misgivings—in a word, cowardice –hound him for the rest of his life.

Jim is a young first mate accused of abandoning an imperiled steamship carrying a pilgrimage of 800 Muslims to Mecca and Medina. Through Jim, Conrad scrutinizes his lifelong obsession with guilt and the possibility of redemption.

Nothing else by Conrad, said the Rev. Sinclair Oubre, a Roman Catholic priest and able-bodied seaman based in Port Arthur, Texas, moved him quite so powerfully.

"What struck me was Conrad's courage in addressing the issue of innocent guilt," said Oubre.

While Jim appears to be the only officer with integrity, he is the one assigned blame.

"In light of the recent case of Captain (Wolfgang) Schroder in Mobile and the criminalization of seafarers in general, it has become even more timely," said Oubre.

Schroder, a German national, was convicted in October 2006 of negligence in the death of a Mobile, Ala., crane operator, who was fatally injured when Schroder's ship, *Zim Mexico III*, struck the pier.

After serving four months while awaiting sentencing, Schroder was released in February of 2007 and told to leave the United States or be deported.

Korzeniowski as timely as the morning headlines.

"Sailors still love a good story," said Dan Elwood, a deep sea deckhand and tugboat mate turned hospital nurse in Baltimore. "I think any seaman would love to have someone like Marlow telling them stories as long as they could have a beer while he talked."

But seamen simply don't sit around refining the art of conversation as they once did.

Oubre, who also serves as president of the Apostleship

of the Sea U.S.A., a seafarers' advocacy group, blamed the reduction of crew sizes, "the ravenous desire for overtime" and a ban on smoking in common areas for estranging sailors from one another at sea.

The end of toleration for alcohol on ships, TVs in the forecastle and quick turn-arounds in port don't help either.

"It's not like you get to stay in Africa for three weeks because they're unloading grain with shovels," said Elwood. "Sometimes you don't even get to go ashore. And anyway, what's left on the planet that's still exotic? There's not much that hasn't been ruined."

A curious seafarer might watch the 1965 film adaptation of *Lord Jim* starring Peter O'Toole, but "the chance of handed-down sea stories becoming great books by men like Conrad and Melville is becoming extinct," said Oubre.

"The great maritime tales will be lost forever and we're all going to die of loneliness."

Like many an old man on the bridge, irritability was one of Conrad's main characteristics. The gout he began experiencing as a young seaman in the Malay Archipelago did not help. He was known to pretend not to be able to hear when certain subjects were brought up in conversation.

Despite his literary accomplishments—he was offered British knighthood in 1923 and turned it down, perhaps in deference to the Polish coat-of-arms to which he was heir—Conrad seemed forever uncomfortable in a world that had not been very kind to him.

Joseph Conrad died suddenly at home on August 3, 1924, falling out of his chair and to the floor.

But he's still out there, said Bunker.

"And he'll always be out there, because he speaks to us."

The Castle in the Sand

OCEAN CITY

*"From Memorial Day to Labor Day you didn't do
anything else but work. The rule in our family was that
our women didn't have babies between Memorial Day
and Labor Day . . .."*
—Adam Lockhart Showell, Castle in the Sand hotel

"And you weren't allowed to die either . . ."
—Lauren Conner Taylor, the Santa Maria motel

T he history of the Castle in the Sand hotel
on 37th street in Ocean City reaches back more than
400 years to an Eastern Shore land grant during the
colonial reign of Benedict Calvert, a child of eight who
served as the Fourth Lord Baltimore.

It winds from the late 17th century, long before
Maryland's Worcester County was carved out of Somerset
County, down to Adam Showell, whose forebears were
among the five families who founded Ocean City not long
after the Civil War.

Showell, 55, tells stories of what used to be—some he
lived through, others he's only heard or read about—in his
office at the Castle surrounded by old maps, family
obituaries and photographs of the days when people
rented their bathing suits on the walls.

[In honor of the family's early history, Adam's sister

and former partner, the late Ann Showell Mariner, belonged to the National Society of the Colonial Dames of America. Ann died at age 66 in January, 2013.]

"Our family goes back to 1683, the land grant was north of Berlin," said Showell, now holding the reins of those who came before him. "My ancestors did very well. They became successful farmers, sending crops and lumber to Philadelphia and Baltimore."

Said a cousin, Ocean City attorney Harold "Chip" Gordy, 68, "We are merchants by birth. It's in our blood."

The Showells moved from Berlin to Ocean City in 1896. The Castle in the Sand has been the marquee business since Adam's parents—John Dale Showell III and the former Ann Lockhart, both deceased—opened the hotel in 1960.

But long before that—since ancestor Colonel Lemuel Showell [1825 to 1902] underwrote the Wicomico and Pocomoke Railroad that first brought tourists to the Maryland seashore in 1876—the family owned some of the most fabled attractions in Ocean City.

[Ocean City was founded in 1875 and incorporated in 1880. The unincorporated Worcester county town of Showell, just east of Route 113 and north of the Route 90 approach to OC, was originally known as St. Martin's, named for the nearby river.

The community was renamed Showell in honor of the colonel, believed to be the richest man in Worcester County before a reversal of fortune in the late 19th century. In 2013, Showell was home to less than 100 people.]

Most memorable of the family's beach holdings was the "Showell block" at the Boardwalk and Division Street: a big chunk of oceanfront anchored by a bathhouse (where late 19th and early 20th century bathers rented swim suits for a quarter); a salt water pool filled via a pipe extended into the surf; a duckpin bowling alley where Chip Gordy filled in sometimes as a pin setter and soda fountain.

"A lot of people didn't know how to swim back then," said Adam of folks who rode the old W&P rail for daytrips to the shore. "They'd rent a bathing suit, hold onto the rope and wade into the water . . ."

Nearby, the Showells owned an arcade and a movie theater where Adam's mother, Ann Lockhart Showell [1924 to 2010] sold tickets. She and Adam's father—a World War II marine named John Dale Showell III—were married in 1947.

Eras change distinctly about every generation or so; from the days of tentative bathers holding onto a heavy rope bolted to the boardwalk—as they did in front of the Showell beach house in the Roaring 20s—through the great storm of 1933 that cut an "inlet" between the barrier island and the mainland to create a sport fishing bonanza.

During the golden age of prosperity and development in the 1950s and '60s—the advent of the "motor hotel"—Adam Showell's parents were at the forefront of Ocean City commerce.   Upon Ann Showell's death [almost a decade after her husband], longtime friend and newspaperman John M. Purnell said: "Mrs. Showell was the last survivor from the glam era of old Ocean City . . .

"She was a glamorous and posh lady who always lived well. She was always stylishly dressed, and you never saw her in a pair of jeans unless she was gardening . . ."

In the days when the resort only operated in the summer months—some 12 short weeks during which a year's income had to be made—Ocean City's prominent families would hold end-of-the-season parties in their homes.

Young Adam and his older siblings—John Dale Showell IV and Sarah Elizabeth Showell along with Ann—

grew up in the midst of bay front soirees reminiscent of Gatsby. At their parents' West Ocean City estate, sold in 2011, they saw resplendent lawn parties of roast beef and oysters and champagne.

At one time, "John Dale" (as Adam's father was known) owned the former state yacht—118 feet, steel-hulled—*Maryland Lady*.

Now in the prime of his middle-age, Adam Showell is old enough to remember the days just before the federal government bought all 37 miles of Assateague Island in 1965; back when men from the old Ocean City families kept hunting and fishing and carousing cabins there.

"I grew up with a rowboat and then a little motor boat," said Showell of his Huckleberry Finn childhood. "I'd just go exploring around and it was a big adventure in my life when I made it across the Wire Pond to this island where I built a fort and camped out."

These days, Adam camps out in a little cottage off of Coastal Highway and 37th street, a former boarding house called the Teresita that his folks bought from George Morse in the early 1970s. There, he keeps the Showell name percolating in business deals, connected to the kin that came before him.

"People love Ocean City," he said. "Their childhoods were spent here."

When the lights came up, everyone had
moved away.

BILL JONES

This one is about Uncle Bill and pickles.

My mother's big brother—Bill Jones [1929 to 2013] of the Dillon Chiefs neighborhood sports teams in 1940s Canton—served in the Navy at the end of World War II and went on to a long career as a letter carrier for the post office.

As a young man, he worked at a waterfront pickle factory in southeast Baltimore. On the Chiefs, named for the street where he lived, Uncle Bill played second for the baseball team and ran the offense as quarterback in football. No league, no standings, no trophies.

"It was all for bragging rights," said Uncle Bill. "One kid on the team was called Joe Dumps. We never knew his real name."

There were many ethnic slurs for the different villages of immigrants in Baltimore in those days: the Polish along Broadway and Uncle Bill's Canton neighborhood near the J.S. Young licorice factory, the Italian families in Highlandtown, Jews along Lombard Street near Little Italy and Irish and Greeks mixed in with all of them.

For some reason, my uncle said, the kids who lived north of Patterson Park, where all sorts of different families lived together, were called "the snot noses." My guess is that they were poor whites with roots to the west and the south of the city.

It was an age of race-driven prudence. Or perhaps old-fashioned politeness taken to an extreme when a black laborer named Wallace hosed down the neighborhood cannery on Binney Street after it had closed for the day. Instead of walking by the neighborhood women who worked the "packing house" as they sat on the sidewalk in their lawn chairs after dinner—my grandmother Anna and her sister Francie included—Wallace kept his distance by walking in the street.

My grandmother's house at 2729 Dillon Street was tiny—just four rooms with a tacked-on kitchen making a small yard smaller by half—and Uncle Bill started taking work at a young age to make his own way. This way, he would not have to ask for anything at home, where his father drank heavily and his mother carried the family working in sweatshops.

As a teenager, before joining the Navy at 17, Uncle Bill worked at a waterfront pickle factory in southeast Baltimore. Between shifts of brining cucumbers, Bill would run up Broadway and catch a movie, sitting down in the crowd only to find, once the lights came up after the show, that everyone who'd been sitting around him had moved—he stunk of dill and vinegar.

I was thinking about Uncle Bill (who took me to my first major league baseball game in 1967, the hometown Birds vs. Yastrzemski's Red Sox) when I interviewed Anna Panzer Majka a few years back.

An uncle of Mrs. Majka's father was one of the early Panzer pickle owners. She told me as much as she could remember about what was told her about Baltimore in the days of sail.

"My grandparents said that the people who owned the old seaman's boarding house owned about eight rowhomes on the same block" along a cobblestoned street on the Fells Point waterfront.

In time, Panzer Pickles would buy those houses one by one.

Wrote Mary Zajac, a true daughter of Crabtown: "My father grew up just blocks from Panzer's pickle plant on South Ann Street in Fells Point, where the sharp, vinegary scent of pickle brine hung in the air when production was in full swing."

According to Mrs. Majka, the men who owned the seamen's boarding house were quiet and kept to themselves. Which is more than neighbors could say about the sailors who flopped there between ships.

Said Mrs. Majka's daughter, Rebecca: "My grandfather owned the Panzer Pickle business a long time ago . . . I think he owned it with his father and brothers . . . it's the only pickle business in Baltimore I was ever aware of. . ."

Turn the fan on, they'll come running

KRAMER'S POPCORN

There is a Baltimore, no doubt better than the truth of it, which only exists in memory.

While my land of the lost—east of President Street, south of Lombard—may not be yours, all is contiguous on the shifting map of vapor we call the past. And because nothing drives memory as powerfully as smell, I nominate this old-time-used-to-be for landmark status: Kramer's Golden Crisp Popcorn Shop, 3728 Eastern Avenue in the heart of the old Highlandtown retail district.

At "the popcorn store" you could buy rock candy weighed on a scale and scooped into white paper bags stamped with a picture of a woman stirring a kettle; chocolate pecan eggs (made "special" every Easter); and of course popcorn—piled fresh in the front window from kernels popped on site and glazed with a caramel that perfumed the Avenue.

By the time Thanksgiving arrived—when the soon to be December air is sharp, scents carry and the past more emotional than usual—the lure of Kramer's was irresistible.

"When business was slow, Mom would say, 'Turn the fan on . . . let'em smell it out there . . . that'll get'em in,'" remembered Dolores Kramer St. Ours, now 87.

"Mom" was the boss, the late Anna Kramer, who'd

learned the trade at the Nut House near Lexington Street downtown and a candy store at 33rd and Greenmount in Waverly. In the 1950s, at the urging of her husband—a butcher named Joe—she opened her own place a few doors away from Epstein's department store.

"The only advertising we ever did was the smell of that popcorn," said Dolores.

"The exhaust fan in the transom spread the news that a fresh batch of caramel—a confection of water, brown sugar, corn syrup, and "real" (not margarine) butter—had been whipped up in a copper cauldron over gas jets.

"I'd make up to five tubs on a Saturday," said Ray Kramer of Ocean City, Dolores's brother. "You could smell it all the way up in Patterson Park."

True to her Polish roots and Depression-era instincts, nothing went to waste.

"If there were scraps on a display plate of fudge or peanut brittle or coconut, Grandmom would come around the corner and throw it in the pot," said Robert St. Ours, Jr., Dolores's son. "If you told her it changed the taste of the corn, she just said, 'Ah, they love it!'"

And if you happened to be a Catholic nun—whether from the nearby parishes of Sacred Heart of Jesus and Our Lady of Pompei or any other—the cash register refused to ring.

"Her orders were, 'Give the sisters what they want, don't you dare take a dime from them,'" said Robert.

Kramer's closed in the late 1970s after "Miss Anna" was mugged waiting for a bus and the spinsters who owned the building—the Metzger sisters—sold to a man who doubled the rent.

The address is now home to Chicken Rico, a wildly successful Peruvian restaurant specializing in birds on the rotisserie.

Crabtown, USA

It's hard to beat the smell of spiced chicken turning slowly over an open flame. Like Miss Anna's popcorn, the scent drifts out onto the Avenue and draws people in.

Albert Prato DeFelice, musician and patriot

EASTER PARADE

"We celebrated Easter the best we could in those days. It was Depression time..."
—Albert DeFelice, eastside kid

T o m a k e i t to Easter Sunday Mass at Our Lady of Pompei Church back when FDR was in his first term and Albert DeFelice was a boy in knickers—"they would whoosh-whoosh when you walked," he remembers—the family passed synagogues and skipped through Patterson Park to get to the corner of Conkling and Claremont Streets.

[The Jewish *shuls* would have been the Anshe Kolk and Anshe Wolyn Congregation on North Chester Street or Tzemach Tzedek on East Fairmount Avenue, not that young Albert would have noticed. All he knew is that the buildings weren't temples and the kids who went there didn't eat pig feet with tomato sauce like he did.]

In time, Albert had graduated from knickers into his Sunday best, "a two dollar pair of white pants" from Barney's at the corner of Eastern Avenue and Conkling Street. By then, with a little push from Luigi—his musical, born-in-the-Old Country father—Albert joined the Pompei concert band on French horn.

"We'd march through the streets of Highlandtown playing John Philip Souza and Italian marches,"

97

remembered DeFelice. "Actually we were just walking, but we were playing marches."

Now 83 and living in Perry Hall, the only thing DeFelice recalls getting for Easter during the rough years following the stock market crash of '29 is a chocolate chicken.

For Italian families from the old Baltimore neighborhoods—and many of the post-war suburbs as that wave of immigration pushed beyond the city—the observance of Christ's resurrection isn't represented by jelly beans and marshmallow chicks.

It's all about ravioli made from scratch.

["All homemade," said DeFelice. "We never bought any food from the store."]

And somehow, said Albert's daughter Cindy, the ravioli were never more delicious than served up by her grandmother in the basement of a corner rowhouse in the 600 block of South Newkirk Street on Easter Sunday afternoon.

"Maybe it was because you enjoyed them with your entire family, all of your cousins, the whole gang," said Cindy. "We always had 25-to-30 relatives on big holidays like Easter."

Cindy DeFelice and a couple dozen of her cousins grew up in the prosperity of the early 1960s. Grandma's house— where Luigi lived with his wife, Anna Prato DeFelice once the economy improved—was at the corner of Newkirk and Fleet streets, right behind the spot where the Samos Restaurant now stands.

In Cindy's scrapbooks are black-and-white snapshots of the DeFelice cousins in their suits and dresses and bonnets lined up against the Formstone of her grandparents' home.

She remembers pet bunnies and live baby chickens in

boxes saved from new Easter shoes—the clothes not from Barneys but Dietz's on the Avenue—shoeboxes with holes poked in the top of the box for the pre-PETA chicks to chirp and breathe.

"Easter dinner was 12 noon for the first shift, mostly grandchildren. Two homemade ravioli filled the plate," said Cindy. "We still have grandma's plates with an embroidery of gold flowers around the rim."

The ravioli on the "good china" was made the day before on the kitchen table. If you have seen the movie *Il Postino* in which Philippe Noiret plays the Nobel laureate poet Pablo Neurda, you will recognize what Cindy lovingly remembers.

"She made the ravioli on her kitchen table. Made a hole in (a circle of) flour and put the eggs in the middle of that," said Cindy. "The she started mixing and kneading but she never let the eggs run out. I was a kid—amazed that she didn't use a bowl!"

The second shift of dinner, including homemade wine, was primarily the "grown-ups"—including Cindy's Aunt Phyllis, a Baltimore Colts cheerleader from the Johnny Unitas and Lenny Moore glory days—and the youngsters who sang in the choir at Holy Redeemer Chapel a few blocks away on Oldham Street.

[Closed by the Archdiocese of Baltimore in 2002, Holy Redeemer was a nearby alternative to Our Lady of Pompei for Catholic families moving east from Highlandtown toward Dundalk after the Second World War. It is now a vibrant Protestant church.]

"After dinner, the kids were shipped off to the Grand Theatre for a 35 cent movie and popcorn," said Cindy. "We'd get back to Grandma's in the late afternoon for another round of pasta and all sorts of people coming and going and then off to another relative's house for coffee and dessert."

Most of those relatives were just around the corner—or more accurately up and down the alley that runs between the 600 block of South Newkirk and Macon streets—where descendents of the Prato siblings settled to be near the streetcar that ran out to Sparrows Point and the steel mill jobs there.

Along that alley you would hear the call on Easter Morning, often from Gene DeCarlo, Sr., who married Albert's kind and gentle sister, Lola:

"Who's got an egg?
Chicken with a wooden leg!
Who's got a guinea-ghee?
Who wants to pick-a-me?"

This is the Easter yodel of Baltimore "egg-picker." Mostly kids, the pickers would roam with dyed, hard-boiled eggs and challenge others to "picking" matches. The top and bottom of an egg was "pecked" against the top and bottom of someone else's egg. If your egg had the harder shell and your opponent's egg cracked on both ends first, you took their egg.

"Grandpa Louie would fool us with a marble egg against our regular eggs," said Cindy. "He always won."

The monkeys were kept in sheds along
President Street

MONKEY ROW

We lived on President Street," said Old Man Cirelli. "There were so many organ grinders and hurdy-gurdy men on President Street that they called it Monkey Row. But I never took a monkey with me. No sir. I don't like monkeys. Bears either."

It's not Maryland crab soup if there isn't a claw in the bowl.

CRAB SOUP

The soup that Manny Anello thinks about when he wants to savor the good old days goes back to Hollins Street, the neighborhood of Mencken, St. Peter the Apostle Catholic Church and the city market where his Irish grandmother bought live blue crabs.

Two indelible memories of Anello's early 1950s childhood in southwest Baltimore are feeding sugar cubes to the a-rabber's ponies in neighborhood stables and watching his grandmother make a huge pot of crab soup.

"It's been emblazoned on my brain since I was three," said Anello, a veteran Arbutus attorney. He told family stories while enjoying a fine bowl of crab/corn chowder at a now closed joint called Larry's on the first floor of his law office.

The chowder conjured images of Anello's grandmother—Josephine Martin Cronise—at the stove in the house at 1223 West Lombard Street near South Carey. There, the extended family lived together.

Grandma [1892-to-1977] was born in Baltimore, the daughter of a B&O railroad laborer at the Mount Clare works. Anello's mother Rose, born in 1916, was the second of Josephine's four children.

Anello—born Salvatore Emanuel Anello III, a 1965 graduate of Mt. St. Joseph High School—lived in the Irish/Lithuanian/African-American neighborhood until he was 10. In those days, he was known as "Little Manny."

Though he often walked to the market with his grandmother to buy the crabs and stood by as she put together her version of the Chesapeake staple, he's only made it twice in the last 30 years.

"It's a big job, not easy to do—she made enough to fill large crab pot," said Anello. "Grandma's secret was putting in two dozen shelled female crabs cleaned and broken in half."

[Authentic Maryland crab soup is always made using whole or half crabs instead of or in addition to crab meat.

You don't see it too often these days and there is a generation who believes that if you don't get half a crab in the bowl, you have not been served crab soup. Some folks just throw in the claws and unscrupulous establishments try to pass off vegetable soup spiced with Old Bay as the real thing.]

An especially unique take using halved crabs is Frances Kitching's "Jimmy Stew," with broth the color of a tidewater inlet. It can be found in *Mrs. Kitching's Smith Island Cook Book* from Cornell Maritime Press. Miss Frances died in 2003.

To be worthy of Grandma's crab pot, said Anello: "All the vegetables had to be growing."

He meant fresh, uncooked produce from the market or roadside stand: lima beans and peas that had to be taken home and hulled; string beans in need of snipping.

"The only vegetable from a can was Maryland white corn," said Anello, taking his last spoonful of chowder and vowing, "I'm going to make it again," he said. "It's on the agenda."

BOSNIAN REFUGEES

Back in the mid-1990s, in the immediate wake of the atrocities in the Balkans, I was compelled by the blight of my Highlandtown neighborhood to offer shelter to about a dozen war refugees.

If the locals didn't appreciate a neighborhood where waves of immigrants had gotten their start, maybe victims of ethnic cleansing would feel differently. It was 1995, the year of my Bosnian Thanksgiving.

Of the people delivered to me through the Lutheran Church in 1995, a few were young single men who had been through the wars; one was a cranky middle-aged woman who the soldiers dismissed as a born malcontent and the rest were the Sadzak family.

The Sadzaks were Mom and Dad, three kids—from toddler to grade-schooler—and a young Bosnian woman in her early 20s who helped take care of the children. For several months after arriving from Montenegro, even though they had a two-story rowhouse to themselves, the entire family slept in the same room. Their nightmares had accompanied them to America.

The soldier boys lived under my roof two blocks away. We had a lot of fun and never talked about the war.

Eldin Cengic was the first to arrive—his eyes lighting up when he saw a jar of peanut butter—and before long we were double-dating a pair of International Affairs majors from Johns Hopkins University, one of them fictionalized as "Lulu" in the short story "The Flap Doodle."

Eldin was soon joined by Dzenan, also in his early 20s and a combat veteran. My cousin—David Mislak, formerly of Dundalk, the grandson of immigrant Poles—gave them $8 an hour jobs packing road salt into shipping boxes in Curtis Bay.

"It was heavy labor and they were good workers," said Mislak, a Baltimorean steeped in Crabtown lore. "They were good workers."

[Mislak's uncle—Alfred Anthony Mislak [1921 to 1960]—was killed at York Road and 43rd Street when a drunken wallpaper salesman slammed his vehicle into Mislak and another man as they tried to push a second vehicle out of a snowbank just before the bar's closed.]

Senad Sadzak, the partriach of the Ponca Street family, got work at a Greektown bakery around the corner from his house on Eastern Avenue.

We found desks so the kids could do their homework and a couple of old bicycles. A group in Upper Park Heights that resettled Russian Jews from the former Soviet Union gave full access to their stockpile of household goods.

And then Thanksgiving—my favorite holiday of the year—rolled around.

On the last Thursday of that November, a good friend of mine—a food writer whose family had come to America from Lebanon a generation before—invited the Sadzaks to her table along the Gwynns Falls.

Even though hosting the Bosnians for the most American of American holidays was "an honor," Anne said she did it more for herself than them.

Crabtown, USA

A Great Lakes Hoosier transplanted to the Chesapeake, she'd spent a half-dozen years in Crabtown but still didn't feel rooted enough for Thanksgiving to be more significant than a quiet meal with her immediate family and perhaps a friend or two.

Anne had gotten to know the Sadzaks in the previous months, in part at a Ponca Street dinner they hosted not long after moving in to show their gratitude. In time, she saw multiple similarities (minus the war) between their experience and her own. At the time, her daughter was about 5-years-old.

"I watched Daisy teach the Bosnian children English as intuitively as I did at her age for my cousins who had come over from Lebanon," said Anne, who by Thanksgiving had challenged herself to give a family she had come to love "the real deal" autumnal feast.

"I even set up a kid's table," she said. "I'd never had enough children in the house to do that before."

I don't remember what we talked about at dinner, true conversation was always difficult unless Eldin—who could translate multiple conversations at once—was around. I'm sure I tried to tell the story of the Pilgrims and the Indians in the Massachusetts colony and I know we said grace.

When the turkey was brought to table, moist and golden brown, surrounded by a bounty to hold three families for a week, Anne handed the carving knife to Senad.

"With a big smile, he set to work expertly," she remembered. "And was delighted when no one else wanted a leg, his favorite part."

I left early to work the holiday night shift on the City Desk—editing stories on the annual Bea Gaddy dinner, unfortunate motorists who'd lost their lives on local roads and, inevitably, some sort of violence, either related to the holiday or just another day of mayhem in Baltimore.

Before I did, Anne unveiled homemade pies in vintage New England Table Talk tins: pumpkin and lemon meringue.

Doling out the slices, she "looked around the table and tried to imagine what the the Sadjaks had escaped. I couldn't let my mind go there, but it was plain to see how grateful they were. I was grateful too."

Before another year had passed, all of the Bosnians I had sheltered had moved to the suburbs. By the time another 15 Thanksgiving dinners had come and gone—celebrated from Baltimore to Los Angeles—the old trucking company at the end of my street was being torn up for three-story townhouses with garages. Gentrification had come to my grandparents' neighborhood.

. . . and Tom Waits is the only voice on the radio

DIVORCE DECREE

The most surprising thing about getting divorced is the degree to which—absent that most perishable of goods, romance, and its favored hostage, sexual fidelity—my ex-wife and I have continued to fulfill our wedding vows.

This is the long road of love, work and friendship that we continue to travel nearly three decades after calling it quits.

Quits—what does that mean?

If you've got kids and you love 'em, it's never quits. I imagine that even the Daddy-Os who hit the road suffer long and tortured nights of exile in a small world where it's always raining and Tom Waits is the only voice on the radio.

My marriage lasted eight years, an exact parallel to the Reagan Administration. Its dissolution in late 1988 was not something I wanted, despite being able to admit now what I could not articulate when I received the sacrament at age 22: I didn't want to be married.

What I really wanted was for Deborah to be married to me.

She was the one who proposed, during a long night of mutual confession in a ratty apartment at the corner of Preston and St. Paul streets. I said OK—pronounced "GERONIMO!"—and the next day we bought a tiny ruby on Howard Street, running down to the tugboats on South Broadway to tell my old man the news.

The ring now lays in a Los Angeles jewelry box owned by Amelia, the daughter born to us within a year of a reception at the Polish National Alliance on Eastern Avenue.

For all the problems that did not reveal themselves until we were flailing around in the deep end of the pool, I believed that we would stay together forever.

Yeah, the trees had grown crooked—the limbs all twisted together, screaming out for pruning—but they'd been planted side-by-side and the roots went deep. Even during the worst of it, I remember thinking: This must just be the way it is.

About a year after saying she thought we should separate—a suggestion I thought was forgotten when she didn't bring it up again—my wife asked me to meet her for lunch at the Women's Industrial Exchange on Charles Street and quietly announced over ice cream that she was through.

And, with the German resolve of her father displacing the Italian passion of her mother, she would not be moved.

The end—energy not destroyed, but changed—was accompanied by all of the heartache and rancor due a couple of kids who'd met at 18, went steady all through Jesuit college, got married in the school chapel upon graduation and then had three children in four years.

She got the house and the mortgage; the newer of the two cars—a gray Chevy wagon; and the monthly payments that went with it—and some peace of mind.

I moved in with my grandfather about 15 minutes away on Macon Street, took the roll-top desk that had been a gift from her in better times, my vast collection of

Johnny Winter records and a hot-air popcorn machine we'd gotten as a wedding present and never used. We never fought over custody of the children—it was clear that our problems were with one another—and signed very simple paperwork without giving what little money we had to attorneys.

About six years into the divorce, after each of us had done hard work on the things we did not like about ourselves, we dated for the better part of a year without telling the kids what was going on.

It was sort of like exploratory surgery: not life-threatening, but not exactly fun.

Around the facade of "dates"—going to hear the remnants of The Band at the old Hammerjacks in Camden Yards, seeing a crappy Roman Polanski movie at the Charles—we explained ourselves to one another, the selves we didn't understand as 20-somethings surfing the big waves of marriage.

The labor of it—stripped of the carbonation of going out with someone new—reminded me of something John Updike had written: It takes tenfold the energy to woo a reluctant wife than to charm a willing girl.

Intrigue, adrenaline, lust—everything that had launched us a quarter-century ago—was not there this time. Instead of jumping off the cliff, we forded the river together, making it to the other side not as lovers but something akin to first cousins.

Judaic law provides a formula—the *kol nidre*—by which one can be released from vows or promises that could not be kept. It is part of the annual Yom Kippur tradition and addresses promises made between a human being and the Creator.

For release from promises made to others, absolution must be granted by the person to whom the promise was made.

Rafael Alvarez

Long before my ex and I tested the waters of reconciliation, I made amends—and had them accepted—for my part in the mess that our marriage became. A year or so after we had dated as ex-spouses, I received the same from her.

Judaism has a second, related ritual—the *hatarat nedarim*—in which the penitent acknowledges that if he'd known he would be unable to fulfill the commitment, he would never have made it in the first place.

That's what I'm talking about.

Neither my ex nor I have remarried. With two of our children away at college and the one with the ruby ring on her own in Manhattan, we have begun taking family vacations again, sharing a week together down the ocean each summer and celebrating a handful of holidays and birthdays, complete with the ex-mothers-in-law.

Sometimes I think the universe brought us together just long enough for our three kids to land on planet Earth. And thus, when each of us is so often asked why we don't get back together again, the response is pretty much the same.

Are you out of your mind?

It was never this good.

Johnny Depp as Baltimore "drape" in John
Waters' film, *Cry-Baby*.

DUCKTAIL DRAPE

A drape was a Baltimore bad-ass from the 1950s who wore pegged pants so tight some had zippers in the cuffs. Shirts came in colors previously reserved for pimps and carnivals. Shoes had Cuban heels and if a drape turned up the collar on his corduroy sport coat, the pattern underneath could be leopard. Unless it was zebra.

A drape had grease in his hair—a cresting pompadour in front, the double wave of a mallard's rear-end in back—and possibly a knife in his pocket. A drape was not a square, knowing better than he knew his homework that Pat Boone was not worthy of the sweat on Little Richard's brow.

A drape was my uncle, Victor "Boopie" Alvarez.

"I had a pair of blue pants with buttons up the side and a yellow jacket. I'd buy all my outfits at Tru Fit on Eastern Avenue without my mother and father knowing it," said Victor, now 80 and living in Cambridge, a million miles away from the days of hanging at the Arundel ice cream parlor near the Patterson movies.

Uncle Vic would leave the house—627 South Macon Street near the Highlandtown epicenter of the drape scene—in dungarees and a t-shirt, his cool daddy clothes in a bag. Then he'd go to whatever house the party was at and change in the bathroom.

Rafael Alvarez

"It was a guy thing," said Uncle Vic. "And the girls loved it."

His then girlfriend and future wife—the former Claire Weigman of South Clinton Street and Sacred Heart of Jesus—was a poodle skirt goodie-two-shoes who fell under Boopie's sway at the Arundel.

A mixed-marriage: a drape and a square.

Brando drapes and Joe College squares are prominent in the John Waters's 1990 film *Cry Baby*, in which Johnny Depp—naturally—plays a drape.

Pete Genovese, the son of immigrants, now 70—was old enough to have been part of the scene before it faded. He once asked Waters if the Highlandtown boys were the true Kings of the Drapes.

"No contest," answered the fabled director.

Genovese also shopped at Tru Fit—which catered to musicians as well as kids hanging on the corner—and remembers that his "best pair of pants had a seam below the pockets on each side, inset with pink.

"They were pegged to a size where I could get my foot through if I pointed them down when dressing, other guys had zippers," said Genovese, who studied his way out of the old neighborhood to become a college English teacher and a writer now retired in St. Louis.

Pete's running buddy back in the day was the late Andy Malusa, a sock-hop crooner who performed under the name Tony Verna. Andy cut a 45 rpm called "Happy Go Lucky Feeling," and Pete—his lifelong friend until Andy passed in 2006—did his best to promote it.

In a world of street toughs, Pete and Andy were good guys, easy-going unless pushed. But they too dressed the part of the delinquent.

"My favorite shirt was also bought at Tru-Fit," remembered Genovese. "It was pink with a lace-up front.

The black lace was like a thick shoelace that went across the front, Wild West style."

The gunslingers of Highlandtown, looking for girls and trouble from Little Italy to Dundalk.

Like many an Italian back in the day—like the father of rock star Frank Zappa—Genovese's father was a barber, operating a shop at 234 South Highland Avenue.

[Zappa, who left Baltimore with his family at age 12 for the Antelope Desert appropriated the drape look in California. The high school portrait of the composer on the back of the 1968 LP *Cruisin' With Ruben & the Jets* bears a striking resemblance to my Uncle Victor, right down to the Bill Haley spit curl.]

"Most drapes wore the duck's ass hair cut but since my old man was a barber, I wasn't allowed such fashion statements," said Genovese. "He did give the haircuts to others, though it always came with a lecture guaranteed to cost him repeat business."

In time, it didn't matter.

"Once we went off with the girls we'd wind up marrying we didn't hang together like we used to," said Uncle Victor. "It all dissipated."

Though you can still see a pompadour on a senior citizen lucky enough to have hair, the drapes were pretty much gone by the early 1960s. And then four brash Liverpudlians made their way across the pond with bangs, guitars and imitations of Little Richard's white woman scream that no self-respecting drape would dare.

That's when barbers really began jumping off of buildings.

It's not because they are Catholic, it's
because *we* are . . .

CATHOLIC EDUCATION

About 50 years ago, at the height of Beatlemania, I attended first grade at St. Clement I Catholic School in what some folks call Lansdowne and others know as Halethorpe.

Delia Dowling, a School Sister of Notre Dame fighting the good fight along Hollins Ferry Road with grace and grammar, just calls it Baltimore.

After second grade, my family moved a few miles south to the more prosperous suburb of Linthicum—once Anne Arundel County farmland where my Polish grandparents picked beans and strawberries—and I never set foot in a St. Clement classroom again.

Until earlier this year. On a cold, sunny afternoon, I was the guest of Sister Delia, who wanted to show a reporter how the parish school—closed in 2003—had been reborn as a middle school for girls: The Sisters Academy of Baltimore.

Founded by women from four Catholic religious orders—the Sisters of Bon Secours, Sisters of Mercy and the Sisters of Notre Dame de Namur in addition to SSND—the school is now in its 11th year.

Independent of the Archdiocese of Baltimore, Sisters Academy represents the best of American Catholicism and the communities of religious women who anchor the faith in zip codes abandoned by almost everyone else.

Declaring that the school exists not because their students are Catholic (most of them are not) but because *they* are Catholic, the Sisters are fiercely committed to children being left behind as the middle class continues to erode and the working class is left to scurry for crumbs.

About to be accredited by the Association of Independent Maryland Schools, Sisters Academy serves some 90 girls in grades 5 through 8 from all backgrounds, many of them African-American and Hispanic.

The good sisters are too diplomatic to say these adolescents deserve a better route to adulthood (mind, body and soul) than the ones offered by most public schools in Southwest Baltimore. But they are quick to point out that 100 percent of their first three graduating classes earned a high school diploma. Of those, more than 90 percent have entered college.

It doesn't cost a dime for the low-income families fortunate enough to have their daughter accepted after a thorough application process, which includes a three week summer program where candidates are evaluated.

I asked my parents if they remembered what it cost to send me to St. Clement when we lived on Daisy Avenue when Dad worked a union job on the Fells Point tugboats in the midst of Lyndon Johnson's Great Society.

Digging into a bureau drawer, Mom pulled out a strange notebook contraption. The size of a pocket calendar and bound with a spiral of old school plastic, it held brown envelopes stamped with "BUDGET ENVELOPE: EXPENSE FOR."

Below that—in cursive handwriting Mom learned during World War II at St. Casimir parochial school in Canton—was the name of each weekly expense, from milk and eggs to the telephone bill and cigarettes. It seems to be financial training wheels for the new housewife.

Crabtown, USA

Their house payment (a "single home," a step up from the city rowhouses in which they were born) was $18.50 a week, three bucks was put away for "heat" each week and the *News-American* "paper boy" got $1.15 a week.

But no budget envelope for the Catholic education they reckoned would propel me and my brothers further up the ladder; only that, said Mom, "it wasn't free."

No matter. Like my diplomas from Mt. St. Joseph High School and Loyola College of Maryland, it can't be taken from me. Just as it is unlikely treasure for the growing alumni of the Sisters Academy.

When I asked Sr. Debra Liesen, the principal and also SSND, why families weren't lined up around the block trying to enroll their children, she said that the school remained something of a secret.

Thus my invitation to re-visit the site of my First Holy Communion at 139 First Avenue and spread word about the Academy's 2015 fundraiser at Montgomery Park in celebration of their first ten years.

"We now have results," said Sister Delia, the school president, referencing graduates who have gone on to private high schools, public prep schools like Western High School (Mayor Stephanie's alma mater) and college.

Academy graduates include Danielle Hipkins who graduated from the Catholic High School of Baltimore and is now a junior at Notre Dame of Maryland.

"We want to increase our name recognition and expand our circle of friends," said Sister Delia, noting that a very special group of friends sponsor a student to the tune of $6,000 a year throughout the four years they are at Sisters Academy.

As Mom might say, that's a lot of butter and egg moolah.

There are many aspects of the education provided at

Sisters Academy—spiritual growth, outreach to others, a "girl by girl" approach to transforming the beleaguered City of Baltimore—that is hard to put a price on.

One of them would be especially appreciated by my mother, who spent much of my childhood vacuuming *behind* the sofa even though I often pointed out that nobody looks back there.

"All of the girls have chores," said Sister Delia. "So they can appreciate cleanliness and beauty."

ABE SHERMAN

Abe Sherman was a legendary Baltimore news seller, born in 1898 and died almost 90 years later. He was known for carrying newspapers from around the world, his service in both world wars [volunteering as a 43-year-old enlisted man in the Good War and the oldest sergeant to storm Normandy] and throwing people out of his store if they browsed too long or he didn't like the way they looked.

"I did a feature on Abe for the *Baltimore Business Journal* about 30 years ago," said William F. "Bill" Zorzi, Jr. "He was only nice to me because he knew and liked my father."

And that's the way the duckpins scatter in Crabtown.

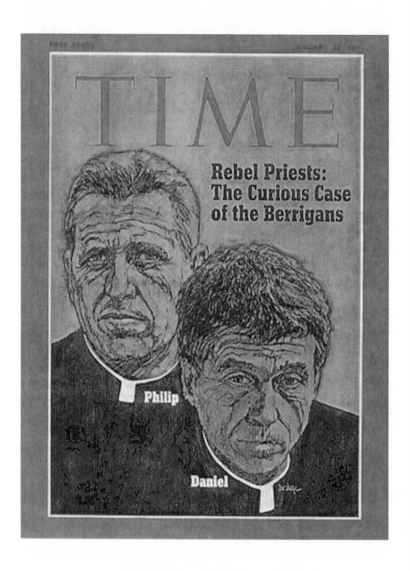

TIME Magazine, 1971

PHILIP BERRIGAN

"I die with the conviction, held since 1968 and Catonsville, that nuclear weapons are the scourge of the Earth; to mine for them, manufacture them, deploy them, use them, is a curse against God, the human family, and the Earth itself . . ."

—Philip Berrigan, 1923 to 2002

It took me six years to write *A People's History of the Archdiocese of Baltimore*, commissioned by William Cardinal Keeler, the 14th archbishop of the Premier See of the United States.

In 2001, having left the City Desk of the *Baltimore Sun* after 23 years of chasing news and odd ducks—the kind of rare, half-baked fowl native to the Patapsco region—the phone rang.

It was Carol "Sue" Abromaitis, the pride of old Hampden and my Loyola College English professor, calling with a pitch.

Was I interested in writing a history of the Archdiocese of Baltimore?

At the time, I was hanging in the Seafarers International Union hiring hall on Essex Street in Canton waiting for a ship. Yes, I was interested.

Over the next half-dozen years, I wrote the book at sea, I wrote it in Los Angeles and Ocean City, Maryland and many a McDonalds in the 3,000 miles between cross-country road trips.

Readers seemed to like it, especially those who learned things about their grandparents and those who discovered that Beatle George Harrison visited the then brand-new Mercy High School on Northern Parkway during the Fab Four's '64 visit to Baltimore.

But the publisher, a Frenchman from Strasbourg who made his living selling Catholic books and calendars and postcards around the world, was angry that it took so long. According to his business model, I screwed up sales.

When the book finally appeared, with the help of literary foot soldiers Rosalia Scalia and the photographer Kirsten Beckerman, two things were missing:

1. My name on the cover, which I am convinced the Frenchmen spitefully omitted.

2. The chapter on Philip Berrigan, a World War II veteran who—not unlike fellow soldier Kurt Vonnegut—became one of the nation's vital voices for peace, spending years in jail for various and ingenious protests.

The long, braided vignettes about Berrigan—who with his brother Daniel was one of the Catonsville Nine: Roman Catholic antiwar activists who destroyed draft records during Vietnam—accompanied stories on St. Peter Claver Church in West Baltimore.

The Berrigans were on the FBI's Ten Most Wanted Fugitives list during the 1970s for committing acts of vandalism against the government: burning and pouring blood on draft records.

Phil's privilege to function as a Roman Catholic priest were taken away by Rome in 1973 and from that point on, his post-clerical ministry was a righteous thorn in the side of the mainstream death machine.

Crabtown, USA

My profile of the former Josephite—anchored by an account of his death and funeral—was deemed inappropriate for a history sold in archdiocesan parishes. Because Keeler was signing the checks (and thus calling the shots, he even gave notes on grammatical lapses) I complied.

You don't forget a man like Philip Berrigan—or the shadow he casts on your own journey as a believer.

I was reminded of the lost Berrigan chapter while appearing as a Spanish conquistador in a production of *Voices of a People's History*, a play based on the work of Howard Zinn at the Patterson Theater in Highlandtown.

I played Bartolomé de las Casas, a 16th-century Dominican priest from my ancestral Iberia. In the wings after leaving the stage as Bartolomé—known as the father of anti-imperialism because of his witness to atrocities committed by his countrymen—I was moved by Mama Kay Lawal-Muhammed's portrayal of Cindy Sheehan.

[Sheehan, the best known antiwar activist of the first decade in the 21st century, went public after her soldier son Casey was killed in Iraq 2004.

"I told him not to go," she said. A fierce critic of George W. Bush—whose perceived cheerful callousness to the carnage enraged her—Sheehan lost a bid for Congress in 2008.]

On stage in Highlandtown, Mama Kay gave powerful voice to Sheehan's indictment of perverse logic: that it is necessary to send more young men and women to die in futile wars so those who died before them will not have been lost in vain.

And in that moment decided to dust off the tribute to Phil Berrigan, who made Baltimore his home from the 1960s until his death at age 79 in 2002.

This is it.

━━━∽∼∾━━━

Philip Berrigan was most closely associated with two Baltimore institutions: the Jonah House antiwar community, founded in 1973 with his wife, Liz McAllister; and St. Peter Claver parish, 1546 North Fremont Avenue in West Baltimore.

[Established in 1888 for African-American Catholics, St. Peter Claver was named for a Spanish Jesuit (1581-1654) who fought for and ministered to black slaves in the West Indies.]

"Berrigan was an associate pastor here during the time of the Catonsville Nine," said the Rev. Joseph Del Vecchio, pastor of St. Peter Claver at the time of Berrigan's death.

The May 1968 raid on the Catonsville draft board made world news and celebrity outlaws—in the resistance mold of Dorothy Day—of Phil and his brother Daniel, a Jesuit priest who turned 94 in 2015.

[Daniel Berrigan and Zinn landed in Hanoi in 1968 as representatives of the antiwar movement to welcome three captured American airmen released by the North Vietnamese government. Daniel's 1987 autobiography is *To Dwell in Peace*.]

The faces of Philip and Daniel and the headline—"Rebel Priests: The Curious Case of the Berrigans"—made the cover of TIME magazine in January 1971.

"I was the traffic cop on the altar for [Berrigan's] funeral Mass because there were so many people who wanted to honor him," said Del Vecchio. "It was an amazing day."

Daniel celebrated his brother's Mass of Christian Burial on Dec. 9, 2002, three days after Phil's death from liver and kidney cancer. The service drew

St. Peter Claver Church, Baltimore

hundreds of mourners, overflowing to the street, to St. Peter Claver.

Vincent Gibbons was one of Phil Berrigan's jailers. After the funeral, the former warden—now deceased—wrote to friends and associates to share his pride that day in being a member of the Catholic faith.

"What an awesome assemblage of deeply committed souls still determined to disrupt the political war machine," said Gibbons, who marched in Memphis in the "garbage man's strike" the weekend of Dr. Martin Luther King's murder and tended to wounded rioters in the chaos that followed King's assassination.

"The church was overflowing and flooded with the wonderful spirit of Phil," said Gibbons. "The procession from Jonah House to the church was much like an ancient Christian pilgrimage."

Gibbons later told this story from his days as warden at Lorton, where he worked from 1976 to his retirement in 1996.

"One night I was advised by the director that I had a 'celebrity' coming [into the prison population] and to be on alert for trouble," he remembered. "When I was told he was [Phil] Berrigan, I released a huge smile. Fortunately I was on the telephone so my reaction could not be seen."

Gibbons was raised in a strict Irish-Catholic home in upstate New York and attended Catholic schools through his second year of college.

He had a grandmother who was a third-degree Franciscan (a lay order); two of his aunts were Sisters of the Holy Name; and a family friend close enough to be considered an uncle was a Jesuit priest.

Gibbons's views on the ways of the world—and what he came to see as Christian hypocrisy in the house where he grew up—began changing in the early sixties when he began reading widely about racial injustice, marched in demonstrations and started to work for voter registration.

"I was filled with the zeal," he said, "of a soul committed to righting wrong."

This good soul was especially anxious to make the acquaintance of spiritual kin—Berrigan—and did so the following day in the prison yard.

"Over the next several months we would accidentally 'bump into each other' and talk about the courts, the criminal injustice system and the ratio of black inmates to white," said Gibbons. "He had lived with that fact in each prison where he was incarcerated."

One morning before dawn, Gibbons was awakened by a call from the Lorton shift commander reporting a problem.

"Phil had to be transported to D.C. General Hospital for treatment of severe abscesses on his legs, yet refused to cooperate with the staff," said Gibbons.

Berrigan balked at wearing leg shackles, which, policy held, were standard—along with handcuffs—for all movement of prisoners outside the walls. Gibbons said he'd be over right away.

Entering Berrigan's room, he instinctively knelt down and asked to look at the injured leg.

"With that I gently pulled up his pajama pant leg," said Gibbons. "It stuck a bit from the oozing of the sores, and I winced at the discomfort I believed I must be causing. It was a hell of a sight. He never flinched."

A hospital was necessary but Berrigan refused the shackles because of the severe pain they caused his wounds and he didn't want to wait in an emergency room with them on.

In the past, Gibbons had seen corpses removed from

the prison in shackles in order to comply with regulations, proposed wrapping Berrigan's ankles with strips of towel. Then he widened the shackles to their loosest notch to be placed over the towels.

"Some prison adventures have good outcomes," remembered Gibbons not long before his own death at age 58 in early 2004.

———

Philip Berrigan was born on the Minnesota Iron Range in 1923 and served as an artillery officer in Europe during World War II. A decade after Hiroshima, he was ordained as a Josephite, the order that ministers to the poor—primarily black—of America's inner-cities.

So maddening could that ministry be—along with the world at large, which Berrigan apparently did not wear as a loose garment—that Phil once asked Willa Bickham of the Viva House Catholic Worker in West Baltimore to make a banner for St. Peter Claver.

It read: "The sting of death is all around us . . . O Christ, where is your victory?"

Brendan Walsh—husband of Bickham, co-founder with her in 1968 of Viva House, and the man chosen to give voice to Howard Zinn at the Patterson just before Thanksgiving 2009—said this at Berrigan's funeral:

"Philip Berrigan was a friend to all the poor of Baltimore City, as well as to all the people of the world who are bombed and scattered, who are starved, trampled upon, imprisoned, tortured, humiliated, scoffed at, dismissed as nobodies.

"He was that rare combination where word and deed were one. Always. Everywhere. Steadfast. Rock solid. Hopeful. One in a million. He was that tree standing by the water that would not be moved."

The aggregate of Berrigan's jail time came to about 11 years. He was briefly a fugitive in 1970 when appeals on his conviction for the Catonsville Nine action failed.

After the end of the Vietnam War in 1975, he began to focus on weapons of mass destruction and U.S. nuclear policy.

In September 1980, Berrigan and seven others poured blood on warheads—as well as banging on them with hammers—at a General Electric nuclear missile plant in King Of Prussia, Pa.

They were charged with conspiracy, burglary and "criminal mischief," in the first of a series of anti-nuclear actions that became known as the Plowshares Movement.

Berrigan wrote, lectured, and taught extensively. His six published books include *The Lamb's War*, an autobiography.

In December 2001, he was released from prison in Elkton, Ohio after nearly a year in lock-up for his final action with Plowshares.

In an essay called "The Trial of Depleted Uranium," written a few years before his death, Berrigan wrote: "The volume of silence over these hellish weapons is surreal, numbing, stupefying. How to explain it?

"Certainly, in their 55-year love affair with the bomb, Americans have not measured the cost of this idolatry: spiritual numbing, social denial, moral paralysis . . . a $19 trillion price tag since 1940 for past, present, and future wars reveals our addiction to war and bloodshed."

And quoted his Lord and Savior: "Where your treasure is, there will your heart be also . . ."

Early one morning, a wicker basket of three
or four eggs in hand . . .

COUNTING CHICKENS

I n *The Beans* of Egypt, Maine—Carolyn Chute's classic narrative of rural poverty—chickens abound.

"... *the layin' hens and green-tailed gamecock feed on the fish guts Beal [Bean] slings into the grass ...*"

The Sunderland fowl of Wittman on Harris Creek just south of St. Michaels do not sup on the gelatinous viscera of fish.

Shiny black Ike (he *do* crow for day) reigns as cock of the walk with Otis, his smaller, nearly identical brother, second in command.

The boys were named for Monsignors Turner and Redding respectively. These soul brothers and the ten hens they service—including a fashionably gray "Appaloosa"—feast on golden cupfuls of cracked corn and ebony sunflower seeds.

Their water is changed twice a day and they roost in a house of glass and wood from which eggs can be gathered without the farmer having to squeeze inside. For the last two weeks of January 2015, I was that farmer, a rookie chicken man collecting 60 eggs on the morning and evening shifts.

The Sunderlands—the former Valerie Kontos, an artist from Baltimore's Greektown neighborhood and husband Truitt, a deep sea chief engineer teaching at the Calhoon

School on the Shore—were far away, helping friends take a sailboat through the Panama Canal.

According to Valerie's sea journal, they were ". . . transported back in time at a traditional *guna yala* village . . . people four foot tall living in thatched roof huts with dirt floors, sleeping hammocks, tribal chieftains," while I savored the best of what the Eastern Shore has symbolized for centuries.

Off the northeast tip of Panama, natives in dugout canoes approached the Sunderland's vessel with fish and lobster and fresh fruit for sale. Some 4,200 miles away, off of Marshall Lane, I steadily amassed brown and white eggs—smeared with chicken poop, still warm from the hen—more eggs than any one man this side of Cool Hand Luke could consume.

And it was oh-so-serene and beautiful, with one moment in particular enchanting to the point of transcendence.

Early one morning, a wicker basket of three or four eggs in hand, I was leaving the "Coop de Ville" (as Tru calls the mobile hen house he constructed) and headed for the big house, daydreaming out past the pier into Harris Creek.

[From that pier this summer, crabs will be caught using the "chicken-necker" method detailed in William Warner's *Beautiful Swimmers*, the 1977 Pulitzer winner for non-fiction.]

As I stood, a light and steady snow began to fall through the pines as a Flying V of geese passed through gray skies, honking like a flock of old men clearing their sinuses in the morning. It was a moment of stillness and beauty, a lifetime of fleeting clarity in every snowflake upon the Shore.

And, like most *satori*, it was fleeting. The geese

disappeared downriver and I trudged up to the kitchen—
Chute's *Beans* next to a knife and fork on the table—where
the spirit gave way to the animal.

Cracking a couple of eggs, I fried up half-a-pound of
Esskay bacon and thanked the God stirring just outside
the window for having the good sense to know how good
I have it.

ELLSBERRY BROTHERS

The Sip & Bite has long been a place to conduct business—serious business, breakfast for dinner business and monkey business.

In March of 2001, the inventive Ellsberry brothers of Baltimore (John and Richard) sat down in a booth at George Vasiliades's hot roast beef emporium at the corner of Boston and Van Lill to chart their family tree on a sheet of loose leaf.

The project had its roots in an off-hand comment the Ellsberry's father made one night in Ocean City when the boys were teenagers.

The old man said, "Did you know that your mother's father was kicked out of the United States when she was a little girl and sent back to Russia?"

And all of a sudden, said Richard, "I had an interest in my family . . . [but] we don't have much more information than orphans because someone didn't think we should know . . ."

STREET DRUNKS

On June 30, 1968, it was a crime to be intoxicated on the streets of Maryland. The formal charge was "found drunk."

The following day, public drunkenness became a medical problem and the Old Line State the first in the nation to codify it as such.

The headline in the Baltimore *Evening Sun* read: "Drunkenness Becomes Health Issue in Maryland starting July 1."

Late in his career, the pioneering Baltimore alcoholism researcher Dr. Max Weisman [1912 to 2000] put it this way.

"Drinking . . . is not the cause of alcoholism, no more than eating sugar is the cause of diabetes. Often, society doesn't separate its attitudes toward drinking, drunkenness and the disease of alcoholism."

With the enactment of the landmark "Comprehensive Intoxication and Alcoholism Control Act"—which immediately became a national model—cops were no longer tossing winos, rumpots and wet brains in the drunk tank.

The legislation stated that inebriates "either incapacitated or whose health is in immediate danger" must be taken to a hospital or detoxification facility.

Now that alcoholics were sick people and not criminals

they were being dumped at hospital emergency rooms. Once there, no one knew what to do with them.

"The medical profession was both prejudiced and ignorant when it came to alcoholism," said retired anesthesiologist Georgina Y. Goodwin [1925 to 2012].

A state survey from the time of the law's passage indicated that less than half of the general hospitals in Maryland would admit a patient with the primary diagnosis of alcoholism.

And the typical nursing staff was not prepared to handle a patient going into delirium tremens.

Thus were planted the seeds of the Tuerk House, Maryland's first public treatment center for alcoholism.

And Wendy Maters—an expatriate nurse who made a deal with God as a teenager to help "those most in need" if she were saved while floundering in the English Channel—was there when they were sown.

"There was no poorer, sick person in the world to me than these alcoholics," said Maters, who ran the University of Maryland emergency room, one of three ERs charged with figuring out the best way to treat alcoholics under the new law.

[The other two were at Johns Hopkins Hospital and the now defunct Provident Hospital in West Baltimore.]

Before Tuerk House?

"Alcoholics were badly treated back then because they were [considered] the dregs of society," said Maters. "The best we could do for a drunk was to "give them [doses] of paraldehyde.

"One for now to take care of the shakes, one for later and send them out the door."

In the immediate wake of the new legislation?

"You couldn't lock people up anymore just for being drunk," said Maters. "They were all being brought to the

ER, and I started thinking, 'All of our stretchers will be used for drunks and there won't be room for anyone else.'

"The first two counselors I hired would come in at night and take [the drunks] to the dining room for a cup of coffee before the bus came to take them to the state hospital."

Others, including the visionary Isadore Tuerk—for whom the project was named, then commissioner of the Maryland State Department of Health and Mental Hygiene—had a better idea.

"They thought there should be a place for alcoholics to detox instead of sending all of them to the state hospital," said Maters.

What was the hive of "let's-get'em-sober" recovery like in the early days of the Tuerk House?

"Talk about a conglomeration of psychiatrists, recovering alcoholics and lawyers!" marveled Maters.

Soon, counselors began noting generational patterns not immediately visible to the untrained eye.

"We learned a lot . . . we began [understanding] the problems facing children of alcoholics, that there was something hereditary involved."

The work of healing the alcoholic was much bigger— vast and circular and baffling in ways that did not hew to predictable arcs—than anyone realized.

"We weren't just treating alcoholics," said Maters. "We were trying to teach doctors how alcoholics should be treated."

It started with five beds in a derelict rowhouse in a rough part of town that has only gotten rougher as the epidemic of addiction continues to ravage Baltimore and large swaths of the nation.

Thousands of recoveries, many more disappointments, an encyclopedia's worth of stories and a handful of miracles have passed since then.

The facility is now established in a former hospital with a fiscal, 2011 operating budget of $4 million. It occupies a building on the grounds of the old West Baltimore General Hospital on Ashburton Street—later Lutheran Hospital, known as Liberty Medical Center at the time of its demise in 1989.

[Originally, the structure was part of a late 19th century campus known as the Hebrew Orphan Asylum.]

The main facility and its various agencies—including a pair of halfway houses named for major figures in early recovery work in Baltimore and a third in Howard County—serve a rotating population of about 300 addicts and alcoholics.

Annually, some 1,200 clients were entering Tuerk House for treatment in the first years of the 21st century.

The folks who wash up at the door have typically run out of options and sometimes have been through tonier rehabs and relapsed in their descent.

Presumably, they arrive with the desire to arrest and treat their disease. Some are merely trying to stay a step ahead of their probation officers or other authorities.

But many have sincerely—and often tragically—come to the end of the line and want help.

"I called someone and said I needed help," said Bobby Marinelli, a city high school teacher who has been in recovery since 1988. "He made a call and that person made a call and there was a bed for me at Tuerk House."

Diabetics need insulin, heart patients with clogged arteries undergo by-pass surgery and a chronic alcoholic or addict—absent a miracle—needs a clean bed in a safe environment in which to begin the long road back to a life worth living.

Crabtown, USA

In the City of Baltimore—where the population of alcoholics and addicts hovers around 65,000, some 10 percent of all residents—detox beds for the uninsured can be scarce.

In any given week, according to the Baltimore Substance Abuse Systems organization—the substance abuse care and prevention authority for the city—only about 7,200 residents are in treatment.

"Tuerk House is at the epicenter of the heroin epidemic in the United States," said Elliott Driscoll, executive director of the program from 2009 to early 2011.

The facility is also in the geographic heart of the scourge, at least on the Westside of town Driscoll noted that Maryland is typically ranked third in the nation in per capita admissions to hospitals for heroin abuse.

"By far," he said, "Baltimore is the most concentrated area of use in the state."

For fiscal 2012, Tuerk House had $4.3 million with which to put as many fingers in the dike against the flood of addiction as possible.

This was not the landscape of recovery funding when Wendy Maters was charged with beginning a "quarter-way" house to bridge an alcoholic's journey from the street to a halfway house and, hopefully, toward a useful life.

In 1969, when Maters began accepting patients for the fledgling program (strictly male in the early years), she had "five dollars per patient per day" to spend on their care. The per diem came through the Department of Social Services.

Audrey Evans, the University Hospital director of nutrition at the time, planned 14-day menus for the early residents—said to be high in protein and certainly packed with calories to put on weight lost to booze—for $1.50 per patient per day.

The five bucks for food and miscellaneous—everything from toothbrushes to shoelaces—was complemented by a state grant of about $45,000 earmarked to pay the salaries of a handful of counselors.

To make that money go further, the University of Maryland kept Maters on its payroll even though she was no longer supervising the emergency room there.

Maters was picked to develop the University Hospital program by the late Dr. Russell R. Monroe, then chairman of the department of psychiatry at the University of Maryland, School of Medicine.

She didn't have much to start with, including an avowed ignorance of alcoholism beyond knowing when someone's liver was shot, when she was thrown on the front lines.

But she had a secret weapon upon which no one could put a price: a dynamo from Hampden named Walter Criddle.

A Korean War tank commando, Criddle owned a used-tire store and was known to his sober buddies—sometimes affectionately and sometimes not—as "the fat flying squirrel."

["For a big man, Walter was light on his feet," said Ed Garbus, a friend who credits Criddle with helping him get sober. "Walter could dance."]

Criddle and Maters: a match made on skid row.

He short and squat and frenzied with a thick head of black hair swept back like James Dean and a love of Corvette sports cars; she tall and thin, a no-nonsense Olive Oyl with a pageboy haircut.

To this day, now 80 and living in Cockeysville, Maters remains the proper Englishwoman. Criddle, who died sober in prison at age 61 in 1991, made up the rules as he went along.

"It was hard to keep up with Walter, I tell you," said Maters, sometimes laughing at the memories, sometimes shaking her head.

However combustible—many was the time Walter railed against psychiatry as the worst thing to which one could subject an alcoholic—they were good people with good intentions and not much money to carry out their mission.

First things first: Where to put the drunks?

Maters's initial attempt to find beds took her to the Salvation Army when it was over near Russell Street where the baseball and football stadiums now stand.

But the Salvation Army had a rule that its guests must work during the day, and that was not what people poisoned by booze needed out of the gate.

"It didn't work out," said Maters, who took her frustrations to an Episcopal priest named Harry Shelley.

The Rev. Harry E. Shelley—a no-nonsense cleric who rode a motorcycle around town—had been a friend and sometimes life raft to Baltimore alcoholics at least since the 1950s.

Shelley's personal ministry to alcoholics began a generation before Isadore Tuerk began his fabled Saturday morning "open house" lectures on the subject at the University of Maryland.

It was the Eisenhower years, a time when scant treatment facilities were available to the average person and well-to-do alcoholics sent to asylums were often said to have suffered "nervous breakdowns."

Upon her husband's death at age 79 in 2001, Shelley's widow—the former Mary Louise Gosnell—said: "I think every alcoholic in Baltimore knew where our front door was."

At the time Maters approached, Shelley was rector at

the Church of the Guardian Angel in Remington and helped coordinate alcohol treatment programs for the Baltimore City Health Department.

Maters: "I was telling Harry about the problems I was having finding a place to get started. And he said, 'You need to meet Walter Criddle.'"

Shelley—with the help of a Health Department colleague named Gladys Augustus, the first president of the Tuerk House board—had trained Criddle as an alcohol counselor.

Once Criddle got involved, the idea that would become Tuerk House began to run under steam, no matter that much of the early energy was high-octane bluster.

Criddle was the sort of guy that Hollywood would cast as the used-car salesman with the heart of gold—the kind of guy who knew a guy who knew a guy that could find whatever you needed when you need it.

[And sometimes whether you needed it or not. Like the time Criddle got "a deal" on some 90 dozen eggs—it could have been ten times that much according to those who delight making the tale taller—and "stored" them in his Corvette until they rotted.]

"I decided that Walter was the person to be our senior counselor," said Maters.

It proved to be one of the most important and far-reaching decisions of her career. Even in a city as awash in eccentrics as Baltimore, one doesn't meet a character like Walter Criddle every day.

"How do you describe a Walter Criddle?" asked Alvin Cohen, a former University of Maryland ER social worker who guided alcoholics to the Tuerk House in the early 1980s. "An incredible human being."

So passionate was Criddle in helping fellow alcoholics put down the jug—including having them sweat out the shakes by working on his ill-fated pig farm in Snow Hill—that some said time moved faster in his presence.

"Larger than life," said Cohen. "He talked in a rapid fire delivery, never silent for very long. He was a conduit for something bigger than himself."

Criddle had gotten sober around 1966, the year the Orioles won the World Series, and somewhere along the line had helped a man with a drinking problem running a Christian outreach program in the city.

That man had the use of an ought-to-be-condemned rowhouse on Lanvale Street just off Greenmount Avenue on the eastside.

And this became the first place where down-and-out street alcoholics in Baltimore found real treatment—including physicals, the 12 steps of Alcoholics Anonymous and various forms of therapy—without having to sing a hymn for a bowl of soup.

"The place was in such terrible shape that your foot would go right through the floor," said Maters, noting that Lanvale Street was the first detox for the indigent. "But I got the pressure off of me to [utilize] the grant. I had the beds."

The place and the program operating inside of it needed plenty of work. Criddle met the challenge with verve if not panache.

"Whatever I needed, Walter would get," said Maters, who learned not to question Criddle on things like getting a bus cheap from state surplus to take drunks to AA meetings.

"I said, 'Walter, that would be nice, but we don't have anyone who can drive it.'"

A mere pebble in Walter's shoe.

"When someone has the kind of charisma that Walter did, well, you know, things happen," laughed Maters. "He believed you always asked for more money than you needed.

"He stirred the pot and I spent a lot of time calming down whatever [tempest] Walter was stirring up with the hospital or the board."

The early board members also learned that not everything was squared away as befitting a program receiving public funds and charitable contributions.

"We'd ask Wendy and Walter for an accounting and they'd promise to have it to next month," said Goodwin, who sat on the board from 1980 to 1995 and again from 1995 2009. "We were never audited, we never brought in a CPA."

The proof was no longer listed on the side of the label but in the pudding.

"Their aim was to help the drunk and that they did," said Goodwin. "Tuerk House was the place to go. People were getting sober."

GRAVEYARD BLUES

"Hey, I remember the misery, motherfuck that fuckin' misery," said the old stevedore, a tear in his eye at the corner Ann and Thames streets. "The people were different then and it's a loss now. It's over for me now. When I want to visit with my family I go down to the graveyard and talk to my mother."

Afaa Weaver, son of Baltimore

AFAA WEAVER

The question—naïve and whimsical, as though beauty really can save the world—floats around Afaa Michael Weaver at the corner of Lakewood Avenue and Oliver Street in Crabtown, ground zero of his childhood.

What is the bridge that Weaver crossed to transform himself from a factory worker named Michael to a heralded poet, disciple of the Eastern arts—*"I am bound by Daoist oaths"*—and New England college professor named Afaa?

Winner of the 2014 Kingsley Tufts Prize for poetry and lauded as the black Walt Whitman of our age (he is lyrical, kind and gentle, even on bad days), Weaver grew up in "the Valley" in far northeast Baltimore when his kin owned a bar called the Apache Lounge.

The area was nice then, back in 1957 when Weaver was six and his steelworker father used union wages to buy 2824 Federal Street for $9,000.

Almost 60 years later—decades in which Weaver survived childhood incest, three marriages, heart failure, profound depression and a razor against his throat in a fight over a woman—the neighborhood is holding on but not so nice anymore.

How did he survive Baltimore when so many of his family and peers—indeed the neighborhood itself in many respects—did not?

Rafael Alvarez

"Creativity," said Weaver, who graduated at 16 from Baltimore Polytechnic Institute in 1968—the year he saw a man running up Harford Road with a rowboat on his head, loot stolen from the old Sears at North Avenue and Harford Road during the King assassination riots.

"Knowing I could write poetry was the light inside of me . . . what helped me make sense of myself and what was going on around me—the hardest thing for me in Baltimore was cultivating and defending my imagination.

"When I come back now, I see what I was up against . . ."

Weaver was most recently back home late last year, in town from his post as professor of English at Simmons College in Boston for his 60th birthday in November and returning a month later to read at the Zappa branch of the Pratt Library in Highlandtown.

"After I gave the [Christmas] reading someone told me that young people in town are teaching city kids mindfulness and none of those kids have dropped out," said Weaver, first exposed to the thrill and discipline of martial arts by way of 1970s kung-fu movies.

"It's all about the mind; you have to be able to have your *own* mind."

When Afaa (meaning "oracle" in Ibo, given to him in 1997 by the Nigerian writer Tess Onwueme) was writing his way out of a South Baltimore soap factory 30 years ago, he wielded creativity against a manufacturing culture that allowed his parents to become homeowners.

"Maybe the price Baltimore paid for places like Bethlehem Steel was what factories do to people," he said. "They stamp you into this numb sameness, a dull conformity," he said.

Baltimore's creative class seems to be growing (when your college degree is worthless, why not throw paint against the wall and call it macaroni?) in proportion to the loss of jobs prevalent when Weaver worked at Procter & Gamble and Bethlehem Steel.

Once there was work in Baltimore and to be an artist was the lot of eccentrics.

Now to be an artist or poet in Baltimore—a weirdo, a drifter, a dreamer—is common but good jobs are scarce.

Is it too harsh to say there is not a poem in the world that might do for Baltimore what Beth Steel once did?

"No," said Weaver. "The American dream is a house, a decent car and to be able to send your kids to a state university. My father was able to work overtime and my mom pinched pennies. That gave us a fairly different life" than what is common around Lakewood and Oliver and many of the old neighborhoods.

Weaver holds an endowed chair as Alumnae Professor of English at Simmons College, editing and translating poetry and prose both into and from modern Mandarin. In 2004 and 2008, he organized international conferences of Chinese poets at Simmons, the first held outside China.

In a telling anecdote on the mindset of the average Baltimorean, he recalls family members refusing to believe that he could speak the language of Yao Ming.

To which he replied: "How would you know that anything I said wasn't Chinese?"

Pushing into his seventh decade, Weaver is contemplating a memoir for an upcoming sabbatical. It would have long passages about the city he left at 33, one of heartbreaking memories and geography he doesn't quite recognize anymore.

"I feel a sense of helplessness when I come back home and I'd like to write something to help people understand how to have faith—how to break free of the things that keep you trapped," he said. "The example of my life is what I want to give."

Rafael Alvarez

In 2014, AfaaWeaver won the prestigious Kingsley Tufts Award for his collection, "The Government of Nature."

Andy Farantos, third generation owner
G&A Hot Dogs in Highlandtown

HOT DOGS

It's the morning of January 11, 2012—a gray, cold Wednesday in Highlandtown—and as people wait outside on Eastern Avenue for the bus, Andy Farantos dumps a stainless steel tray of potatoes on the grill in the front window of G&A Coney Island Hot Dogs, the fried onions and chili sauce landmark started by his grandfather in the Roaring 20s.

Early on in World War II, my uncle Albert DeFelice—actually my father's first cousin as Albert's mother and my father's mother were Prato sisters—waited with a friend for a streetcar on Eastern Avenue just outside of the G&A at Eaton Street.

One of the restaurant's founders—either Andy's grandfather, Alex Diacumakos or his great uncle, Gregory Diacumakos—came out to ask what the boys were doing on the Avenue so early in the morning. Albert said they were headed to the Fifth Regiment Armory to be inducted into the Army. Gregory—or perhaps it was Alex, the G and the A of the hot dog empire—invited the young men in for a breakfast feast on the house.

For the immigrant Greek, as much a thank you to America as a hearty send-off to a couple of kids getting thrown into the middle of a war.

The grill is still in the front window seven decades later and just before 9 a.m., Andy Farantos works it like a keyboard, five dozen eggs at his elbow while 19-year-old daughter Anna—waitress and aspiring model—runs around in Keds with holes in the toes.

The show begins, a cabaret of odd balls and life-long customers who know that the best place to pretend its 1955 is the diner off the corner of Eastern and Eaton Street, next door to the lottery outlet/liquor store and across from one of the city's first supermarkets.

The first guy in the door has a face like George "Goober" Lindsey on a bad day and some kind of not-from-around-here accent, maybe Crisfield or West Virginia.

Goober stands by the grill and bangs Andy's ear about cooking (despite his family's renown for hot dogs, Farantos is a world-class steak and chops man) and the weather; how it always feels colder in the winter if you've been caught in the rain. Affable as only someone with nothing better to do can be, he talks about the weather for a full five minutes before taking a stool at the counter.

Andy shares on the sly that such a man will often comes in, ask for nothing but a glass of water and never shut up. The man promptly proves the Greek wrong by ordering a cup of coffee. Running between the grill and the cash register, Andy has an off-the-menu discussion with a much slower speaking young man—good hearted to the point of naivete, an unsettling, tapered shape to his head—who has saved up to buy himself a New York strip steak on Friday.

Farantos unwraps a rectangle of aluminum foil to show the young man a defrosting slab of prime beef and the regular leaves with a breakfast sandwich in hand and dreams of eating like a king in less than 48 hours.

Crabtown, USA

By this time Goober has befriended a middle-aged African-American woman on the stool next to him.

"My son, he's been sick," says Goober to this perfect stranger. "He's got nerve trouble. Who doesn't have trouble?"

The woman nods—*mmm-hmmm*—and somehow the conversation turns to Goober's art work—how he's been getting back to it lately, how the quiet sketching relaxes him, how, if she doesn't mind waiting for a moment or two he'd like to show her some recent drawings.

He runs across Eastern Avenue and returns with a large sketch book, opening it on the counter while Anna sets a blueberry pie into a see-through cake dish and dear old Dad lays out the first wave of the day's hot dogs, described as "all the way" when served with mustard, onion and homemade chili.

On the counter: drawings of barn swallows, magpies and tree swallows while egg sandwiches fly out the front door.

Beauty found.

Beauty made.

Beauty shared from revolving diner stools at a Formica counter.

Welfare peanut butter.

WILD SQUIRRELS

Spike lived near Tommy O'Dea on Bond Street. Tommy and I mixed it up a couple times but nobody messed with Spike," said Tony Jutchess, son of a Baltimore tugboat deckhand named Whitey. "We hopped plenty of trains growing up. Spike kept wild squirrels in a cage in his room. He fed them from a huge can of peanut butter, I think it was welfare peanut butter."

I'm sure it was originally a good day

LADY LUCK

The kind of woman who avoids black cats and wouldn't walk under a ladder on a bet, Susan Miller wasn't thrilled about getting married on Friday the 13th. But with Valentine's Day right around the corner, she didn't want to wait. And saying "I do" on Monday the 16th was definitely out.

"The last time I got married was on the 16th of the month back in 1980, and that didn't work out so well," said Miller, 40, a Maryland Port Authority police officer who was married at the county courthouse in Towson yesterday to Lloyd Miller, a 47-year-old lumber supervisor at the Home Depot on Eastern Avenue.

"We looked all over for a clergyman who would marry us on Valentine's Day and couldn't find one. We even tried to charter a boat to marry us in the harbor," said Lloyd Miller, who prevailed on his sweetheart to tie the knot yesterday.

It was a bold step on an ominous day. Marlene P. King, a deputy clerk of the Circuit Court in Towson, signed the Millers' marriage license. King blamed the 13th for a drop in weddings yesterday, with only 17 compared with the usual 25 or so on any given day.

King claims she is not so much superstitious as disposed toward misfortune. "I have an insecurity about luck," she said. "It doesn't seem to fall my way."

It didn't fall to Kenny Ziegelheafer on South Schroeder Street near Hollins Market, and he doesn't buy into such foolishness as luck, good or bad.

"I locked my keys in the car," said Ziegelheafer, a carpenter. "I think Friday the 13th was originally a good day until somebody with an agenda turned it all around."

Said Ed Garbus, a state employee: "I almost got hit by a car [downtown] today."

The source of the superstition is usually traced to the passion of Jesus Christ, who was crucified on a Friday after sitting down to break bread with the 12 apostles.

According to Scandinavian mythology, Loki—the god of strife—became an uninvited 13th guest at the Valhalla banquet where the god of light was murdered. And a coven always has 13 members, a dozen witches plus the devil.

"Usually I'll put the date on the board, like February 12, 1998, but today I wrote it out: Friday the Thirteenth," said Dottie Dowling, a history teacher at Parkville Middle School. "Most of the kids didn't pay much attention, but I heard two kids talking about it all day long—they kept saying if you stepped on a crack you'd break your mother's back."

There is nothing random about when Friday the 13th falls, said Jim Fill, a math professor at Johns Hopkins University.

"The Gregorian calendar, which we use in the Western world, was adopted in 1582, and it repeats itself exactly every 400 years," said Fill. "We can figure out how frequently Friday the 13th comes up by looking at any span of 400 years."

Every year, said Fill, at least one Friday the 13th falls. Other years, it occurs two or three times—but no year has four or more.

Crabtown, USA

"Overall, it falls about once every 200 days," he said. "So while I've probably had bad things happen on Friday the 13th, I'm sure I've had my share of bad Tuesday the 27ths as well."

The Thomas Wolfe Memorial of Baltimore

THOMAS WOLFE

"Wolfe unearthed the Earth . . ."
—John Mason Rudolph, poet

It was Stanley Bard who told me that Thomas Wolfe lived in Room 829 of the Chelsea Hotel.

Bard was the manager of the Chelsea at the time, about a decade ago, before a corporation pushed him out. Stanley's father—David Bard [1905 to 1964]—had been part owner of the Chelsea and had known Wolfe.

The towering writer, who died before turning 40 while undergoing brain surgery in 1938 at Johns Hopkins, lived at the Manhattan landmark while working on *The Web and the Rock*, his follow-up to the immortal *Look Homeward, Angel*.

"We had a bellhop here back then named Pernell Kennedy, a confidante of the guests who took care of them personally," said Bard. "After Wolfe died, there was still a pair of his shoes left in the room. Pernell put them in the basement and forgot about them."

In the first spring of this new century, I rented Room 829 for an assignation with a woman from Detroit whom I had not seen for a very long time.

In 2001, the year I left the *Baltimore Sun* to work on cable ships, she wrote to me, confirming things we had both wondered about but never spoke of a decade earlier.

"I am [claiming] small amounts of time for myself . . . today I will have an hour to work on the baseball story. I look forward to being myself in a different time. Even if I never get published, I won't think that the time has been wasted."

After several failures as a playwright, Wolfe was first published at 29 when *Look Homeward Angel* was released on the eve of the Great Depression.

But it was not Wolfe, or any particular writer, that attracted Cookie and me; the mojo magnet is never literature but the strange lives and quirks of *fortuna* that make it possible.

A shared love of Tom and his kin through the ages—Twain, Richard Yates, Tom Nugent—connected us.

"My father arrested Denny McLain back in '68," she said, telling a story—impossible to confirm—she heard every time she went to a ballgame at Michigan and Turnbull with her dad. "Pop let Denny go and we got tickets to every game the rest of the season."

Before our meticulously planned rendezvous at the Chelsea, I'd only touched her twice.

Once underwater at a surprise birthday thrown by her husband; a quick squeeze of her slender foot as she swam by. And once in the vestibule of St. Alphonsus Catholic Church at the corner of Saratoga and Park, around the corner from what long ago had been Baltimore's Chinatown; not far from Abe Sherman's bookstore and the speakeasy where Morris Martick [1923 to 2011] was born.

Martick's Restaurant Francais became home to several generations of young artists as smart and pretty as Cookie but a bit more off center in the way they navigated getting from here to there.

"The night after graduation from the [Maryland] Institute found me in the Mount Royal Tavern drinking my usual 14 beers," remembered Terry Van Tassel a few weeks after Morris's death on December 15, 2011.

"A friend introduced me to a Basque painter named Nieves Saah. She told me that a really cool restaurant downtown was hiring."

In the same way that I had left a note for Cookie to meet me at St. Alphonsus (and later, the Chelsea), Van Tassel's friend said, "Come to 214 West Mulberry around 11:00 a.m. tomorrow and ring the bell. There's no sign. If you want a job, just show up."

"I worked my first lunch shift before I met Morris," said Van Tassel. "I was vacuuming the dining room at the end of a busy lunch shift, intently focusing on sucking up breadcrumbs and made the unfortunate error of disregarding loud pings and grinding sounds from the antiquated machine . . .

"The din from the vacuum as well as my dimwitted hung-over state left me totally unprepared for the attack.

"'STOP!!! STOP!!! Yes, I'm talking to you, miss! You over there with the vacuum! Turn off my vacuum.'

"Numb with horror, I fumbled to find the switch as the din continued. Thundering across the dining room in a rage, Morris pulled the plug and jerked the vacuum cleaner from my hands.

"'What the hell is wrong with you? Are you crazy? You're crazy! You're crazy! You can't work for me Miss, because you're crazy! What kind of person keeps vacuuming when the vacuum makes a noise like that?'

"Morris continued his rant for ten minutes, while I shrank in mute horror. Plugging it back in, Morris gave me the first of many lessons in running a restaurant—how to vacuum the floor."

But back to Cookie . . .

Who one day passed on an afternoon of vacuuming—one of her many household chores in suburban Detroit—to sit at the piano in her living room and play a funeral blues for a mutual friend, a newspaperman from Harlem.

At St. Alphonsus, she stood just outside the heavy doors to the sanctuary—built in 1845 and Oz-like in its vaulted columns; a shrine where old school Communicants regularly participate in the Latin Mass—as pregnant as a woman can be without giving birth.

The church was a stop on one of our chaste strolls around Baltimore, early afternoons where we'd find a bench on the street and I'd read her early drafts of my fledgling fiction. For some reason, she had a Magic 8 Ball in her bag, the classic kiddie oracle the size and shape of a duckpin bowling bowl.

You ask the ball a question, turn it over and through a small window, an answer appears upon which you can chart your fate.

I held the toy in my left hand with my right on the pulsing globe spinning inside her and asked an unspoken question.

Cookie smiled, I turned the ball over and received this answer:

"You may rely on it . . ."

~~~

After that, except for a quick glance at the funeral of another gone-too-soon friend, we did not see one another for nearly a decade. Her life took her back to the Motor City while mine burrowed deeper into all the Crabtown zip codes east of President Street.

One day, a letter arrived, saying how often she had

thought of the stories I'd read aloud to her way back when; tales of an artist who cuts a hole in his grandfather's roof, the Virgin Ruthie arguing with an angel in a hot air balloon above Patterson Park.

Orlo and Leini suffering in Eden.

The letter said she was happy to discover that the stories had found their way to print and that she had finally found the time and courage to take a chance with her own.

I wrote back. She wrote back. Valentine's Day came and went. Then Easter.

Early May arrived with a plan to meet at the corner of Prince and Mott in lower Manhattan, outside of St. Patrick's Old Cathedral.

She appeared with the last light of day and—against the walls of New York's original Catholic cathedral—we kissed for the first time. I broke free and hailed a cab.

"Twenty-third and 7th avenue."

More kissing in the cab and then—at 223 West 23rd up the ancient elevator that the young Stanley Bard used to ride with Pernell the bellboy. We got off on the 8th floor.

"Tom's room," I said as we crossed the threshold and fell into bed.

The first time was gentle before turning wild. The second time was riotous from the start—she called it the climax to a "violent crush."

There's no foreplay like a decade of flirtation and intrigue.

We confirmed all of the mutual, not-acted-upon hunches from years ago—remember this, remember that, I thought for sure . . .—and settled down enough to open presents.

There were books from me and books from her; stories by and about Tom whose centennial had been commemorated the year before with a U.S. postage stamp.

"He'd leave this room in the middle of the night with a new manuscript in his hand, narrative hot out of the typewriter," I said. "And then go walking the streets telling anyone who'd listen: 'I WROTE 10,000 WORDS TODAY!'"

She said that she'd wanted to be a writer since she was eight-years-old—two perfect circles set atop one another. After referencing more incidents from Wolfe's chaotic life—his pain and doubt and the bodies left in the wake—I asked: "Do you want it that bad?"

"I do," she said. "This is the wildest thing I've ever done."

[Baby if you want to be wild, you've got a lot to learn . . .]

We played some more and, just before her return to real life—one Wolfe never experienced, not as a child or an adult—I pulled a brand new Magic 8 Ball from the satchel of presents carried from Baltimore.

I don't remember what we asked this time around, but I can tell you this.

The question I'd posed years earlier at St. Alphonsus has yet to come true.

ISADORE SHOCKET

From the archives of the Highlandtown branch of the Pratt Library: "Oh yes, there was once a Mr. Shocket. Isadore Shocket . . . he had a chauffeur and every day he'd come in right after lunch or we'd have lunch together . . . my father always ended up paying the tab . . ."

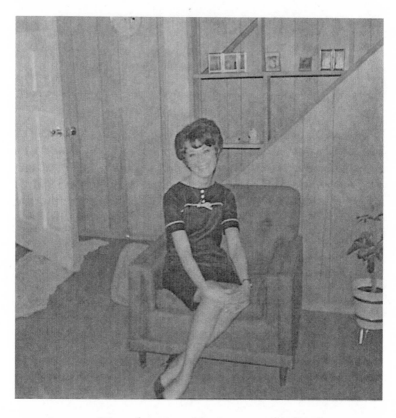

A true Hon hangs Christmas balls from
ceiling tiles with curled ribbon and
thumbtacks.

HEY, HON!

What passions beat within the heart of a true Baltimore Hon?

Not Formica-deep caricatures, but the day-to-day navigated by a strata of Crabtown about which so much fuss is often made.

As my late Polish grandmother put it on many an occasion: "Tain't funny McGee . . ."

To find out what defines a 365-day-a-year Hon, I swung from the branches of my family tree—where the genuine article hangs like a row of *gotchkies* on the line—and scratched the genealogy of an old friend from southwest Baltimore.

"I come from a long line of Hons," said Kerry Ann Oberdalhoff Lessard, a 42-year-old aging into her rightful Hon-ness while laboring to instill those same old-school values in her daughter.

"I die a little inside when she shows no interest in bowling or Yahtzee," said Lessard.

Now of Ellicott City, Lessard's roots run deep in Pigtown and the western edge of Wilkens Avenue near St. Agnes Hospital. With a master's degree in applied anthropology from the University of Maryland, Lessard works as a counselor at Chase Brexton Health Services on Cathedral Street downtown.

Some basic guidelines from the Authentic Hon

operator's manual as inherited and understood by Lessard:

You work hard. You keep a clean house "because you never know who's going to drop by."

[And if some neighborhood blowhard is bending your ear about their aches and pains and grandson who's "on that goddamn dope" you deftly end the conversation by saying, "I got windows to clean."]

You have a traditional deviled egg recipe—wet mustard or dry?—in easy reach for get-togethers ranging from baby showers to Memorial Day cook-outs to funerals.

You hang Christmas balls from the tiles or dropped ceiling of your home—whether rowhouse or "single home"—with curling ribbon and thumbtacks.

You know how to have a good time but you also "know your place." You're not cheap—either in your morals or "pocky book"—or else other Hons "will talk shit about you."

You keep yourself presentable and don't "let yourself go . . ."

[As in, "Did you see Darlene at the bull roast? Boy, did she let herself go . . ."]

You don't "put on airs" without risking a comment like, "I remember her when she didn't have two nickels to rub together. Now she's got a little money and she acts like she don't even know me."

You stand up for yourself and you don't let people shit all over you.

And family is everything.

Of all the Hons from whence Lessard comes, no one quite fit the bill like her Aunt Hazel.

"She was my grandfather's aunt and lived on Eastshire Drive off of Patapsco Avenue," said Lessard. "She and my grandmother [Evelyn Taylor, 21223] are who I think of when I think of a Hon."

Hazel Lyons Shanahan was born in Baltimore in 1920 and died here some 74 years later. Her late husband, James Shanahan, worked for the B&O Railroad, about as good a job as you could get back in the day, said Lessard, when an upwardly mobile apprentice "had really arrived" if she married a cop.

[Lessard's great-grandmother, Agnes "Toots" Taylor, was friendly with a Southwestern District officer who now and then would give her a lift to work in a paddy wagon.]

"I loved going to Aunt Hazel's house, especially at Christmas. My sister and I would be all bundled up and walk from the car into the warmth of Aunt Hazel's living room.

"From there, we'd be ushered back to the kitchen. I remember the linoleum floor and the Formica table covered with a bright Christmas tablecloth.

"There was always coffee going and she would feed us Christmas cookies and her legendary cheese ball—a blob of blue cheese, cheddar and cream cheese rolled in chopped walnuts and, naturally, eaten with Ritz crackers.

"No Christmas season is complete without the cheese ball. But what I loved most of all was listening to Aunt Hazel talk with my grandparents and they usually talked about other people! It didn't matter that I didn't know half of them. I liked feeling like I was in on something.

"I learned the value of mouth closed, ears open [and] I still associate the rowhouse table and the smell of strong coffee with gossip. It's my favorite aesthetic experience. My grandmother [Evelyn] would shoot me a withering look if I acted up and the punishment would have been being sent to the living room and missing the gossip.

"There were lots of tales of people getting drunk and arguing and 'running around' on one another."

[Women who ran around were "trashy" and men who strayed were "no good."]

"Hazel and Evelyn would weigh in on what ought to have been done or said in any situation," said Lessard, known in her kiddie days as Kerry Ann. "Together, they were my Emily Post and Dear Abby. What more did I need to understand what was expected of a Baltimore girl?"

In turn, much was expected of Lessard's daughter, Emma, now a 20-year-old college student who benefitted from growing up next-door to her great-grandparents Evelyn and Bill on Wilmington Avenue.

[Bill Taylor, a *Sunpapers* delivery man back when there was still a "bulldog" edition on Sundays, died May 15, 2011. The last piece of cake he ever enjoyed was a slice of cinnamon at the hospital, a goodie made with love for Kerry's family by my mother—the former Gloria Jones of Dillon Street, a Hon to be reckoned with.

When Bill's betrothed Hon (the former Evelyn Nina *Meyers* got on his nerves—and let's be candid, a true Hon can be a pain in the ass—he'd pretend to acquiesce to her every desire.

"Okay Hon," he'd say, "I'm wrong, you're right. Okay? Jeee-sus Christ."]

Lessard on her daughter: "Without knowing why, Emma has a clear sense of what's right and what ain't, which is what I learned at the kitchen table of Hazel and Evelyn and passed on to her.

"I didn't realize my Hon traits until I was old enough to get some perspective and started to hear Evelyn's voice come out of my mouth.

"It took me too long to stand up for myself. But Emma—who's quick to give an opinion when someone in the family isn't being treated right, who says, 'You know me, I gotta open my mouth'—understood it right out of the gate. I admire that.

"Like I said, she's not much on bowling, but will ask the loudmouth sitting next to us at Camden Yards bashing the O's—'Why the hell did you come then?' She knows there is no greater sin in this town than being a fair-weather fan."

And worse, like the big hoo-hah up in Hamden that occasioned this essay.

"If you try to steal what we have embraced as quintessentially Baltimore—like a Mayflower truck on a snowy night—you will have your ass handed to you," said Lessard.

"And that's just for starters . . ."

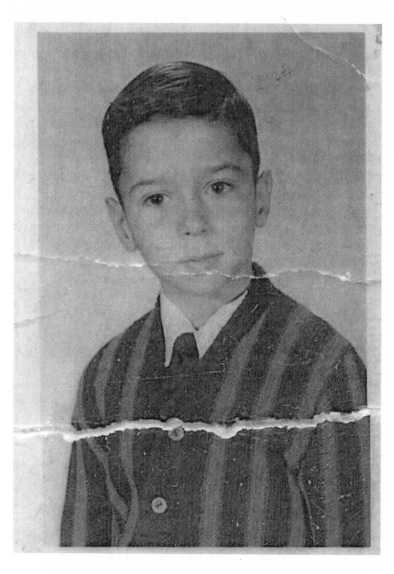

Ralphie Alvarez in the first grade—he
thought he was cool

MARY POPPINS

I thought I was pretty cool back in the first grade—1964, white-hot ground zero of global Beatlemania; knew there was no turning back once I took hold of the Jerry Vale pompadour my parents gave me, combed it straight down across my eyebrows and took a pair of kiddie scissors to it.

For good report cards, I received Beatles and Beach Boys albums, knowing in my six-year-old soul upon first listening to "In My Room," that Brian Wilson was a sad and beautiful genius.

Pretty darn cool until the summer of 2015, lakeside in Rangeley, Maine—reading *Middlemarch* in the sunshine until a rainy afternoon where I decided to manicure an old cardboard box of vinyl LPs. There, I found a copy of the original soundtrack to Mary Poppins movie.

And remembered that, no matter what I may thought at the time, I was still very much a very young child back when Ringo was shouting, "Ah, rock on George, do it one time for me!"

For my birthday that year, my Aunt Sylvia—knowing I was Beatles' crazy—called and asked me what record I wanted. And I said, without pause, "Mary Poppins." She asked me if I was sure and I said yes and that's what I got.

Rafael Alvarez

MARY POPPINS WHEN THE FABS HAD JUST PUT OUT *SOMETHING NEW!*

Half-a-century later, it's good to be reminded that the kid inside the kid knew a few things that the leather-clad rocker waiting to break out did not.

God is an Orioles' fan.

BASEBALL CHAPLAIN

F ather John Bauer has blessed bats
(limiting hitters to one blessing per bat), heard the
confessions of Judas Iscariots in face masks known as
umpires and for years has handed out Holy Communion
to the likes of Rick Dempsey and Mike Piazza along with
ushers and any ballpark employee who asks.

But Father John Bauer—Yankee hater, Highlandtown
boy and, Catholic chaplain for the Baltimore Orioles since
2002, refuses to pray for the home team.

"A woman came up to me at the ballpark and said,
'Father, do you pray for the Orioles?' I told her no, that I
had priorities—to pray for peace, for our soldiers, for the
sick.

"And another lady standing next to her says, 'The
Orioles are sick.'"

Bauer, a Redemptorist ordained in 1956 and now
retired at his childhood parish, the Sacred Heart of Jesus
at Conkling Street and Foster Avenue, has loved baseball
since he was old enough to tag along with cousins to
sandlot games.

He was among the more talented kids to play the
American game in Patterson Park between the Depression
and World War II, starring as a catcher for Engine
Company No. 5 in Fells Point and in the outfield for the Red
Shield Boys Club on Clinton Street, which closed in 2006.

"We never lost a game," said Bauer, though I was unable to apply Casey Stengel's adage—"You could look it up"—to the claim. "In [seminary] I hit over .400 and I could hit the long ball too."

More than most, however, the old priest—born the year the incorrigible Catholic Babe Ruth hit 60 home runs for an obscure team up north—knows that it's just a game. Once a Caribbean missionary, he spent several tours of duty in Vietnam as an Army chaplain, volunteering in 1969.

"The country was at war and I felt left out, so I volunteered. Soldiers need a priest too," said Bauer, who played fast-pitch softball with GIs on bases in Germany, starting each game with a prayer that no one would be hurt and gave last rites to soldiers on the battlefield.

"I was in Vietnam from 1970 to 1971. I flew to different fire bases to say Mass. I saw medics decide who to work on and who couldn't be helped. One night we lost 32 guys. There's a lot of work that people can't do but I found out I could do this.

"One time one of my pilots was killed. And on Christmas, I flew from base to base and celebrated five Masses. Finally they told me, 'Father, we're taking you back now.'"

There are a few things Bauer would like to tell Orioles's manager Buck Showalter, a stickler for the fundamentals who has managed the team since late in the 2010 season, turned around a woeful franchise and was named American League Manager of the Year in 2014.

"These guys don't run the bases right," observed Bauer, having compiled his scouting notes over a decade as the preacher in the box seats. "They touch the base with the wrong foot."

Bauer's approach to getting off on the right foot with the ballplayers is to sit—Roman collar in place—on the bench before batting practice. As the players drift out of the clubhouse to the field, he slides down the bench to make room and asks: "How's the family?"

"One guy comes out, maybe two, and they sit and start talking about other things than baseball," said Bauer. "But by the time the National Anthem is over, I have to be off the field and in my seat."

He took that seat much like Doug DeCinces took over third base for the Orioles in 1976, by replacing a legend. DeCinces had to fill the position of the peerless Brooks Robinson, a statue of whom now graces Russell Street with a gilded glove. Bauer followed the beloved Monsignor Martin Schwalenberg, who held the O's chaplaincy for more than four decades and died in 2004.

Bauer wasn't at Opening Day in 2012, for it falls on the most somber hour on the Christian calendar, 3 p.m. on Good Friday.

But two days later, Bauer was at the ballpark to celebrate the first Mass of the new season on the fourth floor of the B&O warehouse. For those taking notes at home on their theological scorecards, it will also be Easter for right-fielder Nick Markakis.

Because of his Greek heritage, Markakis is widely assumed to be Eastern Orthodox, which often celebrates Easter a week after the Roman Church.

"One year I was talking to him on Easter Sunday and said, 'I guess you'll be celebrating next Sunday.' And Markakis said, 'No I won't.'"

Markakis befriended the affable Bauer, who smiles easily and has small, twinkling eyes beneath the bill of a blue "Vietnam Veteran" ball cap. Bauer baptized both of Markakis's sons—Taylor in 2009 and Tucker a year later—at Sacred Heart of Jesus where the priest was Christened 84 years ago.

Bauer is all but retired, noting that a priest is never really finished with their vocation "until they throw the dirt on you." He holds onto his volunteer gig at the Yard and his assigned seat near the "enemy" dugout because there are only so many priests to go around.

While watching the game play out on the emerald diamond, does he ever regret choosing the altar over the outfield?

"If I had pursued playing ball it would have been over long ago," said Bauer. "Even if I'd have held on and become a manager, I'd be fired. But here I am—84-years-old and still a priest."

In late 2015, Bauer's fellow Redemptorist priests at Sacred Heart of Jesus were remembering him at daily Mass in the petitions for the sick.

The window sills were wooden too.

WOODEN STEPS

When we first moved in we had wooden
steps," said John Woolshleger of the rowhouse his
parents bought at 1106 South Lakewood Avenue, one of
hundreds torn down by the City of Baltimore to make way
for a highway that was never built.

The house was taken by eminent domain in February
of 1967 and the Woolshlegers—mom Margaret, widow of
Frederick—got $2,500.

"The window sills were wooden too," said John, a boy
at the time. "Later on my mom put on the Formstone but
those wooden steps were comfortable to sit on. A lot more
comfortable than the new brick. I told Mom to take the
money. What the heck? They were gonna put a highway
through."

The highway was never built, the blocks where the
Woolshlegers and their neighbors—mostly Polish, families
with names like Jakubowski and Mazurkiewicz—stood as
vacant lots for two decades.

Then a developer came in and put up townhouses.
They now sell for as much as $500,000 each, sometimes
more.

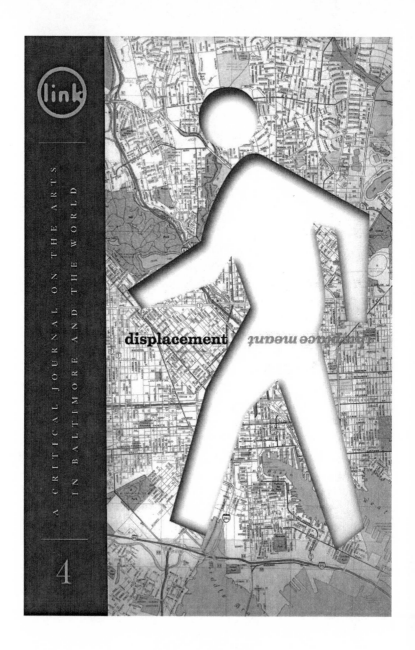

link

A CRITICAL JOURNAL ON THE ARTS
IN BALTIMORE AND THE WORLD

displacement

4

Weird art shit.

GOING MOBILE

"Every summer, my father would pack us all up in the car and we went somewhere. He'd say: 'You can't get lost in America . . .'"

—Wendell Pierce, actor

One of the most important literary experiences of my life did not involve reading or writing.

All I did was stand around and watch.

It was the summer of 1976 and I was fresh out of high school, writing poetry to the melodies of Robin Trower songs, swiping diet pills from the medicine cabinets of suburban housewives and waiting in the old Seafarers International Union hall at Baltimore Street and Central Avenue to catch a ship before starting college.

I was 18-years-old and more than anything in the world wanted to be a writer.

My best friend had an older brother who'd been in the Navy and was a gifted carpenter. That summer, he put a camper top on the bed of a small pick-up truck for a cross-country road trip with his then girlfriend and now wife, the writer Karen Hesse.

One of the last things Randy Hesse did before shoving off was fitting hand-made wooden bookshelves into the back of the truck. I was there—hands in the pockets of ripped up jeans—watching as he drove the last screw and began setting in place books important to him and his sweetheart.

The combination was exhilarating: the printed page, a pretty girl and the open road!

One day, I was gonna do it too . . .

———✦———

Some 25 years after that bi-centennial summer, I finished Christmas dinner in Highlandtown and began loading my '99 Volkswagen Beetle with cases of the Baltimore arts journal *LINK* and milk crates of a short fiction chapbook called *CRABTOWN STORIES*.

[The journal ceased publication in 2006 after 10 issues. I have a hundred cases of them in a second floor bedroom of a Greektown rowhouse and give them away liberally and indiscriminately.]

My journey included no hand-made book shelves, no girl to read aloud to. Just me and boxes of books wedged between a sleeping bag, a jug of water and a tub of peanut butter. Books to be given away to anyone who crossed my path, the VW's neo-Flower Power vase on the dashboard holding two ball point pens and a toothbrush.

Destination: Los Angeles, where I had a lunch date with a Hollywood attorney who'd never met a writer willing to drive 3,000 miles for a free meal, jump back in the car and drive home.

She couldn't know that giving away books born in Baltimore from one end of the continent to other was a bigger thrill than any movie deal she might broker for me.

———✦———

Dec. 25, 2002

The trip began this afternoon, but the giveaway started a day earlier, in the service department of a Volkswagen dealership where I took the Bug for a once-over before the trip.

Crabtown, USA

There, I met a young woman named Angelina Romano Chilcoat and her toddler, Isabel. It was Christmas Eve and we were stuck at the mechanics. Angelina was reading stories to her daughter and it made me wonder if Mary read to Jesus, or whether the Mother of Christ was even literate.

They called my number and I decided to give her a copy of *LINK* No. 6, an issue devoted to the notion of pilgrimage which contained a story I'd written about another teenage virgin who had given birth, a spoiled brat from Baltimore named Ruthie.

By the time I reached Santa Fe, Angelina had forwarded a note: "I wanted to know if Ruthie and her baby would be safe after they stopped running . . ."

And then: "What is *LINK*?"

LINK—a "critical journal on the arts in Baltimore and the world"—debuted in 1996 and its themed issues have addressed such topics as hysteria and the history and future and *idea* of these things we call books.

"What is it?" asked the clerk at a gas station just over the Woodrow Wilson bridge when I handed him a copy late on Christmas Day.

"Weird art shit," I said and he understood with an immediacy that no mission statement could have accomplished.

Dec. 26, 2002

I wake up in the car at 5 a.m., curled across the two front seats with a sleeping bag for a mattress, and hit an Exxon food mart in Roanoke for morning coffee.

Paying for the coffee, I hand the clerk a copy of No. 7, titled "CODE" with binary art on the cover. "Hey," he says happily. "It's about computers!"

South of Roanoke in Marion, Va., I stop at the offices

of the *Smyth County News & Messenger*, once owned and edited by Sherwood Anderson, author of the immortal *Winesburg, Ohio.*

Anderson is buried on a Blue Ridge mountain hillside there, beneath an eccentric tombstone designed by Wharton Esherick that proclaims: "Life, Not Death, is the Great Adventure."

[Personally, I believe that it is both, but that's another story.]

On the grave, I leave a copy of *LINK* No. 8—the one devoted to books—and a copy of *CRABTOWN*, which contains a short story by John Mason Rudolph, a rare book dealer from Baltimore who found himself marooned in Marion after culling through the estate of Anderson's widow, a woman named Copenhaver.

At the offices of the *News & Messenger,* I give a copy of No. 5 to the circulation manager and a copy of No. 8 to Dan Keagle, editor-in-chief, trying to persuade Keagle that a goof from Baltimore going out of his way to lay a literary journal on the frozen grave of a too-often-forgotten writer is worth a few paragraphs in the local rag.

Anderson would have gone for it when he was running the show.

Over the Virginia border at Bristol and into Tennessee, I give copies of *LINK* to a college kid who says his grandmother lives in Glen Burnie and roll into Nashville and the home of Karl Meyer.

Meyer runs a Catholic Worker inspired "House of Hospitality" on West Heiman Street and calls it "Nashville Greenlands." As much as possible, the folks stay with Meyer—young people mostly, those looking for a different way—live off of what they can grow in the large yard.

I met Meyer through an ad he placed looking for someone to help with his hand-written memoirs of 40-

odd years of agitating for a better world. I gave him a copy
of No. 6, handed No. 7 to a man I met in the nearby Belle
Meade neighborhood and gave copies of No. 7 to
Greenlands resident Patrick O'Neill and a young man
named Matt who earns his keep on Heiman Street as an
organic farmer.

The Camden Pubic Library just west of Nashville
received a copy of No. 8 and then I crossed the Mississippi
River, picking up WEVL out of Memphis in time to hear
Sue Foley sing, "Where the Action Is."

Dec. 28, 2002

The action is in Little Rock, Arkansas (birthplace of
Brooks Robinson), where the United States Department
of the Interior has transformed a classic Mobil Gas station
across the street from Central High School into a museum
of the school's 1957 integration by the "Little Rock Nine."

I rolled onto the parking lot on the afternoon of what
would have been the 88th birthday of Pops Staples and
gave a copy of No. 5 and No. 6 to a college girl behind the
museum counter with the marquee name of Spirit Trickey.

Trickey is the daughter of Minnijean Brown, one of the
nine black kids who made history when they tried and
tried and tried again to integrate Central High School,
finally succeeding with the help of federal troops.

In 2001, all nine of the former classmates appeared
together on the Today show.

Before leaving Little Rock, copies of *LINK* were given
to a group of recovering drug addicts working a Saturday
afternoon car wash to raise money for their halfway
house; a peace activist named Debbie Luckom who put me
up for the night on Karl Meyer's good word; and a poet
friend of Luckom.

By 10 p.m., I am in Oklahoma City, where I stopped

207

long enough to down an espresso and check my e-mail at a joint called Java Dave's.

"My dad was a writer," says the guy behind the counter. "When people asked him what he wrote, he'd say: 'Boy, I'll write about an old lady walking a baby seal in a stroller if they pay me . . .'"

He gets a copy of No. 5 and No. 6.

Dec. 29, 2002

Somewhere around Elk City, OK.—not far from the Texas panhandle—I pull into a truck stop to use the bathroom and notice that the door to the stall is scrawled with the words: "NO JEWS."

I complained to the clerk behind the register and the kid scrubs it clean with fingernail polish remover, apologizing, with a fool's honesty, that the epithet had "been up there for a while."

You arrive at places like this—these over-the-road oases—at odd hours to take care of your personal business: brush teeth, take a dump, maybe write out a few bills and drop them in the box.

If you ask, the clerk is almost always happy to make a fresh pot of coffee but sometimes you don't ask just because you don't want to talk to anyone.

And sometimes all you want is for the shit-house to be free of hate while you relieve yourself.

By afternoon, I am in New Mexico and continue to pull off the road to take pictures of old, rusting cars. Leaving crumbs in the forest for the literary anthropologists, I toss a copy of *CRABTOWN* into the back seat of a green Edsel that has weeds growing up through the floorboards.

Dec. 30, 2002

The day begins at the Aztec Café downtown where I

am interviewed about the road trip on local radio by a woman named Honey Harris. I give away three copies of No. 7—one to a cop who gives me a Santa Fe police shoulder patch in return—and grab a Nader-green "NO WAR" bumper sticker for my lime laptop.

At the café, I meet a guy named Leonard E. Hoffman, a realtor and accordion player who will open the reading I do that night with an Allan Sherman oom-pah-pah schtick.

Once a member of "Freddy and the Fuzztones," Lenny remembered visiting Baltimore once and meeting old guys who were gunsmiths and accordion players.

Giving No. 7 the once-over, he spots the name Woody Vasulka and pronounces him the "godfather of video art," a man who hosts a daily, mid-morning salon that is frequented by folks like Laurie Anderson and Hopi Indians whose work is influenced by Andy Warhol.

At the coin-operated laundry that morning, I try to read Vasulka's essay in No. 7, but have no idea what it's about.

At the reading later on, hosted by a guy who lives in a loft behind a shop that sells camper tops for pick-up trucks, I read "Orlo and Leini Meet the Invisible Man" from *CRABTOWN*, give away a bunch of books and buzz on into the night, cruising through Indian reservations on my way west.

Dec. 31, 2002

I roll into Arizona on Route 66 while listening to a cassette tape of Laurie Anderson's *Mister Heartbreak* that I bought at a yard sale somewhere along the way for 50 cents. On it, William S. Burroughs recites "Shakey's Night," as the West moves up before me in red, brown and white.

A copy of No. 5 goes to the Winslow publc library and the librarian gives me a souvenir library card to go with my souvenir Santa Fe police patch.

Earlier—after giving away a copy of No. 7 to the Gallup, N.M. library, I saw one of the best propositions ever plastered on a billboard: "Have you slept in a wigwam lately?"

January 1, 2003

I awake in the town of Kingman, AZ., after going to bed early with a biography of Jane Bowles I bought for a buck in a Santa Fe junk store.

Traveling alone for a week had brought a twinge of sadness on the eve of 2003, alone and anonymous and tired after a 500-plus mile day. But the feeling fades, I have learned, in the sunshine of each new day and the possibilities stirred in the first cup of coffee behind the wheel.

A copy of No. 7 goes to a cashier named Rose at Billy's Gas on Route 66. Later, No. 5 to a guy getting gas near Needles, CA.

[All these gas stations made me think of the years of the Orioles's dynasty under Earl Weaver when you could get drinking glasses with pictures of Brooks Robinson on them at Crown.]

Stopping for a buffet in Barstow, I get my first "no thank you" from a man eating noodles while reading the New Testament. Back in Baltimore, my extended family was enjoying homemade egg noodles dropped into a traditional Spanish peasant stew called *cocido*. I call to wish everyone a Happy New Year and get back behind the wheel.

Los Angeles meets me by mid-day and I give a copy of No. 7 and No. 5 to my hosts: a newspaper couple, Joe

Mathews and his wife Anna Wilde, who report for the *L.A. Times* and *Wall Street Journal* respectively.

They are placed under a Christmas tree topped with a red cap of the Anaheim Angels.

January 2, 2003

"You gotta do something, they ain't never got'em in this world . . ."

—Simon Rodia

Ah, Simon, don't I know it.

Does *LINK* meet the Rodia standard?

Do *CRABTOWN STORIES*?

Rodia, alone, built his magnificent towers in Watts between 1921 and 1954. They have survived official condemnation that they be razed as "junk" in 1959, the L.A. riots of 1965 and the 1994 earthquake.

"Hail to the innocent Gaudi of California!" declared Gio Pomodoro, "who destroyed the myths of Disneyland and movie land in a swift, isolated competition."

Joe Matthews drove me to the wonder erected by the immigrant's obsessive hand.

"I didn't have much awareness of art growing up, just paintings on the walls of boring field trips," said Mathews. "I think art is something I aspire to as a writer, all art is essentially a story on some level."

To Mathews—a California boy who once covered Pigtown for *The Baltimore Sun* as though it were a foreign country—there is no greater artistic spectacle of creativity than the Tournament of Roses.

"The guy who puts it together is a dry cleaner, yet he's shaping a parade that's seen around the world," said Mathews. "They have to use organic material for everything on the floats and he figured out that with shades of crushed walnuts you could create any skin color in the world."

That's art, said Joe as we strolled beneath the spires.

I gave away a copy of No. 5 to a fellow gawker, had lunch with my attorney, dipped a toe into the Pacific Ocean and turned around toward the rising sun and home.

January 3, 2003
LINK No. 6 goes to the public library in Eloy, Arizona. At 4 p.m., I cross into New Mexico on an all-day drive that takes me to El Paso by nightfall, when I pull into a mall to see Scorese's *Gangs of New York*.

Afterward, I stumble out and drive another hour before setting up camp on the parking lot of a truck stop in Esperanza, Texas that has a caged tiger on exhibit.

Draping a sleeping bag across the front seats of the Beetle, I curl up like a fetus, cold and falling asleep with thoughts of the road trip I never took.

It was 1979 and I was 21, just three years away from watching Randy Hesse pull out of his father's driveway in a pick-up truck turned into a bookmobile.

I got it in my head that a train ride to Idaho was the thing to do, making my way to Ketchum to see where Hemingway had done himself in. My parents talked me out of it for reasons that I'm sure made sense to them and I wound up instead on a plane to California, the very comfortable home of my mother's cousin Valerie and Disneyland.

I've criss-crossed the United States many, many times since then and have yet to make it to Ketchum.

January 4, 2003

At 6 a.m., I enter Van Horn, Texas and have my morning coffee in a well-lit McDonald's with a copy of Dorothy Day's *The Long Loneliness.*

I learn that on the night of her first arrest for civil disobedience during World War I, she and a fellow advocate for women's suffrage stayed up all night in their cell discussing the novels of Conrad.

LINK, I decide, must go into the prisons. Later give away a copy of No. 5 and a copy of No. 8 to the Fort Stockton Public Library, about 120 miles east of Van Horn via I-10.

Several hours east of Van Horn is Ozona, which celebrates native son Davy Crockett with a monument to the pioneer in the town square. In Ozona, I bought tuna, crackers and peanut butter for $2.50 at the dollar store and ask myself: Is giving *LINK* in the middle of Texas no different from the Sex Pistols'a ill-fated tour of the American South in 1977?

Why aren't I doing this in Manhattan?

I hit Weimar by evening and make good on the promise to get a room. I give No. 7 to the night clerk, who tells me later: "I liked the part about cloning intelligence . . ."

January 5, 2003

A copy of No. 5 and No. 7 are given to the day clerk before I head off to find a Catholic church to attend Mass in a town of about 2,000 people.

At St. Michael's, a woman named Annette plays the organ in an empty sanctuary and we talk about what it means to be Catholic.

"The laity," she says, "is the future of the Church."

I give her a copy of No. 6.

In downtown Houston. I ask the skateboarders jumping the steps of municipal buildings to direct me to the funky part of town. En route to Westheimer Road, I give two copies of No. 6 and one of No. 7 to the folks at the Houston Bicycle Company, being more generous with the copies the closer I get to home.

A copy of No. 5 and No. 7 go to the cashier of an internet café and copies of No. 7 to a pair of young women dining at the Empire Café—the café manager and a Vassar student smoking cigarettes by herself in the corner, struggling to write a play.

I think of the parable of seed that falls on rock, on shallow soil and that which the wind casts over rich Earth, where it takes root. By dusk, I am at the home of Pati D'Dico and her husband, William Warren, on Pauline Street in New Orleans.

Painters, Bill and Pati own and operate the Waiting Room Gallery next to their house at 904 Pauline Street in the Bywater neighborhood.

"I've been reading *The Bone Orchard Conga*, by Ray McNeice," said Bill of the poet who had just toured Italy and Russia with Yevtushenko and Ferlinghetti. "He's the son of a traveling salesman who died young."

Pati said she hadn't been reading much of anything lately, although she was dipping into Margaret Mead's autobiography at odd moments between portraits of Dick Cheney holding in his breath.

"I'm taking a more political approach in my work because I feel the world is insane and continuing to believe in sound bites," she said. "Cheney keeps having heart attacks because he's been lying to himself for half of his adult life."

Pati and Bill get six copies of *LINK* for themselves and the gallery.

Another copy goes to the public library across the street from their house as I continue to hot-foot it home.

Crabtown, USA

January 6, 2003

Passing Royston, Georgia, birthplace of that peachy SOB Ty Cobb, I pick up WUOG-FM out of Athens and manage to hold the station for a good 45 minutes of psycho-twist garage rock, hearing stuff I'd never heard before: the Matadors; the Sloths, Bunker Hill, Haskell Adkins, and Ramsay Midwood singing selections from *Shootout at the OK Chinese Restaurant.*

No books given away.

January 7, 2003

In Richmond, Va., the cashier at an Exxon station looks at the scrawl I leave on the gas receipt and asks: "Are you a doctor?"

"Writer."

And slipped two copies of *LINK* across the counter before getting back on I-95, just a few hours left to go.

Just what did I accomplish beyond the fun of it?

In an intense fortnight on the road, I gave away 78 copies of *LINK* and about twice as many copies of *CRABTOWN STORIES* to people who otherwise would not have come into contact with either.

It's been over a decade since the trip ended. In all this time, no one who received a copy of *LINK* or *CRABTOWN*—both of which carry e-mail info and old fashioned addresses—has made contact.

If the ink-riddled pulp of a fallen tree is given away along the interstates of America, does it make a noise in a reader's mind?

He drank like a fish and wrote like a prince.

DAVID MAULSBY

"David Maulsby was everything modern reporters are not..."
            —Joe Challmes, now at the City Desk in the sky

"This job is more fun than fucking, especially at my age!"
            —Maulsby, in passing on the City Desk

In a profession that once harbored clever misfits who'd find it hard to hold employment elsewhere, David L. Maulsby [1914 to 1975] was especially eccentric.

A World War II Marine who stormed Okinawa and was never quite the same afterward, Maulsby covered the zoo, drank like a fish and wrote like a prince.

Not enough purple prose for the copy desk?

Simultaneously affable and tortured, Maulsby had the soul of a poet, the heart of a Salvation Army volunteer, a love of animals to rival Doctor Dolittle and the thirst of F. Scott Fitzgerald.

"Don't mess with me," he liked to say, "I was a Marine..."

This is how David Maulsby was remembered nearly four decades after his death by David Michael Ettlin.

Ettlin was just a kid working the lobster shift in the *Sunpapers* wireroom in 1967, not long removed from working as a store announcer for E.J. Korvettes in

Catonsville, when he was befriended by the older, recently widowed reporter.

"Between midnight and dawn were the hours when David was apt to turn up," said Ettlin. "After the bars had closed and whatever adventures he may have unsuccessfully pursued."

Maulsby drank himself to death by his 60th birthday and Ettlin inherited the zoo beat from the older man enroute to a long tenure on late rewrite before retiring as a *Sunpapers'* night editor in 2007. In those 40 years, Ettlin charted the migrations of many an odd duck in the skies over Calvert Street. None flew with more imperfect beauty than Dave Maulsby.

"Some folks merely tolerated David, others had outright contempt. But I loved him," said Ettlin, especially grateful for the $20 Maulsby once provided so the then 21-year-old might self-publish a chapbook of poetry.

[Maulsby's daughter, now 60, recoils from the harsher assessments. "Yes, he could be exasperating at times," said Mary Burwell Maulsby, his only immediate survivor. "But contempt? I don't buy it."]

"I probably worked with more than 200 reporters whose names and faces I've forgotten," said Ettlin. "But David remains a wonderment—joyful, tragic; unforgettable."

David Lee Maulsby IV was born on December 11, 1914 into an old and respectable Baltimore family (in the Faulknerian sense) with deep roots in Harford County and Roland Park.

The first of four brothers (the youngest, Allen, was the last to die at age 82 in 2004), David grew up on Roland Avenue just above Cold Spring Lane. His father passed away when he was young.

Crabtown, USA

Maulsby graduated from the Virginia Episcopal, a boarding school in Lynchburg. Married to the former Mary Burwell Burchard in 1936, he received a bachelor's degree two years later from Washington & Lee University.

A member of the First Marine Division during World War II, Maulsby took part in the Battle of Okinawa, the horrific "Typhoon of Steel" which took the lives of more than 150,000 men. It was one of several things the otherwise engaging Maulsby rarely talked about.

"I think he saw a lot of things he couldn't live with very well," said daughter Mary.

Maulsby's post-combat service in occupied Japan, however, was a warhorse of a different color.

"He told me that when the Americans took over a posh hotel in Tokyo as headquarters, he and another guy got all of the Japanese servants together and taught them that the proper response when an American officer asked for something was: 'Fuck you,' " remembered David L. Maulsby, Jr. 69, a cousin living in Bolton Hill.

[At one time, said Maulsby the cousin, there were four David Lee Maulsbys living in Baltimore, all descendents of the same long-dead patriarch.]

After the war, the Marine gave his young cousin a prized combat knife. The blade is remembered not for the enemies dispatched but the time the veteran accidentally sat on it before an invasion and sliced his butt open.

Maulsby joined the morning staff of the *Sunpapers* not long after his service discharge. While his wife was alive and the children were young, the family lived on Malvern Avenue in Ruxton. Mrs. Maulsby's 1966 death from cancer at age 48 left an overwhelmed father to care for Mary and a namesake son, the late David Lee Maulsby V. And his drinking increased.

"Dad spent the night with Mom's casket at the Church

of the Good Shepherd," said Mary, who has lived in New Mexico since graduating from Washington's Sandy Springs Friends School in 1971. "He slept in one of the pews and burned the wood with his cigarettes.

"He had no regard for any kind of rules . . . rules didn't apply to him."

And what was once merely eccentric was now erratic and less charming.

Maulsby called everyone Ace, listed his religion as Druid, covered police headquarters without trying to hide the half-pint of gin in his back pocket and began all phone interviews with the salutation: "David MAULS-by of *The Sun*."

The *Sunpapers* of Baltimore, once the peerless paper of record in Maryland for everything from Esskay hotdogs to homicides in Essex, has been reduced after some 180 years to a skeleton short on marrow.

Yet once upon a time, Arunah S. Abell's dreadnought assigned reporters to traffic court, a beat for the very green or very jaded, work Maulsby endured in order to follow his instincts when the editors were otherwise occupied.

"Dad hated covering traffic court," said Mary. "But it was the bread and butter that allowed him to do the other stuff."

And the other stuff was sublime. From the Baltimore stripper who died when her snake, both a pet and a prop, bit her; to a baby pig named Noodles taken for walks through Mount Vernon on a leash to the time Maulsby chaperoned a gorilla on the Playboy jet from Baltimore to Phoenix for an assignation of primates.

Such tales became known in the newsroom—whether written by the master or a mere journalist- as "Maulsby stories."

"Dad loved nature and animals—he was a kind, sensitive soul when he wasn't tortured," said Mary, whose memories of the bad times include the he used the family kitchen for target practice. "And he loved people . . . we'd be walking downtown and I'd realize he wasn't next to me anymore.

"When I looked back, I'd see him on a bench talking to a stranger. He had a real gift for picking out the oddballs . . . he was pretty odd himself."

Among those who got the Maulsby treatment in ink and newsprint was an 88-year-old who claimed to have known Jesse James and lived in a derelict laundry truck on a vacant lot. No one knows how he met the guy but after giving the old coot his moment in the spotlight, Maulsby began checking up on the man: bringing him food and water, undoubtedly something stronger.

"He wound up writing the old guy's obituary after finding his nearly frozen body one day," recalled Ettlin. "He came into the newsroom swinging the poor stiff's lantern and wailing: "He was sooooooo cold . . .""

In Maulsby's obit, which ran without a byline after his Nov. 15, 1975 death from throat cancer, it was noted that the reporter had used his own money to bury the man who called a laundry truck home.

Maulsby's services were held at his childhood church, St. David's Episcopal in Roland Park, organized by his son and daughter.

"He gave his body to science and was cremated," said Mary. "We didn't feel that what was left had anything to do with him. His ashes never quite got picked up."

Outside of Albuquerque, Mary keeps a box marked "Daddy's Stories," a cardboard Noah's ark stuffed with yellowed clippings about elephants, hippos, snakes, dogs, cats, bees, pigs, birds and bears. And stories of frequent encounters with strangers kindred to the man who wrote those tales.

"I got a wonderful reminder about Dad one day as I was sitting in a café," she said. "An elderly gentleman rode up on a bicycle above which he had rigged two large gray umbrellas. This was not only to shade himself, but his four parrots and a small dog. He left each bird with a piece of apple and the dog with a biscuit, and came inside the cafe and ordered a coffee and a bowl of fruit.

"I thought of my father, and how fast he would be talking to the man and his animals."

Such conversations—"Can I ask you a question?"—led to gems like this one from June 25, 1963.

"Who killed the black crow? An unidentified man, with the top of a trash can, he killed the black crow.

"Who saw him die? Harvey Zalis, 16, said he had seen and watched the crow die.

"Who'd make the shroud? None from that crowd all murmuring aloud and a small boy with a shovel was turned away when he sought to dig the grave."

Zalis, now in his mid-60s and living in Westminster, admitted that he was the one who dispatched the crow with a lucky toss of a trash can lid.

"I remember the crow, a wood crow, very big. It had been swooping down on people . . . but all I remember about the reporter is a gentleman with a notepad. I was shocked that anyone was even asking about it."

Dave Maulsby asked.

"He had a streak of brilliance in knowing what people would be interested in reading," said John Plunkett, 90, a retired assistant managing editor who joined the paper a few years after Maulsby.

Like the scorching summer day in Crabtown when

Maulsby wondered if it might just be hot enough to fry an egg on the sidewalk.

"It wasn't," said Chesapeake Bay writer Tom Horton, also a newsroom youngster in the early 1970s, remembering Maulsby as "a gentle man with hands that shook . . . always gracious and interested in us wet-behind-the-ears reporters."

["Yes, his hands shook," said Mary. "He was sober for two years. The year before my mother died and the year after. But then he could no longer refrain. He was too sad without her."]

Maulsby was a natural storyteller who knew in his bones that while scandals come and scandals go, few forget golden yarns spun on the wondrous, half-cocked loom that is the City of Baltimore.

Of all the animal stories filed by Maulsby, the best remembered is the 1970 tale of a 300-pound gorilla named Baltimore Jack.

It had it all: sex, jet travel, hope and disappointment, a now endangered species called the Playboy Bunny and the Maulsby by-line.

The Baltimore Zoo, which Maulsby covered with a zeal other reporters invested in bigger game, had sold Jack to its counterpart in Phoenix, which wanted the bachelor ape to mate with Hazel, a nine-year-old gorilla widow.

When the Maryland National Guard backed out of a promise to fly Jack to Phoenix—tax dollars were needed to clear jungle in Southeast Asia—*Playboy* publisher Hugh Hefner offered the services of his private jet, *Big Bunny*.

Sedated, Jack snoozed on Hef's round bed as Playmates stole peeks at him. Maulsby went along on the blind date. Hazel was thrilled. Jack less so.

"What followed was some two weeks' coverage of whimsy and absurdity from Phoenix as David sat by the gorilla cage, fueled by gin and noted, day-after-day, Jack's failure to impregnate Hazel," recalled Ettlin.

"He was Baltimore's shame."

After collecting string on the life and work of David Maulsby for years, I rushed the story into print only to regret it. An early draft appeared in the *Little Patuxent Review* out of Howard County, Maryland and was riddled with rookie mistakes.

The Maulsby portrait was marred by the kind of things—wrong dates, wrong names—that a good city editor beats out of a young reporter. Or else that young reporter ages into his middle years selling insurance.

For this I owe the Maulsby family and Mary Buchard Maulsby—who gave me her time and access to her files— an apology.

A more complicated lament is the effect that reporting the less-flattering aspects of Maulsby's life—much of it related to booze and sex, details too harsh for a daughter's love—had on Mary.

"Yes, he may have been tortured but he rose above it in so many ways," she wrote after the first draft appeared. "He was kind and true and you could see the kindness and sensitivity in his face. He had a brilliant mind, a dry wit and an amazing sense of humor. He loved to laugh, and laugh he did—every day.

"He was extremely perceptive, and could read people like a book. He was a mentor to many, including his brothers. Some of my fondest times with him were early morning walks in the woods, watching rabbits and listening to the birds.

Crabtown, USA

"I wish you could have found some of my father's peers, though most are probably dead," she wrote. "They used to tell me how envious they were of the relationship between my mom and dad when their marriage was in its earlier years.

"It was the kind of love at first sight that lasts a lifetime, even though the drinking often got in the way of their happiness. No one was with him at the moment of his death, but I'm sure she came for him and that he whispered her name in his last breath."

It reminded me of the final lines of Conrad's *Heart of Darkness* in which a bereaved fiancé begs to know the last words of her betrothed.

And a charitable acquaintance allows, "The last word he pronounced was—your name."

And finally, the turkey story.

A Baltimore Carol.

The tale is passed on with the kind of ornamentation that comes with hearing it over several years and many drinks. There is no rebuttal from those on the embarrassing end of the story. Like Maulsby, they are long deceased.

The teller is Joe Challmes, who worked the rewrite desk in Maulsby's final years and whose own death in 2015 made him the last guy to have heard the story from the source.

"In the 1960s, the Baltimore County Democratic machine rewarded all the hacks and political hires, ward heelers and district bosses with holiday gifts," recalled Challmes over a turkey club with old newspaper hacks at Roman's Place near Patterson Park.

"Small fry got a turkey and maybe a fifth of cheap

whiskey. The higher the honcho, the bigger the haul. One year, Maulsby was hanging around with the bosses in the county courthouse along with A. Gordon Boone, county state's attorney and a very big wig."

Boone and Maulsby were Ruxton neighbors. According to Challmes, as everyone was about to leave for the holiday, Willie the elevator man popped in the room, distraught and inconsolable.

"Willie had drunk his fifth and someone had filched his turkey while he was sleeping," said Challmes. "Willie had a family at home waiting for him to bring home the Christmas turkey and was beyond calming down.

"As befits a big wig politician, Boone said all the soothing things [but added] that all of the turkeys had been handed out and poor Willie was out of luck. Boone packed up his case of expensive bourbon and huge turkey and he and his henchmen made to leave.

"From the back of the room boomed a voice, 'GIVE THAT MAN YOUR TURKEY!'"

Everyone turned around: What the hell?

It was Maulsby. Boone tried to side-step the challenge, said that if Maulsby was so keen on Willie getting a turkey, the reporter should buy him one.

Maulsby didn't budge.

"GIVE THAT MAN YOUR TURKEY."

When Boone demanded to know why—incensed at being cornered in a room full of underlings—Maulsby pinned him.

"Because I am the reporter and you are the politician and unless you want to read about this in your Christmas morning paper, you better give that man your turkey."

The next day, a story ran on the freshly-minted humanitarian—A. Gordon Boone—coming to the rescue of Willie the Elevator Operator whose Christmas turkey was stolen by a heartless cad while the victim was hard at work.

"Maulsby," concluded Challmes, "and what a reporter should be."

THANKSGIVING DUTY

My welcome-to-how-we-do-things-at-*The Sun* moment was Thanksgiving 1977 as a new reporter," said M. William "Bill" Salganik, a veteran *Sunpapers* newspaperman and union leader. "I was working day general assignment. I turned in my story and was going home for Thanksgiving dinner.

"Right before I go there's a shooting in the Murphy Homes [on George Street]. I go over to the desk and say, 'You want me to go over to West Baltimore?' And the guy running the desk says, 'Nah, go enjoy your family. It would be news if someone wasn't shot in the Murphy Homes.'"

Berger cookies for a wedding present.

TINNEY / McSHEA

As autumn began its turn for winter in 2009, I drove from Lexington Market in the heart of Baltimore to Lexington Park in St. Mary's County with a bag of Berger Cookies and wedding wishes for dear friends leaping from cohabitation to commitment.

Jason Tinney asked Aileen McShea to be his wife and she said yes.

On the banks of the Potomac—a fiddler next to the preacher, bridesmaids in sunflower yellow—Tinney allowed that he did not trust himself "to make this promise twice."

A harp blowing actor turned writer, Tinney knows that a magician never explains his tricks. And thus I suspect no small amount of stagecraft in the declared distrust.

It is more likely that he will renew the privilege of Aileen's affection with each sunrise above their Monrovia homestead; that his heart more accurately echoes the sentiments of a fellow wayfarer.

"I love you . . . with a love that doesn't bend . . . and if there is eternity, I'd love you there again."

The cookies—discs of shortbread slathered with fudge—shared a table with other edibles from the Free State at a bonfire the night before the ceremony.

The three day celebration—rehearsal dinner/barbecue shindig, the exchange of vows, a barbershop quartet, bagpipes in the mist, crabcakes, and more Americana than a Route 66 gift shop—took place at Woodlawn, a Federal-era estate on the National Register of Historic Places.

Dessert (pies of pumpkin, pecan and key lime) came from the Wildewood Pastry Shop on Three Notch Road in nearby California, five miles south of Hollywood.

[Hollywood and California in St. Mary's County? Who named these places? Someone who got lost headed to the Gold Rush?]

Addressing the dearly beloved and holding back the rains was Dave Sheinin, a sportswriter with a one day minister's license who broke into an acapella "Ave Maria" that moved those of every faith.

[I'd like to see Frank "Rhett Butler" Deford pull that one off.]

"Things that are real are permanent, outliving fads and crushes and whims and that which is unreal," preached Sheinin. "You may be lured by the song of the unreal—that malleable, plastic smile—and it may hold sway for a terrifying moment.

"But you always return to what's real and solid and true."

And that is why I ferried a bag of Bergers from the corner of Paca & Lexington to as far south in Southern Maryland as you can go without getting wet.

To remind folks who gathered from across the country of my beloved Crabtown, the enduring (if sputtering) engine that once drove all commerce in the State of Maryland.

Baltimore—where I was born, educated and have lived all my life—is the permanent capital of my imagination. But others tell me there are rocks to be turned over beyond the Beltway, which I crossed south of Glen Burnie on Interstate 97 before picking up U.S. Route 301 toward the nuptials.

The Southern Maryland Blue Crabs play minor league baseball in Waldorf—opening day just a couple months away—where I turned off of 301 and onto Route 5.

I passed the road to Beantown, home of the physician Samuel A. Mudd, who went to prison for setting the broken leg of Lincoln assassin John Wilkes Booth as the murderer made for his imagined Promised Land of Dixie.

There were signs for the town of Helen (one of my favorite names, along with Alice) and just before the Amish area of Mechanicsville crossed into St. Mary's County, birthplace of the Maryland colony.

[On March 3, 1634, English Catholics fleeing Protestant persecution landed on St. Clement Island aboard the Ark and the Dove.]

Arriving in Lexington Park, I stopped in the Rod & Reel—LOTTERY / BEER / GAS / BLOOD WORMS—for a cup of coffee and listened to a local man say how he wished things in St. Mary's County would "go back to the way they used to be."

I expect to hear that sentiment a lot in the coming months as I wander from Lonaconing to Pocomoke City. What I did not expect to hear before Tinney and McShea were pronounced husband and wife was the "blessing of the Apaches."

"Now you will feel no rain, for each of you will be shelter for the other," said Sheinin. "Now you will feel no cold, for each of you will be warmth to the other.

"Now there will be no loneliness, for each of you will be companion to the other . . ."

A single viewing of *A Clockwork Orange* can
damn your soul to hell.

APOSTLE TIMMY

Timothy Ratajczak is a devout Catholic despite some doubts, a thoughtful screenwriter of Christian films and a Eucharistic minister at the St. Casimir parish where he was baptized some 50 years ago.

"I flirted with the evangelicals for a few years but I missed the sacraments," said Ratajczak, who has been in remission from leukemia since 2009 and received the sacrament of the sick at least once during the struggle.

Asked if the anointing worked, Ratajczak looked up from a Greek salad at G&A Coney Island Hot Dogs near his Belnord Avenue home and beamed: "Every time."

The heroes of Ratajczak's youth were Woody Allen and Mary Avara's favorite hometown filmmaker, John Waters, the lifelong Baltimorean is a man of hard-tested convictions. As a young man, he was good enough friends with Edie "the Egg Lady" Massey to take a bus trip with her to gamble in Atlantic City.

He doesn't linger on the bad—at times, the 1979 Our Lady of Pompei high school graduate is the definition of God's cheerful giver—but admits that "living in a cancer ward is a pretty lonely place."

And Hollywood is a funny place.

Like the way the director of Ratajczak's beautiful 2012 Easter film—*Apostle Peter and the Last Supper*—is

Gabriel Sabloff, who previously worked on *Night of the Living Dead: Origins 3D*.

"I was not consulted on the choice of the director," said Ratajczak, who shares the film's screenwriting credit with Sabloff. "The studio [Pure Flix of Los Angeles] is a producer driven company. They picked the director."

And the star of the film?

Robert Loggia—the guy who played the capo Feech La Manna on *The Sopranos*.

As the Apostle Peter —the fallible fisherman upon whom Christ built his Church, "a guy who really resonates with Catholics," said Ratajczak—Loggia is both subtle and sage. And he surrenders to his fate with a quiet courage despite demonic visions in his death row cell.

"We never intimate to the public that the people who appear in our films share any belief system with the film," said Ratajczak. "We hire professionals. Fred Willard [*Waiting for Guffman*] was in *Holy Man Undercover* because he wanted to work."

No matter the personal faith of those creating the films, the final product is both accurate and sincere enough to carry the Dove Foundation's "family approved." The Dove group is more apt to line up with the religious who taught Ratajczak in parochial school than they would Pauline Kael.

"One of the nuns told us that if we went to see *A Clockwork Orange* you'd go to hell," laughed Ratajczak. "Later on, when I got [*Clockwork* star Malcolm] McDowell's autograph I told him the story. He looked at me and said, 'She was right.'"

Some of the films Ratajczak has written—which include *Hidden Secrets* and *Sarah's Choice*—have prompted viewers to write.

"They were thanking me because the films helped them at a low point in their life."

Timothy sees the spiritual side of his career ("Half of what I write is Christian, the other half is for myself") as his ministry, one as valid as that of his 63-year-old brother, the Rev. Justin Ratajczak OFM, Conv., a pastor in Boswell, Pa.

"Do I hope my films will convert people? Absolutely," he said. "Isn't that what the Lord told us to do—spread the Gospel? Isn't that the great commission?"

A few years ago, Ratajczak—whose day job is director of marketing for a Baltimore area construction company—wrote a screenplay called *Rhapsodies*, something of a love letter to his beloved Crabtown.

"It takes place in Canton and Fells Point and the Inner Harbor," he said. "Baltimoreans deal with problems the same as everybody else, but more so. It's an ensemble film filled with eccentrics."

As it should be.

Ratajczak's seventh movie—*Queen Esther*, a drama on the eponymous heroine of the Book of Esther and the figure upon which the Jewish feast of Purim is based—is scheduled to begin production in early summer.

"We show Esther defeating the anti-Semite Hamen," said Ratajczak, who has also written horror. "It's really a nasty little story."

From Memphis to Cochin is a long, long drive.

WEDDING CHINA

"I got me a nickel smashed flatter than a dime ..."
—Guy Clark

In May of 2011, just before Bobby Zimmerman's birthday, Hettleman gave away a box of dishes delivered to his grandmother's house on Smallwood Street by a handful of ex-lovers: cake dishes, cereal dishes, bowls for stew and pans for pie.

He gave them to his most recent ex-lover in the midst of trying to set up a secret apartment somewhere near Auchentoroly Terrace to get away from her husband, a musician without soul.

Some of the dishes were from Cochin, others from Memphis and a few from around the corner and up the streets.

All once had night before left-overs in them delivered to Hettleman's studio in the middle of the afternoon.

BLUE MONDAY

The voice of El Duke-O fills the small apartment where Joseph Buchanan used to live.

Mr. Buchanan is no more; dead and gone since pneumonia took him at 72. But he is survived by the ghost of his show-biz persona, a piano-playing rambler known as El Duke-O.

El Duke-O's baritone booms from a tape player and rolls through three small rooms in an old folks high-rise on Chase Street, the last gathering place for memories from a half-century in music, a career spanning the footlights of the Harlem Renaissance to narrow gin mills on the Baltimore waterfront.

He croons: *"Blue Monday...how I hate Blue Monday..."*

Beneath a poster announcing a benefit concert for El Duke-O, is Oliver McAphee, a daughter; a son, Bruce Buchanan; and Ernestine Welch, one of the pianist's four wives. They represent El Duke-O's eight children, 20 grandchildren, 15 great-grandchildren and hundreds of fans in a life spent in Rhode Island and Baltimore. They are all listening to El Duke-O's music.

Over the weekend they were sifting through piles of their loved one's belongings, looking for keepsakes to donate to the Eubie Blake Cultural Center on North Howard Street in the city's old shopping district.

El Duke-O plays blues by Muddy Waters and country

by Merle Haggard along with Gershwin's *Summertime*, as the family takes a moment from the scrapbooks to weep along with their memories.

"It's hard," says Ms. Welch, the wife for whom Mr. Buchanan wrote "Ernestine's Out Tonight," a 45-rpm single still on the jukebox at the Newport, R.I., Elks Club, and the only record he ever made. "It's hard knowing he's dead when it sounds like he's right here."

Ms. Welch stares out a glass balcony door that looks east over the city, her right hand balled up and banging against her knee, in time with the music, as if she is holding on to keep from breaking down.

"My mother used to have a rooming house in Newport, R.I., and the owners of the local nightclubs used to engage her for rooms for their entertainers," she says. "I met him I guess it was in 1950, when they sent him to my mother's house for a room. He was good-looking; I loved the way he sang and played, and I wasn't above swooning."

Her advice for young women prone to swooning over musicians is to think twice if they are also prone to jealousy.

It was in a Newburyport, Mass., club, Ms. Welch remembers, that Mr. Buchanan began getting notice for his tribute to Louis Armstrong. Word of the act reached the trumpeter and Satchmo dropped in on Mr. Buchanan one night to catch the show.

On a coffee table in front of Ms. Welch lies a souvenir from the visit: a trademark, sweat-stained white handkerchief signed "Louis Armstrong."

Said Ms. Welch: "We used to walk arm-in-arm with Ella Fitzgerald."

El Duke-O's final notes were played out in a spare apartment on Cathedral Street adorned with photocopied pictures of a young and saucy Billie Holliday.

Crabtown, USA

A small shelf of books includes *Outwitting Arthritis* from which El Duke-O learned that if he wore gloves while playing it would cushion the pain of hitting the keys and a row of empty liquor miniatures lines a mirrored shelf on the wall.

On the floor: a homemade sign that reads: "The Living Legend Celebrating 55 Years in Show Business—1930 to 1985—appearing here . . ."

The last place El Duke-O appeared—after the big time of backing up for Billie Holiday, Duke Ellington and Sarah Vaughn and working for 10 years as a fire dispatcher in Providence, R.I.—was a joint called Dave's Pub on the corner of Lexington Street and Guilford Avenue.

"If you were there you heard the old tunes," says Bruce Buchanan, who came down from Providence to see his father buried last week at Mount Zion Cemetery on Hollins Ferry Road. "He was the kind of guy who liked to take people all the way back."

Olivera McAphee listens to her father's voice—a voice that came to Baltimore in 1981 to rest and ended up lifting spirits at the Cat's Eye Pub and the Peabody Book Shop and Bier Stube—and knows he never made it as big as he wanted.

"I think he was heartbroken more than bitter," she says. "He didn't get the kind of bright star that he wanted, but you don't get to be the age he was by being too big a fool, either."

The triangular shaped building across from
Zeppie's.

WATERFRONT POULTRY

A note from a stranger in exile from the ribbons of Holy Land that roll east of President Street toward Sparrows Point.

"Dear Mr. Alvarez: I'm not from Baltimore. I'm from the FOOT OF BROADWAY. I graduated from Archbishop Curley in 1977.

"My grandmother had a poultry store where she sold live, and very recently alive, chickens to the other Polish speaking immigrants. My family's store was on Gough Street, two doors from Broadway. It was known as Eva's poultry in the 1940s and '50s just as I came on the scene.

"Before that my grandmother sold pets—rabbits, puppies, kittens, birds, ducklings, most notably monkeys, and of course chicks—then the shop evolved. I played in the cages and sat in the storefront window. We lived upstairs. My grandfather worked the tugboats next to the Recreation Pier, My father and mother used to stroll near the Pagoda when they were dating.

"My grandfather, father and uncle ran their business out of the triangular-shaped building across the street from Zeppie's saloon. I remember playing there, feeding the coal stove and watching the watermelon boats outside.

"There was a calendar on the wall with a topless woman. How could I forget that?

"I am now 2,000 miles away and 7,000 feet higher and

about to teach my Sunday-morning ski lesson, but a more perfect morning would be to walk past John's Bargains, and spin on the outside seat of Prevas Brothers, eating a hot dog with ketchup.

"About 12 years ago, I got the *Fountain of Highlandtown* out of the library and never returned it. I paid the fine and shared it with my mother who was astonished at stories that seemed to be written from her life.

"It was one of the last books she read before developing dementia . . ."

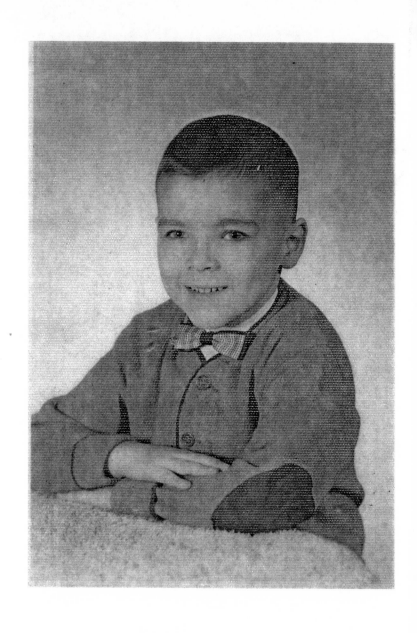

I try to see the face of Christ in them . . .

CATHOLIC BOY

"I'm very conscious of my faith when I'm working but I fail at it every day. Failing and trying to do better the next day; to me, that's what it means to be Catholic ..."
—Leo Ryan, Jr., the altar boy who grew up to be a judge

Leo remembers the first time it dawned on him that the Archdiocese of Baltimore was a big deal.

It's like the day the kid obsessed with baseball finds out that Babe Ruth was born on Emory Street just south of Pratt. This was back about 1969.

"All of the altar boys from the Shrine got on a bus for some big event at the Basilica, we were all in our cassocks and surplice," said Ryan, a bookworm who grew up reading the Catholic Encyclopedia as closely as he followed sports columnist and former St. Jude Shrine usher John Steadman (1927 to 2001) in the *News-American*.

"I clearly remember being struck by the weight of the history. There's a pride as a Catholic belonging to the Premier See," said Ryan of that long-ago bus trip from Herring Run Park to downtown, the temple of books called the Pratt Library on one side of Cathedral Street, the Basilica of the National Shrine of the Blessed Virgin Mary on the other.

"I remember we saw Cardinal Gibbons's hat hanging

from the ceiling," said Ryan. "Just hanging there, disintegrating."

~~~

Leo Ryan is the kind of guy who takes a library copy of Thomas W. Spalding's scholarly history of the Archdiocese—*The Premier See*, published in 1995—to the beach. And then, surrounded by those creasing the clichés of Balducci, Patterson and Brown—has the nerve to call it "a page turner."

"I couldn't put it down," said Ryan, who for decades has spent the first two weeks of each August in Ocean City, ritually making gallons of crab soup and keeping it chilled in Fisher's Popcorn tubs.

In Baltimore, he has been a parishioner at Immaculate Conception in Towson since 1991. At the shore, he attends Mass at St. Andrew's, just south of the Delaware line on 144th street.

Brother Spalding, a distant relative of 19th century Baltimore archbishop Martin John Spalding, joined the Congregation of the Brothers of St. Francis Xavier in 1942. He died at age 78 in 2003. From Spalding's work—which includes a biography of his famous ancestor—Ryan absorbed the history behind the grandeur he experienced on that long ago school trip to the Basilica.

Among the facts, many firsts.

* Baltimore was the first diocese in the fledgling nation called the United States, 1789.
* The site of the first ordination of a Catholic priest in the United States, 1793.
* The city where Saint Elizabeth Ann Seton—the first native-born citizen of the U.S. to be canonized (1975)—founded the Daughters of Charity in 1809.
* And where, in 1885, the Baltimore Catechism was

written and adopted as the standard text for Catholic religion teachers in the United States. Formally, "Catechism of Christian Doctrine, Prepared and Enjoined by Order of the Third Council of Baltimore," the text endured in classrooms for nearly a century.

Did someone say the Baltimore Catechism?
Quick now: Question No. 574.
What is a Sacrament?
"An outward sign instituted by Christ to give grace," answered Ryan with a smile, still the smartest kid in class. "It's still a good answer."

Ryan was enjoying a glass of juice at a *patisserie* on Charles Street one fine Sunday morning in the spring of 2014 after a nostalgic visit to the Basilica for early Mass.

Those good answers, the guidance of his parents—along with the influence of his uncle, the Rev. Kennard S. Muller, 80, of St. Ignatius in Hickory—helped turn the altar boy who wore the surplice into the man who wears the black robes of a Maryland District Court judge.

From the bench—to which he was appointed by Governor Martin O'Malley in 2010—and throughout the rest of his life, Ryan believes that he "can't profess to be Catholic and not be able to forgive . . . as hard as that is sometimes."

The labor of administering justice in District Court, said Ryan, is sort of like practicing medicine in an Army M.A.S.H. unit.

"My court isn't presented with the kind of controversy that lends itself to dilemmas" that would pin Ryan between the secular laws of the state of Maryland and his Catholic conscience, he said.

"I try to treat the people who appear before me with

dignity," said Ryan. "I get impatient with some of them and when I go back in chambers I know I have to do better. I try to see the face of Christ in them."

That face is rarely a pleasant one, often having more in common with one on an early 16th century panel by Hans Holbein the Younger—"The Body of the Dead Christ in the Tomb"—than the radiant visage of the risen Messiah.

The intent of Holbein, as understood by the likes of Dostoevsky (whose works addressed crime, punishment and salvation) was to show the Son of God having suffered the fate that awaits us all.

The challenge facing Ryan—who has later been thanked in public by a few folks he dealt with in court—is to punish when necessary and help correct when possible.

"I put one guy in jail for a while and he said, 'You're the only one who understands me.' Some people need to go to jail and some need to be lifted up," he said. "I get a sense from some people that no one has ever told them they're worthwhile or that they can change.

"Sometimes I tell people things that I believe come straight from Catholic orthodoxy: 'I believe in you . . .'"

It's a Maryland thing.

THANKSGIVING OYSTERS

"My husband says I eat stuff that would make a billy goat puke ..."

—Lorna Meyerson Sotoloff

L et the record show that Sotoloff's husband is allergic to onions, is cool to crustaceans, and grew up in Philadelphia.

And Lorna—Woodlawn High School Class of 1977—is a Baltimore girl through-and-through and, as such, eats sections of lobster other people throw away, the "squiggly parts" of a steamed crab (the "mustard" and guts), and, of course, oysters.

Especially oysters. And especially at Thanksgiving.

"I'll have about 10 to 12 people for dinner this year," said the Reisterstown resident and ultrasound technician at Mercy Hospital. "If I didn't have oysters on the menu, they'd be sad."

Not disappointed, frustrated or angry in the way that only relatives can get over the holidays.

Sad.

Between plates of raw oysters at Cross Street Market, long retired newspaperman and South Baltimore epicure Jim Keat claims not to know "anyone foolish enough" to ruin an oyster by cooking it.

But Sotoloff is serving a chowder to be reckoned with, one she believes might teach the ink-stained dog a new trick.

"I was thumbing through my Thanksgiving folders and came across the recipe," says the bivalve buff who buys her oysters by the pint—$10.99 a jar—from the Blue Point Crab House in Owings Mills.

"It's sort of a combination oyster stew and corn chowder. It's good because I can make it ahead of time. And I'll make an oyster pie while my husband cooks the turkey and works on his sweet potatoes."

And while the oyster dishes mark the Sotoloff Thanksgiving as a Maryland affair, a side dish from Lorna's childhood will make it indelibly Baltimore: kielbasa with sauerkraut. Unlike the oysters, few in her extended clan—foodies known to take pictures of groaning plates—would be sad if Polish sausage went missing one year.

The Sotoloffs have a teenage son—Harrison—who appears to straddle his parents' palates. The kid is a big fan of rockfish and though he won't eat an oyster raw, he does enjoy them cooked. Lorna is confident, however, that he will slurp in time.

"It's a Maryland thing," she says.

Sotoloff learned to slurp while going to bull and oyster roasts with her family as a kid. "I like oysters steamed, stewed, cooked, fried, raw with sauce, and naked," Sotoloff says. "My favorite is a recipe from an old boyfriend, a gourmet. He poached oysters with champagne and cream. Pretty decadent."

There is one way, however, that Sotoloff has never eaten an oyster—an old-fashioned, most unpredictable way that isn't encountered too often these days: a freshly shucked raw oyster accompanied by a tiny parasite known as the "pea crab."

"Oh my God," Sotoloff says. "I know nothing about this oyster crab."

The *Pinnotheres ostreum*, the oyster crab or pea crab, lives inside the shells of certain Atlantic coast bivalves and is particularly abundant in the Chesapeake Bay. At less than an inch across—with a jagged stripe on its tiny shell—the pea crab resembles a spider, according to lifetime Eastern Shore resident Joyce Clarke Heiser, an elementary-school bookkeeper.

"When I was a kid, we had lots of oysters growing up in Box Iron," the 64-year-old Heiser says of her hometown, about halfway between Snow Hill and Girdletree in Worcester County. "It was a real treat when Dad would open them up and there'd be a little, tiny crab there."

It was, Heiser says, "crunchy."

It's a century-old story that oysters aren't as plentiful as they once were, already on a serious wane when Gregory Lukowski, son of my father's best friend Jerome, and I were kids together down Bill Miller's shore in Edgemere.

"Partying didn't stop down the shore just because summer ended," said Gregory, now a Chesapeake Bay pilot. "Beer drinking and seven-card stud—jokers wild—just transitioned with the seasons.

"I remember one particularly brisk autumn day arriving at Mr. Bill's and noticing the half-barrel grill all fired up. I was just a kid but I knew it was too cold for barbecue. What were they up to?"

["They" when Greg and I were young and pretending to be Brooks Robinson and Paul Blair, were always the grown-ups. "We" were "the kids."]

Continued Lukowski: "Next to the grill was a bushel of oysters and a bucket of water. Oysters, yuck . . . don't like those.

"Wait a minute! They just dumped some oysters on the grill and covered them with sopping wet burlap bags soaking in the bucket. After a few sizzling minutes . . .

. . . steamed oysters! Hey, they don't look so yucky. Drop a few in a bowl of melted butter and garlic. Should I dare try one?

"I've been hooked ever since," he confessed and has passed a love for the delicacy onto his sons Zak and Sam.

Billions of oysters lay on the bed of the Chesapeake in the 19th century. The rape of the bay is lyrically documented in William W. Warner's 1976 gem, *Beautiful Swimmers*.

A yardstick for how much over-harvesting has depleted the local oyster—despite occasional reports of a comeback via artificial reefs—is that Heiser only pays a dollar less for a pint on the Eastern Shore than Lorna Sotoloff does in suburban Baltimore. There were oyster packing houses in Girdletree when Heiser was growing up after World War II, but no more.

A dollar more or less won't keep the delicacy from joining bowls of mashed potatoes and cranberry sauce on Heiser's table this time of year.

"I'm not crazy about oyster stuffing, but we'll do some fried oysters around Thanksgiving," says Heiser, whose brother, Bob Clarke, a former chancellor of state colleges in Vermont, brings Cabot cheese and maple syrup to the family's gathering. In exchange, he expects oysters and soft crabs waiting for him in his sister's freezer.

"I fry my oysters in a light egg wash with just a little milk, salt and pepper, and some cracker meal," Heiser says. "We eat them off the plate or on sandwiches."

One aspect of enjoying oysters is in play for Sotoloff, a daughter of Israel, but not Heiser, a gentile.

According to Jewish dietary law, all shellfish—along

with pork and mixing meat and dairy is *treif*—forbidden.

"Obviously, I don't keep kosher," Sotoloff says. "The reason I shouldn't be eating seafood isn't [religion], it's cholesterol."

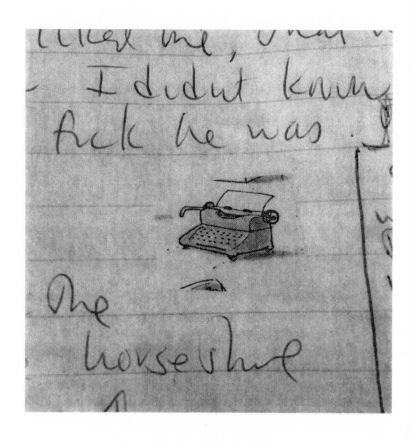

If it cuts good, paste it.

OBSESSIVE COLLAGE

Our obsessions do not seem as peculiar as once feared—all alone, doing math that only makes sense to us—until someone else comes along, particularly someone admired, who shares the eccentricity.

Imagine my glee upon leafing through the *Paris Review* and discovering that me and Satchmo –the immortal Louis Armstrong—are brothers in collage.

While gigging between the four corners of the world, the trumpeter cooled out between shows by decorating reel-to-reel tape boxes with pictures cut from newspapers, magazines, and personal correspondence.

The results—presentations of bright, floating color often depicting the man and his horn—are preserved in the Louis Armstrong Archives at Queens College, Flushing, N.Y.

What especially interests me is that Armstrong created collage to relax from his main form of expression; that few people knew about it and he didn't have to worry about being good at it—all he had to do was enjoy it.

According to the illustrated feature in Issue No. 184 of the *Paris Review*, Louis apparently wasn't good enough at it for his wife to let him hang the work in their home, thus his move to tape boxes.

My practice of this ancient art—collage from the

French *coller*, to glue; a medium traced to the invention of paper in China—emerged as the unexpected and profoundly comforting surprise of my middle age.

Until I spend a little cut and paste time with my morning coffee (a ritual meditation dependent upon fading technologies) I can't quite get on with the day. And it calls loudest during stress, when there is something more practical—such as turning in a story on time—to be done.

Faddists might call what I do "scrapbooking," except that my versions appear to be cobbled together by a lunatic. My children have warned that one wrong move by dear old Dad and my quiet passion could be the slam-dunk "Exhibit A" in my committal.

The evidence is stacked in milk crates: marble composition books fattened not with old photographs but photographs of things that are old: televisions when they were pieces of furniture (often cut from news stories about octogenarians without health insurance); postage both new—love the "50's Fins & Chrome" series—and cancelled; and obits of long-ago baseball players.

Pieced together around decades of my journal entries, it makes for a strange encyclopedia currently running to 40 volumes and captioned in a script that has shrunk as I've aged, as though I were a lost sibling of R. Crumb.

Crackers?

You'd have to ask Louis or his misses. All I know is I'm rarely more serene than when fooling with dollar-store markers, a ruler, transparent tape, old newspapers, and scissors.

The scissors are small, with plastic handles; the kind found in a third-grade art class. Squeezed between my thumb and forefinger, the pressure of the blades is reassuring as I shear photographs in one long, curving motion; the tool gliding around the image of a loved one destined to become stationery on which I'll send well wishes to another loved one.

My preferred canvas is a postcard. In the way that a story unfulfilled until it is received, my ceremonies—echoing an age when light was caught on cellulose and humans delivered correspondence from heavy sacks—are incomplete without a daily walk to the mailbox.

Affixed with a 35-cent mainsail, I launch my 4-by-6 inch visions on voyages to kin I don't see often enough, friends with whom I share other passions, and random, never-to-be-seen-again wayfarers who crossed my path long enough to stand for a photo and give their address.

Many of the images are cut from snapshots taken with an ever-present disposable camera. The cheap plastic boxes shoot beautiful 35mm film, still the choice of artists and old school professionals.

Bought at gas station mini-marts—a "FUN PAK" for $6.95—the disposables are pointed at food in preparation, presentation, and partaking. The pictures are later combined with carefully peeled and re-affixed butcher shop stickers documenting that 1.01 pounds of thick-slicked bacon cost $5.04 in Los Angeles in late 2008.

I'm especially keen on photographing rock 'n' roll t-shirts—sometimes vintage, more often department store retro-wear—worn by the aforementioned passersby.

"Excuse me," I'll say if someone walks by behind a faded image of Freddie King or Foghat. "Can I take a picture of your shirt?"

If the stranger is game, somewhere down the line they'll receive a collage combining the picture of their shirt (no heads, just neck, arms and 100 percent rock 'n' roll), a photocopy of an album cover by the band, and maybe a quote from a deceased band member snipped from an old copy of *CREEM* magazine.

Other hand-cropped images—self-portraits of myself with people I know, the camera held at arm's length—are married to scraps found on the street. Kids may swear that they lost their homework, but America's alleyways suggest something else.

Not long ago, I found what appeared to be the entire contents of a homeless person's pockets, complete with the business cards of social workers, addresses for shelters and soup kitchens, and a citation to appear in court on a street infraction resulting from not having access to indoor plumbing.

All of which I bring home (sometimes after a stop at FedEx Kinko's where color copy machines add ribbons of depth to flat images) to be filtered through my laboratory before being sent back out into the world.

"My mother doesn't understand most of them, I have to go over and explain," said a childhood friend over the course of his father's recent death, my mini-mosaics intended for big smiles during dark days. "But keep 'em coming."

In order to keep them coming, I must practice a discipline more elusive than collage: patience.

My throwaway cameras pile up more quickly than I can afford to have them processed. Because I don't label them, part of the fun is reaching into the grab bag for one and ferrying its secrets to the drug store.

Another week passes before the pics come back—never one-hour processing, because immediacy, overvalued in our culture, robs the process of its natural course.

Writing to a friend in 1953, Armstrong said: ". . . my hobbie *[sic]* . . . is using a lot of Scotch tape . . . to pick out the different things during what I read and piece them together and [make] a little story of my own."

264

Crabtown, USA

You can find me setting up portable studios of tape and ink and paper in coffee shops, saving the sticky sections bordering sheets of stamps to make frames for pictures of road signs snapped from the car—Amelia, La., for my daughter; Ralph, S.D. for my Spanish grandfather—on cross-country road trips.

An unadorned envelope appears naked to me.

What a wonderful world.

Help me in my disbelief.

BALTIMORE BELIEVE

The mystical, beleaguered, enduring City of Baltimore and its mortal enemy: The Monster that Ate the City of Baltimore.

A poor-to-working-class town rich in history and the culture of generations of freed blacks and immigrants.

An eccentric and too-often-trash-littered landscape festooned with banners, bumper stickers, trash cans and t-shirts that declare, in simple black-and-white: BELIEVE.

And an angry and grown-up-too-soon girl pinned against the hood of a Ford Taurus in the Remington neighborhood telling her brain damaged, tattooed boyfriend: "Junior, I don't believe a fucking word you say."

Good to the last drop.

BOSNIAN COFFEE

The photographer Frank Klein IV invites me to his house in Mencken's neighborhood the day before what would have been my Spanish grandfather's 108th birthday. He serves Turkish coffee, the beans ground finer than fine—double super fine as I have seen the process described on sides of Ann Page spice tins—before we walk through the neighborhood with notebook and camera.

Klein—who grew up on a farm outside of Hancock in the Keystone State and dropped out of Loch Raven High School—learned how to brew like the Ottomans while working for non-governmental agencies in war-torn Bosnia and Serbia in the 1990s.

He uses a brass pepper mill and grinds and grinds and grinds for a good 20 minutes while we talk in his kitchen.

"Bosnian coffee is taken black," he said. "Put sugar in and it's Serbian."

Hey, get those things out of the sun.

DEVILED EGGS

". . . golden dollops of silken delight nested in alabaster boats . . ."

—Billy Driscoll, Hamilton boy

When Toni Clark was married more than 60 years ago, she received a honeymoon surprise in Virginia Beach from husband Clyde Clark, known to all as "Skeets."

"He bought me a cookbook," said Toni.

Growing up in the 600 block of South Newkirk Street (now Greektown, a part of Highlandtown then simply known as "the Hill"), Toni left it to her sisters to learn old world Italian recipes from their mother, Mary Starteri Reda Adornato (1896 to 1964).

The honeymoon gift from Skeets—a man with his appetite on the future—opened the kitchen door for Toni, who "didn't learn to cook until after I got married."

Methodically adding to that first book of recipes, she amassed a culinary repertoire gleaned from a cookbook collection that would number more than 500 volumes.

"I had cookbooks from the gas company and the Western Maryland Dairy," said Clark, who for years lived on 48th street in Dundalk before moving to Forest Hill in Harford County. "An older man who lived near Essex used to come by every couple of weeks and buy them from me

271

for a dollar . . . five dollars for the big ones. My heavens, he bought a lot of my books."

What the old man from Essex didn't get was Toni's collection of handwritten recipes, which she has willed to her niece, Cindi Hemelt Gallagher; a fat file of dog-eared and vanilla-stained index cards from friends and relatives that includes the anchor of any reasonable buffet: THE DEVILED EGG!

"I like'em real nice and creamy," said Clark, who pushes the hard yolks through a strainer for the proper consistency. "I don't like'em lumpy."

After whipping up a dozen or so for generations of baby showers and summer cookouts, holiday cheer and funeral receptions in church basements, Clark confessed that she hadn't made deviled eggs in over a decade.

But Leo Ryan, a Baltimore County district judge, enjoyed them just this past Labor Day. In a move unthinkable in his parents' generation, the 50-year-old Ryan consumed STORE BOUGHT deviled eggs.

Which, he says, is better than none at all.

"We went boating on the bay and were asked to bring lunch, so my wife and I stopped at Pastore's on Loch Raven Boulevard to get Italian subs for everyone," said Ryan.

In the chill case, along with the other dairy items, Ryan spied packages of deviled eggs—two halves for $1.29—and tossed them in the cart with a bottle of Stewart's root beer.

Although Ryan—a resident of Towson by way of Shrine of the Little Flower on Belair Road—believes that "deviled eggs need to sit on a buffet table for at least a few minutes to reach peak flavor," he made concessions to his cravings.

"They looked too good to resist," he said. "I ate them in the car on the way to the marina. My wife wasn't happy that I didn't save one for her."

Crabtown, USA

With a little prodding earlier this summer, Toni Clark came out of deviled egg retirement and was back on her game at a birthday party in the alley where she grew up with a score of first cousins between the Great Depression and World War II.

For my son Jake's 26th birthday in July 2009, Clark brought a plate of beauties covered with plastic wrap.

[It's the rare cook who covers their deviled eggs with foil although the real pros use closable Tupperware holders to transport a dozen of the goodies.]

"It's very simple to make deviled eggs," said Clark. "You hard boil the eggs, cut them in half and take the yolk out. You put the yolks in a bowl with mayo. Some put them in a mixer but I strain them by hand.

"And I use apple cider vinegar and just a tip of a teaspoon of regular [yellow] mustard."

[In some circles, the wet versus dry mustard debate rages when it comes to deviled eggs. But not around here.]

"Sprinkle with paprika and then you can decorate them anyway you want," said Clark. "Maybe a slice of baby gherkin, real thin across the top."

Dundalk girl Airin Miller, a promising fiction writer recently graduated from the writing program at Virginia's Hollins University, remembers deviled eggs at picnics with her mother's city police colleagues and childhood family reunions.

Los Angeles screenwriter Noelle Wright said the appearance of sliced white ovals filled with bright dollops of yellow heralded a night of suburban fun for her parents and their friends outside of Detroit in the 1970s.

"I always knew my folks were having a swanky party when the deviled eggs came out," said Wright. "They took their place right next to Swedish meatballs and bacon wrapped water chestnuts!"

In the Donnelly family, Mary Frances—daughter of Gene Donnelly, former spokesman for the archdioceses of Baltimore and Wilmington, Del.—remembered her "Nan" serving deviled eggs at the annual Preakness party.

"It was always there with other classics, like aspic," said Donnelly, known as "Frannie."

And then there's the case of the deviled egg HOG (every family has one.)

This little piggy is the former Nancy Lee Hiebel, whose parents were part of the original wave of dreamers rehabbing houses in Ridgely's Delight during the early years of the Schaefer Administration.

Now Nancy Lee Mitchell—an Ellicott City middle school teacher and lead singer for the Plastic Magi rock band—young Nancy said she had no choice but to thieve deviled eggs.

"No one in my family made them," she said. "I'd have to wait 'til I was dragged to company picnics or family reunions. But once a huge round platter of those little devils were in front of me, there was no stopping.

"I always felt guilty eating so many because I knew they took a lot of effort to make—at least that was my mother's excuse for not ever making them," said Mitchell, whose band opened for the immortal Fleshtones in 2009 at Blob's Park, the Bavarian beer garden in Elkridge that has seen tens of thousands of plates of deviled eggs come and go since the 1930s.

Said Mitchell: "I'd always think, 'I wonder how many I can get away with eating without anyone noticing?'

"When I got older and could drink beer at these less than thrilling social gatherings, I became bolder. I'd wait till the party had dragged on a little bit and eye up the plate of eggs.

"If there were at least one-third of them left, I would loudly declare: "Hey, I'm eating all the deviled eggs!"
And proceeded to do so.
Baltimore poet MiMi Zannino was so moved by the memory of the delicacy within her large, close-knit family that she composed an ode to deviled eggs in honor of her mother, Maria.

ANGEL FOOD

A golden globe lives within this
white oval casing, but if you slice
the shelled whole from pointy end to its
wider bottom, an open-heart lies
cupped in two less-than-perfect halves.
Admire this hard-boiled miracle, then lift
one half and press your thumb lightly
on its back until the half-heart tumbles
into a bowl soon filled with a dozen
other crumbled yolks.
As you crush the soft golden flesh
begin to douse it with mayonnaise, a
touch of mustard, a splash of
Worcestershire, a dash of salt and pepper.
Hand-whip it, then dip your finger
into its center. If it sticks, raise that digit to
your wagging tongue and test what you have
created from all these broken hearts.
Scoop and fill the fleshy white cups with
your golden concoction. Now split a
pimento-stuffed olive and press it like
a belly-button onto each golden mound.
Sprinkle this plated wheel of deviled eggs
with paprika, fill the gaps between with fresh
parsley . . . offer it from the bottom of your heart.

MiMi knew she was grown up when she began making deviled eggs without supervision, which she could do "by the time I was a teenager."

True adulthood arrived when she was designated "official deviled egg" contributor to Zannino family gatherings.

"My latest spin-off of Mom's recipe is to fold Maryland crab meat into the yolk," she said, noting a preference for back-fin from the J.M. Clayton crab house in Cambridge, where she lived for several years.

"I then sprinkle Old Bay instead of paprika on the finished eggs and top each egg with a generous pinch of the crab meat."

Mama Zannino, however, prefers what MiMi calls "the pure recipe—hers . . . so I make both."

Mild paprika, your average supermarket brand (anyone have a number for Ann Page?) is the standard spice sprinkled over deviled eggs, more for the eye than the tongue in that mild teeters on the edge of bland.

Western civilization long ago adopted the *deviled* to mean highly spiced food, with the phrase in use for years before turning up in English literature during the mid-18th century.

Thus, the use of hot paprika—or even smoked—would give the eggs a rung in culinary hell.

A *New York Times* food writer once suggested the simple addition of tomato paste to the yolks that would not only "tint" the filling but "add a sweet, fruity flavor [to] balance out the spicy part of the equation.

In they are called *œuf mimosa* and finely chopped parsley is mixed with the yolks and mayonnaise.

In Spain, where the locals are fond of adding hard

boiled eggs and canned tuna to everyday salads, there is an appetizer known as "Salmon Stuffed Eggs," whose recipe can be found in Penelope Casas's 2003 book of tapas recipes published by Knopf.

And those wild and crazy Hungarians mash hard-boiled yolks and mix them with milk moistened bread, mustard and parsley before refilling the cavity.

In a move apparently unique to Hungary, these concoctions—when served as an entrée—are then baked, topped with sour cream and served with French Fries.

The global approach to deviled eggs includes fillings made from nuts, wasabi, chutney, capers, caviar (as they do in the Netherlands), spinach, and poppy seed.

Germans are known to add a touch of anchovy, which the average American has never even liked on pizza. And new wave foodies sometimes load the hollow with hummus.

"I'd be strung up if I brought deviled eggs with hummus in them," said Mary May Maskell, deviled designee for a large Baltimore family of Irish-Catholics: 11 siblings and their offspring capable of devouring 72 deviled eggs in a matter of moments.

"Sometimes my brother Bobby puts an olive on top of his and everybody's like, 'What's with the olive, Bob?'"

The family recipe—rooted in Germany—is the legacy of Maskell's "great, great aunt Lil," known as "the legendary cook."

Mary Elizabeth "Lil" Benzinger [1860 to 1945] was the sister of Maskell's father's grandmother. It was Benzinger's grandfather, a German, who began the family line in America.

"They have to be just like my mother [Agnes Ripple May] made them," said Maskell, 50, of Parkville "with a hint of vinegar" from yellow mustard.

A dental hygienist and alumnus of the Institute of Notre Dame, Maskell believes the tradition will continue through her niece Jeannie, 41, and has noticed a trend: the younger generation isn't interested in the work it takes to make a plate of deviled eggs—"a lot of time and effort"—but appetites have not waned.

"I really like watching people enjoy them," she said, looking forward to making a batch for Thanksgiving. "But if I don't hide the eggs as soon as I arrive, they're gone in ten minutes."

Like many Baltimoreans, Toni Clark assumed the once ubiquitous deviled egg was red, white and blue through and through.

"It's really an American dish," said Clark, who has no memories of her mother ever making deviled eggs amidst the mountain of pasta that came out of the basement kitchen of the Adornato house at 638 South Newkirk Street.

The scholarship of Mark Sohn supports the deviled egg's place in Americana. A professor of Appalachian studies at Pikeville College in Kentucky, Sohn has documented the place of honor deviled eggs hold along the mountainous region of the eastern seaboard.

"No mountain dinner is complete without deviled eggs," writes Sohn in *Appalachian Home Cooking*, published in 2005 by the University Press of Kentucky.

Down south, the yolks are sometimes mixed with crushed bacon or pickle relish and the mayonnaise of choice is Duke's.

Like so much of what we now think of as All-American, the deviled egg landed here from foreign shores, its appearance preceding not just the United States, but the discovery of the New World. It harkens back to ancient Rome.

In elite circles of the Empire, according to *Cooking and Dining in Imperial Rome*, edited by J. Dommers Vehling, "boiled eggs [were] seasoned with broth, oil, pure wine, or are served with broth, pepper" and an onion/garlic substitute called silphium.

The earliest recipes for the dish we might recognize as a forerunner of the deviled egg appeared in medieval Europe. These eggs were stuffed with cheese, sweet spices, sauces made from pine nuts and raisins.

By the 16th century, it was then common for cooks to remove the yolk of a hard-boiled egg and mix them with hot stuff like mustard and cayenne before refilling the egg.

Some recipes called for eggs to be boiled not hard, but medium and filled with pine nuts, honey, vinegar, pepper and something called "lovage."

I'm lovagin' it!

———

Finally, a page from the deviled diary of a hale fellow well met with twinkling eyes and insatiable appetites.

"By nature, I am not a deviled egg man," writes Bill Driscoll, a longtime public servant at Baltimore's City Hall. ."But I have learned to eat them like oysters, one gulp and gone.

"My ex-wife's family was dominated by good Germans, hearty eaters all. They loved heavy food. Her mother, Irish as Paddy's Pig, was, oddly enough, a good cook.

"She somehow adapted to the German way. It was there, in the ample bosom of her food loving family that I was introduced to the delights of that ovoid delicacy, the deviled egg.

"I like a simple mayo whipped yolk and a dash of

paprika and [because] deviled eggs are an outdoor summer treat, are best kept chilled. Thus, I approach deviled eggs cautiously, especially at potluck cookouts.

"I have an unfounded fear of mayonnaise gone bad."

They call me the working man, I guess that's
what I am.

BLUE COLLAR

*"My parents and their friends had blue collar attitudes
even though they no longer had blue collar jobs ..."*
—Richard Yeagley, filmmaker

So, a Baltimore kid from Loch Raven
Boulevard gets a film degree in his own backyard—
Stevenson University, 2007—and heads for Tinseltown
before the ink is dry on the diploma.

Once in Los Angeles—getting an apartment and an
assistant's job, hustling like a million other greenhorns in
the Land of Broken Dreams—he decides to make his first
film.

What do you think it is?

A documentary about skilled labor in Baltimore.

The Tradesmen: Making an Art of Work—which
premiered this spring at the Charles Theater—is an 88-
minute celebration of brains, brawn and the building
trades in Crabtown, USA.

Wrote Shannon Dunn for a local website: "Yet another
Baltimore boy is wearing his heart on his sleeves, then
rolling them up to make a film set in his hometown."

That boy is a personable and seemingly unflappable
perfectionist named Richard Yeagley, then 26, who made
Tradesmen for approximately $60,000, most of which
was financed by a fellow Baltimorean he befriended at an
Orioles/Angels ballgame in Anaheim.

Rafael Alvarez

"My dad's a mechanic, he fixes high-end hospital beds," said Yeagley, discussing the film over a plate of braised lamb at Ikaros restaurant in Greektown.

Having constructed a piece of work likely to last as long if not longer than anything recently erected in Baltimore, Yeagley said that while he identifies with the blue collar ethic that permeates Baltimore, he couldn't build a deck or lay brick to save his soul.

Nor could most of his college-educated friends.

Such thoughts—and the financial help of retired businessman Bryant Waters, Boys Latin class of 1974—brought *The Tradesmen* to the screen.

The film features a stone mason—we see him sweating over the jigsaw of a flagstone walkway, hauling heavy buckets of sand by hand; a carpenter, auto mechanics, union officials running vocational schools in the absence of such training in public education; a handful of artists who employ tools typically found on construction sites and Yeagley's uncle, the legendary plumber to the Baltimore arts world, Chris Jensen.

[Jensen—as pure a Baltimorean as there is, a neighborhood clean freak known to chase down people who toss trash near his home at Howard and 28th streets and give them a piece of his combustible mind—was featured in an earlier documentary by Stevenson graduate and Archbishop Curley high school teacher Nick Brownlee. That film is called *The Prince of Poopy*.]

Mixed with footage of people working—you can hear the difference in vocations in the sound of a power saw versus a mason's trowel—are a handful of talking heads explaining how the United States went from a country that built things to one whose economy is enslaved to consumption.

Of special note is Judith Lombardi, former associate

professor of sociology at Stevenson, who pointed out that many of the privileges Americans of all political persuasions take for granted today—such as workplace safety and the five-day work week—were triumphs scored by organized labor.

"It's obvious that [Yeagley] is a doer and not a dreamer," said Waters, who said he was "hugely impressed" by the film and despite Yeagley's optimism wasn't much concerned about whether or not his investment is recouped.

"I never really understood the impact such a movie could have," said Waters. "I was never a blue collar worker, but I always found comfort in their presence."

And that, Oriole fans—an inexplicable comfort in the presence of people who simultaneously build and *are* the foundation of this town—is the essence of the eternal Baltimore.

"My grandfather owned a very successful [Baltimore] contracting company [C.J. Langenfelder & Son] from the 1950s through the 1970s," said Waters. "They built highways, bridges and tunnels and had a large maintenance contract with Bethlehem Steel."

With pride, Waters notes: "He had an eighth grade education and started off driving a truck for an excavating company."

No wonder he feels at ease in the presence of men and women who sweat and sometimes bleed for a living.

GLOBAL LINK

From the rail of the Global Link, McComas Street, South Baltimore, where I worked from the late summer of 2001 through Christmas, waiting—in the immediate wake of 9/11—to go to sea.

"What do you know?," I wrote in that year's journal. "A ship is actually moving , a container ship out of Hamburg pushed into the channel by a tug that slowly backs off, gliding backward through the Baltimore morning, tooting her shrill whistle as she let's go . . ."

He who laughs last.

MISTER POE

"In the quivering of a leaf—in the hue of a blade of grass—in the shape of a trefoil—in the humming of a bee—in the gleaming of a dew-drop—in the breathing of the wind—in the faint odors that came from the forest—there came a whole universe of suggestion . . ."
—Edgar Allan Poe, "A Tale of the Ragged Mountains"

The rascal genius Poe turned 200 in 2009, moldering beneath a landmark gravesite at the corner of Fayette and Greene Streets.

"We stand here in a cemetery, a place of remembering, surrounded by the famous and the forgotten," said Jeffrey Savoye, secretary and treasurer of the Poe Society of Baltimore.

"Among the mayors, generals and merchants, the tomb of one person is known around the world—dismissed by some but cherished by many, many more—and that is the tomb of Edgar Allan Poe."

Savoye was graveside with Justin Wert, a Poe scholar from Piedmont Virginia Community College in Charlottesville; Wert's literary mentor, Benjamin Franklin Fisher, a professor at Ole Miss; Jeff Jerome—curator of the Poe House at 203 Amity Street, visited by Jorge Luis Borges in 1983; and a few others, most known to one another as well as a passerby or two on a bright autumn day.

"As is our tradition—stretching back to the dedication of this monument in 1875—we are gathered here to place flowers on Poe's grave in remembrance of this unique American genius," said Savoye.

Afterward, Wert presented a paper in the Poe Room of Enoch Pratt Free Library headquarters on Cathedral Street, a hallowed room set up with a sheet cake bearing the number "200" on the frosting.

Wert's presentation, the 87th annual Poe lecture in Baltimore, was "A Tale of the Ragged Mountains and Mesmerism." On hand to listen were a trio of freshmen from the Maryland Institute, College of Art who wandered in after their teacher told them to go out into the city and find an adventure.

They laughed in all the right places—like the part about vampirism, leeches applied to the sides of the head and a doctor named *Temple*-ton; but a better show was the night before when Savoye, Wert and Fisher dined at the Bamboo House on York Road in Timonium.

Over sesame chicken, the "bird's nest" entrée, sliced beef with asparagus and a couple of Manhattans, the devotees told stories of Poe scholars—such as the academically generous Thomas O. Mabbot; hangers on; quacks who believe the poet's enemies had him chased down and murdered; and gentlemen like Alexander G. Rose, a longtime officer of the society who died in 1995.

"It would have been fascinating to have met Poe," said Savoye. "I'm not sure I would have liked him. He was needy and always making demands on people."

It has been 160 years since Poe's death and 170 since "The Fall of the House of Usher," was published in *Burton's Gentleman's Magazine.*

[The story has twice been adapted for film: in 1928 and again in 1960, starring Vincent Price and directed by the

Roger Corman, the man who brought you the Ramones in *Rock and Roll High School*.]

His bones picked over ravenously, there is little original scholarship, if any, left to do on Poe.

In the absence of new information—and because he wrote about the perverse, the bizarre, the grotesque and the arabesque—Poe and his brief, difficult life are often exploited to support every emotional and artistic fantasy of the garden variety crackpot.

[Savoye, said that attracting younger members to the society is difficult, noting that adolescent boys tend to be interested in Poe around the 5th or 6th grade—when "The Tell-Tale Heart" is assigned in school—before moving on to more urgent desires.]

"I've had people quit the society," he said, "after they find out that he never wrote under the influence of drugs or alcohol."

Live better, work union.

ON STRIKE

It was exciting to be an eight-year-old kid in Baltimore in 1966. The Orioles won their first World Series of the modern era behind the slugging of Frank Robinson, the defense of Brooks Robinson and the pitching of Dave McNally. A guy named Moe kept things loose in the clubhouse.

Every day, something new and strange came blaring out of WCAO, the AM pop station—red doors painted black sailing through the theremin vibrations of blossom worlds—while a blizzard dumped 20 inches of snow in the backyard.

And my father—Manuel Alvarez, a tugboat man on the South Broadway waterfront—went on a six month strike with the Seafarers International Union.

Three local towing companies were hit, with picket lines going up outside of the City Recreation Pier in Baltimore where the tugs docked in the last years of Fells Point as a true seaman's village of brothels, pickle factories, coffee wharves and an evangelical soup kitchen called the Port Mission.

During the strike, bay pilots trying to dock ships without the aid of tugs damaged or destroyed several piers, although vessels carrying military cargo to and from Vietnam were serviced by the tugs.

The work was performed by all parties, from

stevedores to management, out of patriotic pride. Tug crews accepted no pay for this work. The strike of '66 lasted for six months.

"I remember Mom cleaning other people's houses for money and my parents agonizing over whether or not to apply for food stamps out of pride," said Gregory Lukowski, who followed his tugboat mate father down to the waterfront and eventually became a Chesapeake Bay pilot.

"Christmas was lean," said Lukowski of 1966. "And the winter seemed extremely cold."

The strike ended with basic hourly wages set from $2.71 for deckhands to $3.23 for captains.

Not much by twenty-first century standards, even in the Great Recession. But it was a good buck when overtime, holiday pay—even a relic known as triple time—were factored into the crews' salaries.

"That strike guaranteed us a five-day workweek and put an end to the company using us as casual labor," Dad recalled.

"When that contract expired, we went on strike again and did better. Before it was all over, we killed the goose that laid the golden egg."

Today, none of the major tugboat firms in Baltimore are locally owned. When the out-of-town companies succeeded in defeating the union in the late 1980s, my father went to work in a hardware store until he was old enough to collect Social Security.

I grew up with the expectation that I would go to college and learn to do something that didn't involve shovels or wrenches or, as the old man often said when we were doing chores around the house, "picking 'em up and putting 'em down."

Crabtown, USA

His skilled-labor wage put us in a brick rancher in a solidly middle-class suburb where most of the other fathers worked at Westinghouse and the moms who weren't teachers more or less stayed home. For a few years, my mother kept track of inventory in the shoe department at Sears and was home before we got out of school.

The same wage that put us in with the white-collar families paid tuition for my brothers and me at a Catholic high school. Mom still remembers "75 bucks out of every paycheck" going to the Xavierian brothers at Mount Saint Joseph High School.

That union wage had my back as I worked my way through Loyola College. And it bought the 1978 Ford Granada—bright green with white Landau roof—I drove to the clerk's job I'd landed on the sports desk of *The Baltimore Sun* on my way to becoming a newspaperman.

And if all of our middle-class achievements went to hell, there was always that working-class safety net: the waterfront.

When the economy would go soft and things got tough at Bethlehem Steel or the Esskay meatpacking plant or even Westinghouse, work typically remained stable around the port.

"There's always something down the waterfront," Dad would say, even though the last thing he wanted was for his boys to be pulled into the labor pool, however plentiful, along the Baltimore harbor.

Always something has been something close to nothing for almost 25 years now.

<hr />

Season two of *The Wire* was about the last days of being able to follow in your old man's footsteps to make a living.

It was, said David Simon, a 12-episode wake for the "death of work"

Before HBO gave the green light to *The Wire*, Simon was considering this as a subject for his next fly-on-the-wall book: a narrative account of life on Baltimore's diminished waterfront.

The story could have been set amidst the ruins of any number of manufacturing plants that once made Baltimore one of the biggest producers of goods in the world: the mammoth carcass of Bethlehem Steel's Sparrows Point shipyard or the breweries that announced one's arrival in East Baltimore.

Once upon a time there were even factories that made umbrellas and hats and bread and licorice.

But the second season was set in the middle of the place that made so much of the other commerce possible: a commercial port dating to the 17th century.

The harbor waterscape is the star of the first scene when McNulty, banished not just from homicide, but from terra firma itself, rides the police boat with Officer Diggins of the marine unit.

McNulty points out the Beth Steel Sparrows Point complex where his father worked until he was laid off in 1973. Diggins says his uncle was a supervisor there until he got the ax in 1978.

Some 30 years ago, the largest private employer in the Baltimore area was Beth Steel.

My grandfather, an immigrant from the Galicia region of Spain, was a shipyard worker during World War II when—to beat Hitler and Mussolini and a cat named Tojo—the yard launched Liberty ships almost daily.

To slide those ships out of the cradle and into the Patapsco River, three shifts of unionized workers, many of them recent transplants from Carolina tobacco fields and Appalachian coal mines, worked the Beth furnaces around the clock.

When Beth Steel went bankrupt in 2001, robbing several generations of pensioners and their widows of benefits thought to be good to the grave, my father was dumbstruck. His comments are documented in Deborah Rudacille's 2010 memoir of mills, *Roots of Steel*.

In my father's youth, it seemed as though Bethlehem Steel alone kept solvent the Highlandtown neighborhood where he grew up and a half dozen other communities around it.

A sausage factory might come and go, but no one could imagine Bethlehem Steel no more. When the steel mill was eventually bought by a Russian company, Pop was beyond disbelief.

Rooskies owning Bethlehem Steel?

For a while, and then they went belly-up too.

Today, the largest employer in the metro area is Johns Hopkins Medical System and it's sibling University. For the average Baltimorean, making beds and taking blood does not pay as well as making steel.

And while Hopkins helps their entry-level employees get high school equivalency degrees to train for better jobs, at "the Point" there was on-the-job advancement for smart workers without education.

When my grandfather started his career at Sparrows Point—some 40 years honored by a stainless steel plaque engraved with a picture of a ship, a testimonial that hangs today in the front room of his old rowhouse where I live— he was shoveling slag for a dollar a day.

At the time of his retirement in 1970, he was a skilled machinist with no more formal education than four or five elementary grades in the village where his father worked with oxcarts.

He sang that sad, raggy tune like a fool.

GRIEVOUS GOOFY

"I work myself to death just to fit in . . ."
                                        —The Who, *Quadrophenia*

A year before the Watergate hearings, when I was a freshman in high school, I took a yellow school bus from Linthicum to Mt. St. Joseph in Irvington. On Hollins Ferry Road in Lansdowne, the bus stopped for a single student, a funny looking kid with fish-white skin, freckles and splayed teeth. We called him Goofy.

Goofy had a rough time on the bus. I don't recall anyone hitting him, though some shoving probably occurred as he ran the gantlet looking for a seat. What I mostly remember is the moment he came aboard when a bus full of boys—all Catholic, headed either to St. Joe or the recently (and unnecessarily) defunct Cardinal Gibbons High School—erupted in calls of "Goofy! Hey Goofy! You're a goof, Goofy."

It got so bad that one day the bus driver opened the doors and said: "Get on the bus, Goofy."

After freshman year, I began to carpool with older guys in the neighborhood and, though we both stayed at St. Joe through graduation in 1976, I no longer paid Goofy much mind. I was busy trying to be cool. I'm not sure what he was doing.

But I never forgot him or the bullshit he endured for no other reason than the way he looked.

Rafael Alvarez

After returning to Baltimore from a lucrative but artistically bankrupt exile in Hollywood in 2009, I sometimes drove my sister-in-law's father to Arbutus for dialysis. The ride took us by the very corner where Goofy waited for the bus.

Though the corner was always empty, I'd see the specter of Goofy with his canvas, drawstring book bag. And remember words that would surely get someone fired today: "Get on the bus, Goofy."

I often thought that if given the chance—grandiosity masquerading as faith in the search for a very small needle in a very large haystack, I'd try to make it up to him.

I love the wayback-machine that is Arbutus and for a time picked up side work there writing about crab soup, fire department parades and majorettes. One day in late June of 2011, I was assigned to write about a food pantry for the poor.

The story was what we used to call a "quick and dirty" on the *Sunpapers* City Desk. Pop in, ask questions of anyone within arm's reach, be sure the photographer gets a good shot of the main character, run back to the office, pull clips from the morgue to see the last time the place was written about, double check names and dates and bang out 8 to 10 paragraphs. Daily journalism.

The pantry was going through a hard time—those who had once donated food now needed food themselves, reminding me of tales I'd read in *The Grapes of Wrath* while driving across Oklahoma during the 2008 presidential election.

I asked my questions, browsed through the free book section and put up with a lady who said, after giving good quotes, "Please don't use my name," as though people going hungry in the suburbs were a state secret.

300

Crabtown, USA

And this: the sight of a bearded, disheveled man with one of those orange-tinted homeless tans walking back and forth between the free clothes room and shelves of canned goods, a guy helping out in little ways.

He looked familiar but I didn't know how or why. I thought he might be someone from rooms I frequent in order to stay on the right side of a good thing. Figuring he was as good for a quote as anyone else, I walked up with my notebook and said: "I think I know you."

Without going through "Where did you grow up?" and "Where did you go to high school" he put out his hand and told me his name, first and last.

If a miracle brought me to that moment, a greater one kept me from blurting out, "GOOFY!"

It was none other.

And he had no more recollection of who I was or being in the same class as me than I can remember what Mom served for dinner some random weeknight in 1972.

[I knew, however, that just because John didn't remember me 40 years down the road did not lessen the pain we put him through when it happened.]

John was living in a homeless shelter on the grounds of Spring Grove State Hospital in Catonsville and took the bus to the Arbutus church pantry a few times a week to trade chores for food.

"I like helping," he said. "Once you start, you want to do more."

He said he was a laborer on disability and had been put through the financial and emotional wringer by an ugly divorce. And then he confessed to a lot of the same problems I once had, problems with solids and liquids that lead, if you are lucky, to the aforementioned rooms of hope.

I asked if I could give him a ride to where he lived, a

place where breakfast was always cereal with 2% milk and he sometimes ate ravioli cold out of a can. He said that a lift to the bus stop would do and as we hopped in, my mind began churning.

How to apologize without making him feel bad again?

"Who did you hang around with at St. Joe?"

"Nobody," he said. "I was a left-out."

John hadn't related a time of exclusion—we never let poor Goofy play in any reindeer games—he used a pronoun:

He was a "left-out."

"Well," I said, pulling over to the bus stop on Sulphur Spring Road. "If I ever did anything to hurt your feelings, I apologize."

John thanked me, took a couple of dollars I'd fished from my pocket, shook my hand and closed the door behind him.

One onion for dinner.

SIP & BITE

"This life make me very strong . . ."
—George Vasiliades, patriarch

George Vasiliades was born on the island of Karpathos during *katochi*—the Nazi occupation of Greece.

He grew up so poor—no shoes, malnourished, not a pencil to use in school—that dinner was often a couple of roasted onions.

The plate in the center of the dinner table often held a single onion.

"Greece was poor because of the war. We had real hunger," said George, born near the village of Olympos on March 29, 1942. "If you had onions you were better off than other people."

Better off than so many others—300,000 people in Athens alone—who starved to death during Greece's "Great Famine" of 1941 and 1942; long months in which trucks went through the streets picking up the dead.

George was three years old when the war ended. The withdrawal of the Germans led almost immediately to the *antartopolemos,* a guerilla led civil war pitting Communists against the Greek National Army. Another five years of chaos and deprivation ensued.

Today, the business that hungry kid founded in Baltimore—the Sip & Bite restaurant where you are likely sitting over a good hot meal as you read this—uses 100 pounds of onions a week.

That is nothing compared to the tons of onions and potatoes—not to mention warehouses of eggs and wheat fields of toast—that Vasiliades has gone through in his more than half-century as one of Baltimore's champion grill cooks.

George worked almost every day of those 50 years and he and his loved ones have never missed a meal.

"When I come here I didn't know what a tip was," said George. "I had clothes, shoes, food and was making maybe $15 a week. I think that maybe we come to heaven."

This is George's story, the tale of the diner he started at the corner of Aliceanna and Boston streets, first on one side of an alley called Van Lill and then on the other—on the Baltimore waterfront.

It's about the way the neighborhood changed around him from working people—can factories, lumber yards, stevedores and tugboat men—to wealthy senior citizens and young professionals wandering from pub to pub in college sweatshirts.

How liver and onions stepped aside for Eggs Athena.

A tale of the son and his young wife who took over the joint—fixing it up, making it sparkle and shimmer, bringing the last century into a new one with a little glitz and show biz—after George fried his last egg and retired to play cards in a Greek coffee shop up the road.

This is once upon a time in America.

George Vasiliades had an uncle—also named George, born in Greece in 1901—who was already long in Baltimore when the family back in Karpathos was trying not to starve to death.

Crabtown, USA

The older George wrote letters back to the village telling of his life in the New World. If the streets were not paved with gold, the plates were heavy with food.

Anyone who had relatives in the U.S. "were wishing to come to America," said George, recounting the long and arduous journey his father took to get here, paving the way for the rest of the family.

Wishing to get to the United States and landing here are not the same thing.

Point of origin: A mountainside wheat field in Karpathos.

Destination: the Moonlight Café at the corner of East Baltimore Street and South Broadway, about halfway between the waterfront and Johns Hopkins Hospital. The diner was owned by Uncle George, a man came to the States about the time World War I ended, dug coal for a while and found his calling, as so many expatriate Greeks do, making a spatula sing.

Uncle George was intent on bringing the rest of the family over, beginning with his brother Antonios, a farmhand/stone mason and the father of young George. In early 1956, Antonios got word from Athens that his paperwork was in order. It was January 6 and he had four days to report to the embassy.

And thus began the ordeal, with the clock ticking on the chance at a visa, of finding Antonios on the mountainside to tell him the news.

Young George, then 14, and his brother Bill, were dispatched like Hermes, the messenger of Olympus. Their father had four days to get to the American embassy in Athens.

"The phone call came about 7 in the evening and my father was in the fields with my mother, about four hours away. He had to catch a ship to get to Athens," remembered George.

•

George's grandmother suggested he sleep for a few hours before making the journey and about 10 p.m. that night he set out with "only the moon" to guide him. The brothers George and Bill traveled a narrow dirt road in the pitch.

"We were scared," he admits.

After a few hours down the road, George—wearing raggedy shoes with the front open from wear—tripped over a large stone and ripped the nail on his big toe. It was well before dawn.

They happened to be near a cousin's house, where a man came out to see what the commotion was and wrapped a rag around George's bleeding foot.

The boys were given goat milk for strength and walked another hour before finding their parents encampment near the wheat fields.

[It was not unlike the Poles and Polish-Americans in Baltimore's Canton neighborhood—many of whom would eat at the Sip & Bite in their golden years—who spent Depression-era summers in the strawberry and bean fields of Anne Arundel County, picking crops and living in tents.]

"My father heard us calling for him and he knew the embassy had called. He knew!" said George, excited by the memory. "He threw his bag of seeds on the ground and went back to the village. He had to catch a ship."

Bill and George accompanied their father to Diafani (or "transparent," named for its clear, pure water) on the northeast coast of Karpathos to catch a ship to Athens.

"The ship never came," said George.

A fisherman was leaving port in a small boat and agreed to take George's father on a trip from Karpathos to Rhodesto Athens. About an hour into the journey, in rough seas, the engine failed and the boat began to drift.

Crabtown, USA

And drift and drift, with no word from Antonios, who by this time had missed the embassy appointment. He had left with the fisherman on Friday night. With no sign of them by Saturday morning, calls went out to all points between Karpathos and Rhodes.

"My grandmother just sat at the window looking at the sea and crying, 'He's dead, he's dead,'" said George."

After three nights at sea without food, the storm had pushed the boat to Tylos, about six hours from the destination. Antonios and the fisherman were picked up by a passing ship that took them to Rhodes.

Antonios made it to Athens, anxious and terribly late. Only to be told he was a known Communist, an easy brush people used to paint their enemies in the wake of civil war. It took three months to clear up the mess. A few days before the Greek Orthodox Easter of 1956—April 23rd that year—Antonios came to his village to say goodbye. He left his wife and children with promises to bring them over as soon as possible.

The boy who tore the nail off of his toe while racing to give his father a message?

He got a new pair of goodbye shoes from Athens, black patent leather.

And the priest came to give a blessing of farewell to a stone mason headed for a life of hard work and plenty over a short order grill.

"I come to Baltimore on a Friday and on Monday I'm working at the Moonlight . . .

—George Vasiliades

The names George and Antonios run through the Vasiliades family like the Aliakmonas River runs through Greece.

In 1958, at the Moonlight diner, there were two Greeks named George: the uncle who first came to America and his teenage nephew who'd landed in New York on a Greek passenger ship called the *Olympia*.

Soon Antonios sent back to Greece for his wife Calliope and the rest of their children: the older son named Bill and 12-year-old Maria.

[Antonios died in the mid-1990s at age 82. Calliope died in 2010 at age 95.]

Reunited in a big village called Baltimore, the Vasiliades family set up house in what is now Greektown, first on Newkirk Street and then Macon.

In the 1950s, it was simply called "the Hill," a section of East Baltimore near the old City Hospitals between the edge of Highlandtown and Dundalk.

Shoulder-to-shoulder with his father and uncle, George worked at the Moonlight from 1958 through 1965, often saving the 20 cent bus ride home from Broadway to Highlandtown by walking home in good weather.

Now 70, George twinkles at memories of the two hospitals the Moonlight served, Johns Hopkins and the long-defunct Church Home and Hospital, where Edgar Allan Poe breathed his last in 1849.

He took classes in English for a couple of months, worked his way up from dishwasher to short-order cook and, for a while, smiled George, had a pretty nurse for a girlfriend.

In 1965, now in his early 20s, a confident young man well-acquainted with diner life, the nephew was ready to cut the tomato-stained apron strings of his uncle.

George the younger, though he never did any of the serious cooking at the Moonlight, set out on his own. A Greek who delivered roasted coffee in bulk to restaurants around the city took him aside one day.

Crabtown, USA

"He says, 'George, I have a place for you . . .'"

The opportunity stood about a mile to the southeast, at the corner of a then-industrial Boston Street and a narrow lane called Van Lill, an area of lumberyards and piers of nearly-derelict work vessels called "bum boats." The diner was owned by a Greek named Kalandros and he wanted to sell.

The original Sip & Bite was on the west side of Van Lill, which is where George started. A few years later it moved to its present location—2200 Boston Street—on the east side of Van Lill.

It was previously a bar called Muggins Boat House and the Vasiliades brothers bought the building for about $6,000. George and his brother and the employees walked all of the equipment across Van Lill street and had the grills going before you can say "pigs in a blanket."

"In the early '60s I lived on the second floor of Muggins," said Bonnie Hockstein, whose father, George T. Lennon, owned the joint. "I ate at the Sip & Bite every day. They had the best rice pudding and always saved an order for me and a slice of watermelon."

George was told by Kalandros that the diner made $1,700 in receipts a week, a damn good payday when you could get an egg sandwich for a quarter. To prove it, Kalandros let George run the register before a deal was made.

Kalandros stayed on long enough to teach George and his brother Bill to cook and then the Vasiliades boys were on their own.

Eggs and pancakes are one thing. A nice brisket—unless your grandmother's name is Esther—is another.

"Every special is hard to learn if you don't know how," said George. "We did quality so we never had leftovers. I made beef stew in a big pot, 20 gallons at a time. I used to work breakfast and lunch, get off 3 o'clock in the afternoon, sleep a couple hours and come back to the grill."

The restaurant did well enough for George to return to his village in 1968, a successful man of 26 with a business in America, and propose to a young woman named Irene.

"I worked for my uncle for a few years and then I never work for anybody but myself—60 hours a week in here," said George. "Anybody who works hard in this country can make it. You can become anything."

<hr>

When the neighborhood was still industrial—with the Standard Oil Company off of Clinton Street and the American Can Company had three shifts going around the clock—a man would come in to order food for his co-workers.

Fifty bacon and egg sandwiches and 50 cups of coffee to go!

Today, when the Sip & Bite is banging—a line out the door, a busy rush lasting up to five hours, late on a Saturday night or Sunday morning breakfast—there is no time to sweep the floor or empty the trash.

Thus the floor behind the counter is often covered with egg shells. There are 30 eggs per restaurant tray and ten trays per carton. At the Sip & Bite, it is not unusual for cooks to use 17 cartons of eggs between 8 a.m. and just before lunch.

The current Sip & Bite—gleaming with Route 66 diner chrome and flat-screened TVs on the wall—looks mightily different from anything an old Boston Street sea dog would recognize.

The 21st century changes were made by George's son

Crabtown, USA

Antonios—"Tony" named for his grandfather, the man who hopped a ride with a fisherman en route to America—and his wife Sofia. The new generation took over from Tony's father in 2007.

Before they did, a good 20 years ago, George gave the place a facelift of his own.

To cheer the place up with suburban colors and new booths, George closed the restaurant for two weeks in January of 1992, an unprecedented move for a guy who wished there were more days in the week plus an extra hour so he could be open 25/8.

One of the changes was a handicapped-access ramp. One of the things left behind was the green, office furniture chair by the meat case for parties who couldn't crowd into a single booth.

When the place re-opened with mauve molding and $135,000 worth of improvements, George held a finger in the air and declared with pride: "I haven't raised my prices one penny, not one penny! Where you going to go to eat a meal with two vegetables and good portions for $5? No place!"

No place now extends to the Sip & Bite of today, with the balance shifting more toward dining experience than diner.

[Tony got rid of the clear glass meat case beneath the cash register, where old-timers could view the flank of cow destined to become an open-faced hot roast beef sandwich.]

The year of big changes—the tongs passed to a new generation—was 2012; the year of sexy chrome, award-winning gyros and *spanakopita* added to the menu, feature spots on Guy Fieri's Diners, Drive-Ins and Dives show.

[While Tony and Sofia take off on Tuesdays, George

never took more than a nap. When Tony got into some legal trouble in 2015, George came out of retirement, put his apron back on and re-opened the true love of his life on Tuesdays]

When he's not playing cards with his peers or zipping around East Baltimore in an inconspicuous clunker, George sometimes drops in on his bacon-and-egg empire. His son is often at the grill while daughter-in-law Sofia charms the customers.

George watches now, claiming to notice a mistake or two (nothing more than another way of doing stuff he's done the same way all his life) while quietly busting the buttons on his sport coat with pride.

He looks over the plates of strawberry waffles and BLTs rolling off the grill and finds it good; a simple man you'd never know is worth a pretty penny, in his mind just a poor boy from Greece.

George Vasiliades raised a family, educated his children—Tony has a master's degree in biology, son Christos is an attorney, daughter Maria lives in Greece—helped others when he could, and gave to his church.

"I did what I was supposed to do," he said.

Who could forget?

THE ALAMO

For every story in the City of Baltimore during the winter, there are a baker's dozen to be had down the ocean between Memorial Day and Labor Day.

Here is a glimpse of a handful of snapshots—caught like flies on sticky paper when my family vacationed at the Hitch Apartments in Ocean City before our vacations became air-conditioned—over the opening holiday of the season.

"Remember when you guys were little . . ."

This was said by a woman bicycling down the Boardwalk early Sunday morning, May 30th, to a relative bicycling beside her. That simple phrase, "Remember when you guys were little . . . remember when we used to . . . ," is the essence of Ocean City, where my family has vacationed all my life.

Each summer creates singular memories—lots of good, some bad (from a rained-out weekend to pedestrian tragedies)—to be rolled out across summers yet to come.

That prompt, "Remember when you guys were little . . ." arrives the moment I approach the Route 50 bridge connecting Worcester County to the ten-mile sandbar that becomes Maryland's second largest city during the summer.

It hits when I see the light bulb sombrero of the Alamo Court Motel.

317

This is the kind of place where Tom Waits might sweat through a long weekend writing a few new songs about dime store watches and rings made out of spoons.

It's where my family spent a long week back around 1971 with our cousins, the Adornato family.

Maddeningly close enough to the ocean to smell it, but not close enough to see it.

"Your cousin Stevie ate a grilled cheese sandwich every morning," my mom remembered, unable to recall why we stayed there, only that "it wasn't a happy time."

But this past weekend—40 years down the road from our Alamo summer—was happy, a contented couple of days; just Mom and Dad and me at their condo on 87th street. The only thing we had to do was what we wanted to do, and that's what we did.

As the hotels and Coastal Highway began to fill up, a guy staying next to my folks' place, Al Vojik, sat on the porch and talked about growing up in the neighborhood near Johns Hopkins Hospital back in the 1940s.

"We used to call Bocek park [Edison Highway and Madison Street] the clay hill," remembered Vojik, retired from the defunct General Motors plant on Broening Highway. "You'd dig out a little cave in the side of clay and play forts."

There was a swamp behind the clay hills—a neighborhood now in ruins that travelers see from the Baltimore to New York Amtrak line—which may have given the area the now-forgotten name of Swampoodle.

I spent most of Saturday working on a not-quite-there-yet short story at the new Ocean City library on 100th street.

Opened in 2008, it's a building designed to look like exactly what it is: a big house of books at the shore. And it replaced one that had been at 14th street and Philadelphia Avenue since the early 1960s.

Crabtown, USA

The library has always been an important part of the resort. In 1984, I received a letter from Watterson "Mack" Miller, a West Ocean City octogenarian famed for his swimming prowess and less-known for having debauched away a great newspaper inheritance between the world wars.

Mack was a janitor at the Castle in the Sand hotel. We became friends when I wrote about his old man and the sea ventures (more Johnny Weissmuller than Santiago) two and three miles beyond the waves.

During my visits to his shack on the fishing docks he told, with no noticeable regret, of a grandfather who wanted him to take over the family business, the *Louisville Courier-Journal*. Mack, known as Wock to his family, was more interested in beer steins and beckoning skirts, drinking his way across Europe before washing up penniless on Maryland's Eastern Shore.

We talked God and booze and books.

"I ordered *Ironweed* at the [14th street] library," wrote Mack after I'd offered my copy. "I noticed that the author got his start as a feature writer for the Albany paper . . .."

Leaving the stacks on 100th street with Mack on my mind, my eye caught the Library of America edition of the U.S.A. trilogy by John Dos Passos, who died in Baltimore on September 28, 1970.

Tom O'Grady wrote that ". . . Dos Passos used libraries with a rare passion, and he used them perniciously. He drained them of all their worth. And when the organ was dead, a new life was born of its energy.

"In the years before his death, Dos Passos could be found almost daily at a small wooden table deep amid the stacks of the Peabody Library in Baltimore."

In a library armchair on 100th street, I read a chronology of the writer's life—"I've always thought you should concentrate on paddling your own canoe," he said of literary envy—before leaving for a nap and dinner with my parents.

["That's the whole secret: to do things that excite you," said Ray Bradbury in the Spring 2010 *Paris Review*. "Also, I have always taken naps. That way, I have two mornings!"]

Mom fried shrimp in a light tempura, accompanied by salad and fresh green beans left over from a rib dinner the night before a few miles over the Delaware line.

While my father did the dishes, Mom and I took an after-dinner walk, and I chatted up a Moldovan waitress at Layton's on 92nd street as she poured me a cup of coffee. Her name was Marina and it was her third summer working the resort.

[When I covered the beach for *The Baltimore Sun* in 1983 and 1984, most of the foreign workers were Irish. Now the majority, like the barmaids at the Alamo Court, arrive from the former Soviet Union.]

"There was this little drunk boy in here this morning," said Marina, "and he knew that Moldova was next to the Ukraine."

I was pleasantly surprised, as Americans don't seem to be interested in much beyond the surface of things, particularly at the beach.

At the Bookshelf bookstore on 81st street, "literature"—Dos Passos and his kin across the centuries—is beyond a wall of crap printed between embossed covers and hidden in a chest of drawers.

"People who know books know to ask for the classics," said Ann Hansen, who has run the store for years with her husband Roy. The couple was still cleaning up from a May 8th ceiling fire over the holiday weekend.

"The only other people who are interested are students

with a summer reading list and the foreign kids," said Ann. "Young people from other countries want to read the classics they've already read in their own language in English."

From the old bedroom bureau, I selected *Billiards at Half-Past Nine* (1962) by Heinrich Boll and closed the drawer like a coroner sliding a stiff back into the freezer.

I probably won't get around to reading the Boll anytime soon (the greatest reading list in the world is made up of the books you intend to read next), but promise to shelve it out in the open and give it some air.

Near the register was a stack of Anne Tyler and I bought *A Slipping Down Life* (published 1970, released as a film in 1999) for my mother. I paid $3 for each.

Later, on the Boardwalk, Dad bought Mom a small bucket of Fisher's popcorn for $5.50, and she will munch the caramel corn and read Tyler's tale of an odd, shy girl named Evie on the porch while the neighbors work sudoku puzzles and sip iced tea.

Golden-agers on vacation until high school graduates and those who thought they were going to graduate invade the shore.

On the boardwalk: in the summer of 1973 I had to have a Faces t-shirt. (Rod and Ronnie, in my teenage head the equal of Mick and Keef long before Rod got lost in the American songbook.)

The next summer, only an image of Robin Trower's *Bridge of Sighs* LP would do.

The popular t-shirt this year judging by the racks rolled out onto the boards? Sexed-up liquid speed in shiny cans: Monster, Rock Star, Red Bull.

Rock is dead they say.

Not dead–or even scarce–are Boardwalk preachers. Standing in front of Biblical sand sculptures across from the Paul Revere smorgasbord, the believers take turns reading the gospels like Flannery O'Connor, minus the irony, with an oceanfront view.

Sunday morning: May 30, 2010, just a block or two away from the memorial to the world's firefighters, came the story of the death of Lazarus from the book of John.

"Take away the stone . . ." he said.

Not far from the spot where the word was delivered is a bench with a small brass plaque. Nearly all of the benches along the Boardwalk are dedicated to someone who loved Ocean City, bench after bench of tributes by someone who loved that someone.

The bench I shared with a kid wiping the sleep out of her eyes before the Sunday morning shift at the Ripley's Believe It or Not museum (this year with "Mirror Maze and Laser Race!") is dedicated to the memory of Linda "Lynnie" Galyon.

It reads: ". . . hearts, roses, hugs and kisses . . . forever my love . . . Michael."

How often will Michael sit on that bench this summer overcome by memories as waves crash behind him, while sunburned families push on with Thrasher's fries in one hand and another on a stroller as the rides of the carnival go round and round?

ORIOLES

Earl Weaver | MANAGER

Brooks always covered his face with his glove when Earl went berserk so no one would see him laughing.

EARL WEAVER

"I don't even think about it anymore . . ."
—The Feisty Bantam on the glory days

If he is to be believed, Earl Weaver was talking about how he was tossed out of 97 baseball games, the American League record, and whether the modern game would long tolerate his antics.

The Hall of Fame skipper would un-holster his pointing finger and go nose-to-nose with the umpire, turning his cartoon bird cap around backwards to get closer to the enemy, a style sported by Earl long before it became entrenched in street culture.

My personal favorite was Weaver's slow, methodical covering of home plate with dirt—usually by foot, but at least once with his hands—knowing that if his team was taking it in the rear by bad calls, the ump would have to bend over as well to whisk the dirt from home plate.

His favorite line to umpires?

"You're here to fuck us."

Jerry Jackson, one of the many sons of Baltimore sportswriter legend Jimmy Jackson, used to "run quotes" for his old man and Gordon Beard of the Associated Press when young Jackson was learning the newspaper trade in college.

325

"Back in those days, the only reporters using any kind of taping devices were radio and TV people, who my dad affectionately referred to as 'EAs'—Electronic Assholes," said Jerry. "When an EA stuck a microphone too close to Weaver, he would deliberately drop F-bombs and every curse word known to man.

"So the quote would be: 'That cocksucker Palmer was fucking outstanding tonight.'"

The old school newspaperman could edit the quote for publication. The EA had nothing to use.

The salty son-of-a-bitch was in Baltimore from his Florida home in 2009 for a charity tribute to Brooks Robinson and claimed not to think about his volcanic antics anymore. But there is one baseball memory—which did not occur on land, much less the field—that I will never forget.

It's what the poet Dean Bartoli Smith calls "bleeding orange."

When I was in middle school, the Baltimore Orioles and the way the organization approached the game, from owner Jerry Hoffberger on down to batboy Jay Mazzone, were the class of the American League, Earl's histrionics notwithstanding.

In those days, my father was in the prime of his career (far younger than I am now) as a chief engineer on the Baker-Whiteley tugboats at the foot of Broadway.

The rest of the crew from his boat—the America, broken up for scrap at the end of the 20th century—are now dead.

And the Orioles, who other teams tried to emulate from the front office to the farm system, have lost more games than they've won for more a dozen years in a row, finishing many of those years in last place.

But it was a different story in 1968. Fells Point was in

transition from a true seaman's village of bars and boats, brothels and bums to a bohemian enclave of bars and boats, bongs and bums. And, inexplicably, a handful of Baltimore Orioles began going down to Thames Street to take late night tugboat rides and have a few beers with my old man and his bunkies.

Brooks wasn't one of them; he may have been too busy helping Crown gasoline make sure all Baltimoreans had a cabinet full of water tumblers with the Little Rock legend's picture on them.

But my old man (all his life more of a fisherman and crabber than a sports fan) always said Paul Blair was on board along with a few other guys.

I rode my share of tugboats as a kid, but was never around when the ballplayers visited. The outings were arranged by someone who knew someone who worked for the team and in 1968 that someone passed my fake red leather autograph book around the clubhouse.

[The '68 Birds finished 91-and-71, a dozen games out of first place. It was the year Baltimore radio jock Johnny Walker went to Africa to get a Witch Doctor curse on the rest of the American League and—in a feat that will likely never be equaled—Denny "Farfisa" McLain won 31 games for the champion Detroit Tigers.]

The autographs Dad brought home from the tugs were so extensive they included Clay Dalrymple, Gene Brabender (can you imagine having that name in high school? BRA-bender!) and "Racetrack" Ralph Salvon, the rotund trainer who would come out with a can of freeze spray when a player fouled one off of their ankle.

[Salvon, an Orioles trainer for more than 30 years, died at age 60 in 1988 of heart disease.]

When I was a young clerk on the horserace desk of *The Baltimore Sun*, Salvon would call the moment a race went off at Pimlico to get the name of the winner. I was in a fallow baseball period at the time, too busy chasing bluesmen and deadlines, and never asked Salvon for tickets in exchange for the inside dope.

In the depths of the paying-no-attention to baseball years, I asked guitarist Buck Dharma of Blue Oyster Cult to sign the same book backstage at the old Civic Center on Baltimore Street. After flipping through the pages, the guy who penned "Burnin' For You"—with the great line, "time to play B-sides . . ."—scribbled, "For Rafael, who has Boog Powell's autograph."

[When I took the book to school to show my friends, a kid obsessed with drawing scenes from World War II—American planes bombing Nazi tanks—signed the book. In school we knew him as Gordon Allis. Some 40 years later, we resumed our friendship via Facebook and shared Coney Island hot dogs at G&A. He now calls himself Ray Allis and I hope to get him to sign his middle-aged name beneath the one from childhood.]

Along with the Oriole autographs, Dad came home with stories about having a few cold ones with the ballplayers and the excitement my heroes found in sailing from the Broadway Recreation Pier over to Locust Point and back.

And the one guy he always talked about was Paul Blair, the All-Star centerfielder—always No. 6 in the hearts of true O's fans (Sorry Melvin Mora!)—and the only Oriole outfielder to win a Gold Glove, collecting eight during his time on 33rd Street.

At the tribute to Brooks—which included living legends from Wes Unseld to Artie Donovan—Blair was front and center, willing to talk to anyone who wanted to chat and doing so knowledgeably about everything from Curt Flood and the reserve clause to the way major leaguers play defense in the 21st century.

Crabtown, USA

"In my era if you played [good] defense you could make it to the big leagues," said Blair, 65, and looking sharp in a sharkskin suit. "I always caught the ball with both hands."

I had but one question: What was it like to ride tugboats in the Baltimore harbor 40 years ago?

"Wasn't me, man," said Blair, noting an aversion to the water and an inability to swim. "I wasn't riding any tugboats."

―――――――

In December of 2010, a blogger for the *New York Times* wrote that Orioles's Hall of Fame manager Earl Weaver had died and gone to heaven. He was, in fact, at home in Florida.

"Well I'll be damned," said Weaver when contacted by a reporter in Pembroke Pines.

Heaven was also relieved.

Some three years later, on January 19, 2013, the Terror of 33rd Street could not be reached for comment when news broke that he had died on a cruise for Orioles fans at age 82. This time it was true. Earl was gone.

"The smartest baseball man I ever met," eulogized baseball writer Tim Kurkjian. "The great Earl Weaver."

Orioles fans—*la famiglia di negro e aroncione* as the late groundskeeper and Earl's gardening friend Pasquale "Pat" Santarone might say—arrived early at Camden Yards on April 20 to pay their respects.

The ceremony was held between games of a double-header against the Los Angeles Dodgers. Speakers included Earl's son Mike, a spitball image of the old man in stature and voice, baseball Hall of Fame president Jeff Idelson—who said Cooperstown once offered tomato plant "starter kits" in honor of Weaver and Santarone's

Memorial Stadium love apple patch—and the immortal third baseman Brooks Robinson.

"When Earl would come out on the field to argue [with the umpires] I'd put my glove over my face so nobody could see me laughing," said Brooks, gray and kind and dignified.

Earl Weaver was a card—Rick Dempsey said the 5-foot-7 inch manager once stood on a box to better scream in his face—but he was no joke. His winning record in 17 years of managing, all with Baltimore, was 1480 wins and 1060 losses. He won four American League pennants and the 1970 World Series.

In Earl's last World Series, 1979 against Willie Stargell and the Pittsburgh Pirates, the Birds were down to their last inning. The Orioles had won 102 games that year, were favored to win all the marbles and had jumped out to a three games to one Series lead. But on October 17, 1979, with just a few at-bats left for the Os in game seven, the outlook wasn't brilliant in Crabtown.

"Earl knew by the 8th inning they were going to lose," said William Bertazon, 67, then a Baltimore City police officer assigned to the home team. "He was pacing the dugout cursing and some of the players were laughing at him.

"He sat down and pushed his hat all the way back on his head and said to me, 'You know what? We're gonna lose this game cuz these guys don't have any heart.'"

As a memento of that autumn shipwreck—the Orioles lost the game 4 to 1 and the Series along with it—Earl gave Bertazon a copy of that day's line-up card, which the aging cop still cherishes at home in Belair.

The 1979 World Series was a tragic collapse, just like the team's loss to Pittsburgh in the 1971 World Series after being up 3 games to 1; just like the improbable calamity of the 1969 Series when Gil Hodges and the Amazin' Mets ran over the Birds in five games.

And Earl—according to Dempsey "one of the toughest, most miserable human beings" to don a major league uniform—hated every moment of it.

"When I die," Weaver once said, "put on my tombstone, 'The Sorest Loser Who Ever Lived.'"

The tugboats saved my life.

WATERFRONT URCHIN

Allen Baker, who grew up without a whole lot of adult supervision in Dundalk, couldn't ride enough tugboats.

In late March of 2012, he pulled up to the foot of Broadway, the home he carries in his heart, as a mate aboard the Barbara E. Bouchard, a seagoing tug that sails out of Melville, New York. She was hauling 120,000 gallons of gasoline from Carteret, New Jersey on the Staten Island Sound to a refinery in Baltimore's Curtis Bay neighborhood.

"I practically lived at the end of this pier," said Baker. "From the time I was 12, I bet I took 50,000 photos of the boats and ships that went by."

"This is one of the very few places left where you can tie up and just hop off into a neighborhood," said Baker, whose family lived a block away at 722 South Bond Street before moving to Dundalk when Allen was six.

"Everything is behind fences now," said Baker. "The [modern] waterfront is walled off. The public can't get to the ships anymore."

Song of Solomon across the graveyards of
Baltimore

THE DEAD

The names speak from gravestones across a gnarled hilltop like characters in a blues opera:

Emanuel Snell, husband of the young Ruby.

Maggie Valentine.

Bessie Mae Hythe.

Almeater Watson, who met his Maker on July 13, 1962.

Have you yet to encounter a soul named Almeater?

If not for months of hard labor by inmates wielding machetes as though the 2500 block of Hollins Ferry Road were the Amazon, one might have searched the grounds of Mount Auburn Cemetery for days without encountering Mr. Watson or hundreds of his subterranean neighbors.

The oldest African American burial ground in the metropolitan area and a National Register of Historic Places landmark, the Westport graveyard lays across a rise at the corner of Old Annapolis Road and Waterview Avenue.

Originally known as the "City of the Dead for Colored People," it is the final resting place for a host of celebrated black Baltimoreans, from slaves who took northbound rides to freedom on the Underground Railroad to *Afro-American* newspaper founder John Henry Murphy. Mount Auburn has also been, for decades, a botanical nightmare, its tombstones enveloped in a wild morass of timber, trash, rampant overgrowth, and tangled vines as thick as hawser line.

The fence around the cemetery was cut, rusting to pieces, and falling down. Dogs and rodents scavenged unhindered for God knows what, roots had pushed some coffins up toward the sod, and security was nonexistent.

In the match between Mother Nature and the Sharp Street United Methodist Church, which has owned Mount Auburn since the cemetery's official founding in 1872, nature had long been declared the victor. The congregation didn't have the funds to put more than a dent in maintaining the 33-acre grounds, long relying on volunteers to "bring lawn equipment," as a sign on a graveyard shed suggested.

"I've cut a lot of grass and I've cut down a lot of trees," says Clarence Wayman, a member of the Mount Auburn board of directors and the man in charge of the current landscaping project—a job so long overdue he expects it to cost some $2 million.

The work started last September, when a truckload of short-timers from a Department of Corrections boot camp in Jessup began showing up at Mount Auburn with machetes and an unarmed guard. The prison labor is gratis, part of a public service program instituted by Maryland Secretary of Public Safety and Corrections Gary D. Maynard. The outreach includes work at military cemeteries in Crownsville, Garrison Forest, and Cheltenham, as well as tree planting and general neighborhood clean-up.

Asked if unrestrained prisoners brandishing 2-foot machete blades should give the public pause, Cornelius Woodson, the director of the inmate program, compares them to similar inmates—those on good behavior not long from release—working in kitchens with knives.

Crabtown, USA

"Our inmates are bringing the cemetery back to life," he says, with neither pun nor irony. "These guys are minimum-security inmates without much time left on their sentence. We believe they are trustworthy."

Apparently, so does the Sharp Street congregation, established between Pratt and Lombard streets in 1787 as the first African American Methodist church in Baltimore.

Sharp Street's Rev. Douglas Sands bought the machetes that help expedite the seemingly endless bushwacking, and a handful of prisoners were invited to Thanksgiving services last year to receive certificates of appreciation. Some of their families received gifts from the church at Christmas.

Since work began, Sharp Street's Wayman has been trying to locate his kin—Caroline County cousins several times removed named Bessie and Arthur Chapman, buried some half-century ago and now lost in the weeds. But so far they have eluded him. "I hoped I might just stumble upon them,"

Wayman says. Soon perhaps—after a commercial landscaping firm is brought in. "First we had to clear the land," Wayman says. "Then we'll go to grading and stump grinding. When all of that's done, we'll have to find the money to fix the fence."

In the early 2000s, volunteers from Morgan State University are to join the rescue effort. Students from the schools of engineering and architectural design will right toppled headstones and use cemetery records and sonar to align markers with the proper graves. It won't be foolproof—for that there would have to be exhumation—but it will be a big step in the right direction.

Right now, the most impressive and easily accessed grave at Mount Auburn is that of Joe Gans, the "Old

Master" who held the world lightweight boxing title from 1902 through 1904 and again from 1906 to 1908.

Just inside the main Waterview Avenue entrance at the corner of Nevada Street, Gans's marker was restored in 2005 by the International Boxing Hall of Fame, to which the Baltimorean was inducted in 1990. It's a monument worthy of a champion lauded by boxing historian Nat Fleischer as the greatest lightweight of all time.

Not so with Anthony L. Brown, born in 1953 and deceased a mere nineteen years later. Tony Brown was one of the stand-out Dunbar High School basketball players and a member of the Poets' 1971–72 team, which went undefeated in his senior year.

Brown received offers from most of the major basketball colleges in the country, including UCLA, only to be stabbed to death by a girlfriend before choosing a school.

He is buried beneath a couple of short two-by-fours nailed into a cross, painted white and inscribed in black marker: *Anthony L. Brown, 11.18.53–03.28.72—Better Known as 'Tony the Tiger.' Dunbar Basketball Star*.

Below the newly cleared ground, entwined with Tony and Almeater and Bessie and the rest of these very quiet Baltimoreans of color, lie Mount Auburn's perennial enemies: the deep roots of honeysuckle, poison ivy, thistle, small trees, and other assorted brush, all waiting for the warming earth to send forth new growth and reclaim their territory.

REAL DEAL

Why is writing about Baltimoreans—the ones who don't know that they are characters and would be insulted at the suggestion—such a thrill?

It has something to do, as Gary Giddins wrote, with the nature of a genuine eccentric.

You can never be sure if they know how strange they seem.

For each unsung Everyman I either found or was led to—Doughnut Frank, Johnny X and Ted the Clown—a dozen more went to the grave with their story untold.

But there was a woman in late middle-age who used to take the bus from South Baltimore to the corner of Light and Redwood every day for lunch who said: "The living God will winnow your good intentions."

And the man in the business suit who came to the same corner on foot with a brown bag lunch and said, "I worked just enough to keep the family just behind."

I know you don't want to hear it, but I'm
going to tell you anyway.

GLORIA JONES

The most surprising revelation about my mother, the thing unknowable when I was a kid but undeniable now, is that somewhere inside of her, a nine-year-old pushes the buttons that make Gloria Alvarez go.

That's right, I was raised by a fourth-grader who has taken up permanent residence inside a Linthicum senior citizen who no doubt is sitting in the kitchen rocking chair right now, crocheting an afghan for a friend or relative (after slyly inquiring about their favorite color) while watching *Little House on the Prairie*.

At least until someone calls up to say she's in the paper and then she'll yell to my father out in the living room: "MANUEL, BRING THE SUNPAPER IN HERE!"

A 9-year-old with the voice of a train whistle and the heart of a lion.

She's a woman with the comic instincts of Joe E. Lewis, whose smile she often compares to her own; a product of old school Catholicism who not only believes she recited enough prayers at St. Casimir in Canton to cover several lifetimes but has declared—with unblinking, childlike faith—that her current incarnation will not expire.

[There is evidence to suggest she may be wrong on that last point, but I assure the Reaper he'll have a schoolyard fight on his hands.

Mom long ago whipped lung cancer, has figured out enough about herself to "tell it like it is" (you don't want to be on the receiving end of that reality check) and, to stay fit, does up to a hundred fast walk laps around the basement each morning while pumping cans of string beans and creamed corn in the air.]

Evidence supporting my "newborn raised by ornery member of Little Rascals" thesis continues to trickle out. I once saw Mom put her hands over her ears when someone—probably me—tried to point out an alleged flaw in her character.

[At the same time, like all the best kids you knew growing up, no one is more fun when she is "on."]

Putting a secret inside of my mother is like dropping a kernel of corn in hot oil: Sooner or later, that baby is going to pop!

Mom has confessed to hiding candy bars in the kitchen cabinets—eaten in solitary glee, in front of the TV no doubt—after we were put to bed. I will bet you a bag of Utz potato chips that she only pulled this stunt when my sainted father, the only grown-up in our house, was working a night shift.

Being a good mother, she made sure her three boys ate their vegetables. And being a good mother who is a world class cook, there was always homemade dessert—my favorite is graham crackers layered in chocolate pudding, cold milk poured on top —to reward us for making that evening's "clean plate club."

But clandestine candy bars in the recesses of the spice cabinet?

A classic kid's crime defended with a trusty kid's rationale.

"I can't help it," she has said in situations both funny and sad. "That's just the way I am!"

Crabtown, USA

For the longest time, I didn't even think I had much in common with my folks. Then I learned that what I thought was distinction was simply passing fashion, both intellectually and, you know, the platform shoes and plaid butterscotch bellbottom phase from 1973.

Now I know that much of what I think and do, I get honestly.

Unlike Mom, a scorekeeping stickler who assigns invisible Xs to those who cross her, I try not to assign blame, or as Mom says, "throw shit in the game."

So when I act in a way that upsets me, I am calmed by the knowledge that it runs in the family.

If I find myself echoing some of Mom's qualities that I dislike in myself (she may not be able to help it, but I am determined to get a better handle), I pause and wonder how my dad might handle the situation.

The ability to pause before acting (or in my family, speaking) is a key difference between children and mature adults. I'm pretty sure Mom's remote left the factory without that button. I wasn't born with it either, but have spent plenty of money on replacements.

I'm not sure she'd admit it, but if you asked Mom her biggest surprise about more than years of motherhood it might be that, even with some rocky bumps in the road, the family never swerved into the ditch.

Some of this fear, hopefully dispelled by now, lingers from her Depression-era childhood.

But no matter what happens, us kids just keep coming back. Maybe because there's no better ally when you're in deep *caca*.

If I spend more than one night in my old bedroom in

343

a row, Mom gets on the phone to my Aunt Sylvia and announces: "The boarder is here again!"

Then she laughs, hangs up and asks me if I'd like "a nice fried ham and cheese sandwich."

The most important thing I have learned about my mother is her need to be recognized for the one-in-a-million human being that is Gloria Theresa Mildred Jones Alvarez.

If she makes you a scarf or a homemade cake —hell, if she even sends you an email saying she went to the fruit stand and got "some good tomatoes for sandwiches"—the clock starts ticking on your obligation to confirm receipt of her thoughtfulness.

So here it is Mom, heartfelt thanks for the whole fabulous ride; one that, according to your way of thinking, will never end.

Happy Mother's Day, hon.

Ah, Gibby, we hardly knew ye . . .

METRO EDITOR

"Life's a deadline . . ."
—Gilbert L. Watson III, 1944 to 2015

I knew I was working for a true newspaperman—
the kind glorified in expired epochs when every
city had a Sunday paper as thick as Aunt Myrtle's ankles—
on the day that Bob Bauman, Maryland's moralizing
Congressman from the Eastern Shore, was arrested for
soliciting sex from a boy prostitute.

It was 1980 and I'd only been on the City Desk a few
months, a 22-year-old agate clerk drafted from the sports
department. As an editorial assistant pitching in on obits
while taking dictation from reporters in the field, I had a
front row seat to everything that moved.

At the center—galloping behind breaking news faster
than the nags I covered in sports—was Gilbert L. Watson
III, the metropolitan editor called Gibby by his mother
and some of the more impertinent young reporters.

The teen hooker went by the name "Eddie Regina,"
and was from a family of Hooper's Island watermen.
Chesapeake Bay reporter Tom Horton got a lead on Eddie
and arranged for a meeting on the State House steps in
Annapolis.

Watson took out his wallet (stuffed with phone
numbers and reminders of things he usually forgot to do
while chasing stories), plucked his American Express card

347

and gave it to Horton and Annapolis reporter Karen Hosler to cover whatever was necessary.

"Our job was to pick up Eddie, get him into the closest hotel and start the tape recorder," said Horton. "We pulled up and there was Eddie, waiting.

"Before we could get out, a big car pulls up, a bunch of guys in suits jump out and cram Eddie into the car. We started following it down West Street and Hosler said, 'I know where they're going.'"

The goose chase led to the local FBI office where the reporters were told to get lost. It seems that Eddie had been hustling the game three ways, "using us and the feds to blackmail Bauman," said Horton.

Back on the desk, upon learning that his quarry had been poached, Watson went nuts, or, as he liked to say of other, less composed colleagues, "rolled right out onto the launch pad."

Convinced that the feds were tapping *The Sun's* phones (in fact, they were tapping Bauman's) Gil ordered rewrite man David Michael Ettlin to get then FBI-spokesman Lane Bonner on the line.

"Angry and insistent, Watson sounded incredulous at the denials on the other end," remembered Ettlin. "But what was so beautiful was Gil's passion for this wonderfully sordid and amazing story.

"How could you call yourself a newspaperman and not love him?"

In the spring of 1983, Watson called me into his office. to say he was sending me to Ocean City to cover the beach that summer. It was the break a rookie yearns for—the freedom to follow my instincts, a beat that established my byline—all of it orchestrated by Gil Watson.

Crabtown, USA

A decade later, Gil and I were still at *The Sun*, each of us chafing under new management in our own way—he with stoic dignity, me less so. While wandering the city for eccentric narrative, I'd made the acquaintance of a 74-year-old former Block dancer named Jean Honus who lived alone on Barney Street in South Baltimore.

"Even when I was 50 I got a better applause than a lot of the young ones," she said, remembering her last bump and grind at Blaze Starr's 2 O'Clock Club.

Honus loaned me some 8x10 glossies of platinum-blonde days when she was billed as the "Jean Harlow of the Block." I filed the story and left for a month-long vacation in Thailand.

Upon my return I found a wire basket full of pink "memo" slips the phone clerks used to take messages. They were all from Jean Honus demanding the return of her photographs. I couldn't find them and Honus began accusing me of selling the pics to dirty magazines.

Watson's solution was transcendent: Send Alvarez to a hypnotist and regress his sorry and forgetful ass back to the moment he last saw the photographs. Just like the cost of Eddie Regina's would-be hotel room, the bill was charged to *The Sun*.

In a trance, I remembered writing the story in a part of the newsroom under renovation (they were constantly re-designing the paper and the building in those days while driving herds of talent out the door) and found a couple of the missing photos.

Honus was hardly pacified, but she stopped calling. And Gil Watson loomed larger as the only person on Calvert Street I would ever call mentor.

The last story I'll tell about Gil Watson did not involve

him. Until his 2015 death from pneumonia at age 70 in his native Chestertown, I hadn't thought about it for a long time.

After Ocean City, I learned the craft of rewrite from Ettlin, a position best played up to the moment, and sometimes after, the paper was put to bed.

Then, a bunch of us would play middle-of-the-night basketball at a church gym in Canton to which I had the keys. Post-game, we'd drive to the foot of a pre-gentrified Clinton Street to drink and get high and listen to music from dashboard radios.

One night, I was in the company of a guy from sports who would go on to become a rabbi in Israel, a Fulbright Scholar from Scotland and a handful of summer interns. Crashing the party were officers from the city's southeastern police district.

With my open container of Wiedemann's as probable cause, they found what is now legally on sale in Washington State and Colorado. The future Torah scholar was also alleged to be "in possession of" and we were hauled away while everyone else went home.

In the lock-up, I flushed my press pass down the toilet, used my one phone call to tell the City Desk I wouldn't be in for my Saturday shift and thanked the God of drunks and little kids that the sergeant on duty that night didn't recognize me from police reporting.

When I returned to the newsroom, I was called into a supervisor's office and grilled about why I'd missed my last shift. Certainly there were enough professional gossips that night on Clinton Street for word of the arrest to have raced through the paper.

I stonewalled with "I had a family emergency" (boy did I) and eventually the subject—like the charges—was dropped.

Crabtown, USA

But had it been Gil asking, I would have told him everything, probably more than he needed to know because I would have wanted him to know. After some feigned anger and real disappointment, he would have laughed and called me an idiot, advising me to get my shit together and keep my mouth shut.

And then he would have said that he'd take care of it. Because that's what a real newspaperman does.

I guess you guys be partyin' all the time.

JAIL TIME

The first question that many JHU undergraduates get when they sit down to tutor inmates at the Baltimore City Detention Center gets right to the bottom line: "You guys getting paid for this?"

Nope, not a dime. For a few hours each week, a group of Johns Hopkins students goes to jail to work on the three Rs and anything else the men and women on the inside care to learn. In this way, by coming back week after week, the tutors eventually earn the inmates' trust.

"They know we don't have to be doing this," says Dennis Pang, a senior, who, along with junior Rufus Arnold, is co-president of the university's Jail Tutorial Project. "They say, 'How come you aren't studying or partying?'"

The students study plenty, party now and then—though perhaps not as much as non–college graduates might think—and make time between pursuing majors in subjects like biology and political science to share a bit of what many once took for granted.

"I've been very fortunate to have been provided with countless opportunities, like access to high-quality education," says Haziq Siddiqi, a sophomore from San Jose, California. "I don't want to just leave inmates with a notebook filled with everything there is to know about the GED. What's important to me is leaving them with a resolve to take positive ownership of their life," he says. "This is a group that many people have neglected."

Though at times it may seem fruitless—a guy who is studying for GED tests one week may be transferred to another facility the next—the Homewood students say they wouldn't make the effort if they didn't think it made a difference.

Lucinda Chiu, a sophomore, is a double major in neuroscience and anthropology. Well-grounded in the hard sciences, she is also a classical musician and knows that not everything can be measured.

"If you judge the 'difference' or 'impact' I am making [based on] how many successfully pass the GED after I finish tutoring them, in the majority of the cases, I have made no difference at all," says Chiu, who grew up in Needham, Massachusetts, a suburb of Boston. "But to see attendance [grow] from sporadic to consistent and motivated to meet with me week after week and the smiles when they understand a concept that had been stumping them for so long, or in the moments when they start to realize the potential they have to succeed . . ."

All of it, says Chiu, is more than enough for her to believe she is making a difference.

The Hopkins undergrad tutors are divided evenly between male and female. Inmates who receive tutoring are from the general population as well as subgroups made up of substance abusers working to maintain sobriety and a group of men with mental health issues. Tutoring in this last group is done in the presence of a psychiatrist.

"My group is still waiting for our background checks and fingerprints to get approved before we go in [this year]," says Chiu a few days before Halloween 2014. "Last year, I helped women work through word problems involving math—such as how many $4 shirts can you buy with $29?—as well as addition of mixed fractions."

Many in the current tutoring crews have been going behind the prison walls off the corner of the Fallsway and Eager Street for a couple of years now, including summer sessions.

With pen and paper—the course work all in their heads—they walk below the forbidding nickel-gray pyramid atop the nearby 19th-century Maryland Penitentiary (now known as a "transitional" center) to share their time and expertise.

Though mixing the personal with the professional is discouraged, some overlap is inevitable.

"Once," says Pang, "I helped someone fill out a student loan application." Says Arnold, "I called a guy's mom for him on Mother's Day."

Behind prison walls, old-fashioned communication remains vital as the tutors break from course work to help inmates write letters to family, to lovers, to attorneys and judges.

Arnold, an anthropology major who preps inmates to take the GED tests, says that of all the JHU tutors, he is the one whose background most echoes that of the men they are trying to help.

"I grew up in a high poverty area where 95 percent of the children qualify for free [school] lunch," he says, a Native American who grew up on the Makah Reservation on the far northwestern edge of the Olympic Peninsula in Washington State. "We have similar drug addiction rates as Baltimore City."

During the fall, Sunakshi Bassi taught a tutorial in fractions and decimals.

"Before I joined the Jail Tutorial, I was very sheltered. I knew very little about the criminal justice system," says

Bassi, a senior pre-med political science major from Annapolis, Maryland. "After I got involved, I signed up for a class called the Constitution and the Criminal Justice System. I've decided to write my senior thesis on prison health and its relationship to the Constitution."

This is the latest generation of Hopkins students to tutor inmates at what was once known as the Baltimore City Jail, a project that is now in its fourth decade and among the longest-running public service projects on the Homewood campus.

The work was launched in fall 1980 by Bill Tiefen-werth, who was mentored in the world of good works and social justice by the fabled Hopkins chaplain and poet Chester L. Wickwire (1913–2008). Originally operated under the auspices of the Chaplain's Office, the program is now sponsored by the Center for Social Concern, for which Tiefenwerth was the longtime director.

"I looked for humility" in the volunteers, says the retired Tiefenwerth, now an Open Society Institute fellow and the executive director of Veterans in Partnership, a program that connects middle school students with military veterans through the study of science, technology, engineering, and math. "I didn't want our students to contribute to the disappointment these people had already experienced."

Of course, there have been a few calculating resumé polishers along the way—there always are, says Tiefen-werth—"but the nature of the work we do melts the hardest of hearts."

eastern
avenue
gateway to
the stars

☆ ☆ ☆

If it ain't decent, and it ain't right, stay
the hell away from it.

CHARM CITY

Baltimore in a nutshell?
It's a pissed off, grandmother with a rag tied around her head, squirting down the sidewalk with a hose, grumbling about how kids today are rotten and the world is going to hell . . .

Raymond Douglas Davies

MOVIE STARS

I am a laborer in the steward department aboard the cable ship Global Link, docked off of McComas Street and across from the *Sunpapers's* printing plant in Port Covington, a reporter's notebook in my back pocket, mop in hand.

This is my first ship since I sailed in the engine room of the *S.S. Mayaguez* (of Khmer Rouge infamy) back in 1977, saying goodbye to Deborah Rudacille pierside in Dundalk.

Had planned a fun night on shore with the best of friends, a trip with Senor Guantes to see Ray Davies in Falls Church, Va., but it sold out.

Note from the rock & roll future: In 2001, I was driving a New Beetle with license plates that raved: THE WHO. A half-dozen years later, in Los Angeles after giving up ships for screenwriting (easier on the knees, harder on the nerves), I began criss-crossing the continent in a Toyota pick-up truck with plates that said KINKS.

My adventures in Hollywood led me to another Kinks story, one impossible to imagine when I was scrubbing Captain William Dowd's toilet and making his bed aboard the Global Link. In 2008, not long after the Writer's Guild of America ended its strike against the studios, I was approached by Kevin Bacon to develop an idea for a television series.

Rafael Alvarez

Though based on a true story, I didn't think the idea was very compelling—worlds collide when a Long Island preppie discovers a hip-hop star in the bowels of St. Louis, leading both to glory. But the strike had been long and brutal and I was broke.

"I'm your man," I said. And thus commenced several months of hanging out with Bacon in New York and Los Angeles while shopping the idea from a treatment I worked up.

The white protagonist was "The Maverick," the black antagonist a rapper called "Consequence." There was the Maverick's loyal girlfriend—an NYU French major named Jeannie (*mais bien sûr*)—and my favorite character, "The Mentor."

From the failed pitch—*"The Mentor is Harry Edelman, in his 60s. Based on legendary producer Ahmet Ertegun, Harry not only sees a lot of himself in the Maverick, he smells pelf in the pudding. Consequence's debut album sells more than ten million units."*

I spent a couple of months with Bacon and his obnoxious friend on whom the show was based.

Somehow, maybe after watching pedestrians in Manhattan nudge each other and point to the star as we walked to an out-of-the-way Italian restaurant, the subject of celebrity came up. I said that the only person I'd met in Los Angeles who'd impressed me was Frances Kroll Ring.

In her early 20s, Kroll worked as F. Scott Fitzgerald's secretary—his last—and took dictation for the unfinished novel *The Love of the Last Tycoon* before the writer's 1940 death in Los Angeles.

My daughter Amelia and I shared bagels and orange juice with Kroll at her home. Talked books, took notes, shook her hand and said goodbye.

"Kroll," said Fitzgerald biographer A. Scott Berg, "is

the last real witness, along with Budd Schulberg, to Fitzgerald as a working writer."

"A living connection," said author Steve Erickson in the *Los Angeles Times,* "to an American culture that cared about writing and literacy."

Is there a living movie star that can touch that?

The conversation about celebrity continued over pasta. On the way out after the meal, I spotted founding Kinks front man Ray Davies at a side table. I hung behind just long enough to shake Davies's hand and thank him "for everything."

Joining Bacon outside on the sidewalk, the actor fixed his gaze upon me and said: "I thought you weren't star struck, Rafael."

"I'm not," was my quick answer. "But that wasn't some movie star. That was RAY FUCKING DAVIES."

The Bacon project went downhill from there. He never wanted to star in the show, was only interested in producing, perhaps directing.

Nary a network or cable station thought the idea worth buying, even after some studio big wig —surmising that I was the weak-link in the chain—sent down word that I was not to talk any more while the idea was being pitched.

But back to Guantes.

Born Richard James Snyder to a U.S. Army field band musician stationed at Fort Meade Guantes has been my Rock & Roll best friend since the early 1970s. It was in his bedroom that I first saw a sign proclaiming the Rolling Stones to be "The World's Greatest Rock and Roll Band."

And believed it.

Without a concert to go to, we did the next natural thing and hung out at a record store on Ritchie Highway in Glen Burnie. I bought a Dylan tribute album in honor of Zimmie's 60th [*A Nod to Bob*, Red House Records] and, in lieu of being in the same room as Ray, a re-release of *The Kinks are the Village Green Preservation Society.*

Then, as witness to our age and perhaps wisdom gained since the days when we'd stay up all night whoopin' and hollerin' and carryin' on, we repaired to a strip mall coffee shop. There, we had just as many laughs over espresso as we once did with National Premium and, as Scatman Crothers once observed, "nine kinds of what-have-you."

How many times had we paid good money to see Johnny Winter play the same eight songs?

More than a hundred.

Would we do it again?

Tomorrow, if not sooner.

I told him about my routine on a ship docked across the channel from the *Sunpapers* printing plant. How, just weeks after 9/11 we rarely left the dock and I was sort of like the Jetsons' maid Rosie without the figure.

And Guantes, a career Teamster, supplier of industrial rugs and uniforms and known to clients as "the Rag Man," told this tale.

"One of my customers, a black fellow who cut meat all his life, died the other day. His co-worker says to me, in that way that way that only older black men can, 'That cancer will walk you right to the cemetery. Might be a slow walk, but it will walk you right in . . .'"

I just want to make enough to buy this town
and keep it rough.

DOCKING SHIPS

Back in the mid-1970s—when the original Pride of Baltimore was being built alongside of the Maryland Science Center—a captain at the long-gone Curtis Bay Towing Co. would dock between 40 and 55 ships a month.

Fells Point was still rough back then, with the Port Mission on South Broadway trading soup for souls and locally-owned tugboat companies—Curtis Bay along with Baker-Whiteley Towing—tied up at the Broadway Recreation Pier.

A captain coordinates the securing of a tug or team of tugs to a ship and proceeds to slip the behemoth into its berth with glove-tight accuracy.

Imagine parallel parking a 30,000 ton Lincoln Continental. Now imagine doing it in a blizzard.

"We were blind," said Captain John Evans after a huge snowstorm in February of 1979. "Once you get within 300 to 400 feet of the pier, your radar is no longer of any use. The wind was blowing a gale and the snow was pouring down. Zero visibility.

"One of the tugs," he said, "was used solely as a seeing-eye tug."

True hospitality is a cool drink on a hot day.

AUNT DORIS

A life doesn't get more authentically Baltimore than the one Doris Geng lived for 87 years. Unless you put it alongside the one experienced by her first cousin, Milton Farson, who grew up with Doris on the same South Baltimore streets during the Great Depression.

Doris Connelly Geng died on September 16, her mother's birthday. Milton Grant Farson, who regularly marveled that he had outlived all of his friends and most of their children, passed away on November 6, 2011.

"My mother was Sadie and her mother was Esther, they were sisters," said Milton not long before he died. "Esther run a bar on Cross Street and she handled herself like a man. You didn't mess with her."

The bar was called Jenkins Café at 20 East Cross Street between Light and Charles. After the bar was sold in the 1970s, it became a hipster hangout called Lush's.

Doris's mother worked the bar. Her "gentleman friend"—Edward Jenkins, a handsome "eye-talian" with an American name whom everyone called "Wop"—was a bookie who did business in the back.

Doris was born at 140 West Ostend Street in 1923. Because her mother served drinks at the saloon from eye-openers to last call, Doris and her sister were raised by an aunt named Blanche and her husband Harry.

"I grew up doing my homework in that bar," said Geng's granddaughter Denise Horn Domingo, whom Doris raised as a daughter. "I have a big [backyard] thermometer from there—it says, 'Compliments of Esther Jenkins,'"

"My grandmother could be a very stubborn woman who had to have her way. But I admired her for that."

Milton, born in 1919, spent his early years at his mother's grocery in Elkridge and the long-lost farmland that surrounded it. When his father skipped out on the family, Milton's mother moved the kids to 936 South Paca Street.

More than once, he said, he had to go to the downtown courthouse as a kid to report that his father wasn't giving the family any money.

Good-hearted by nature—Milton more of a softie than Doris, who could be a rough customer when necessary— they grew up with the kind of want—sometimes true hunger but more often the desire to simply have *enough*— that made them empathetic to others.

"My mother ate lard on black bread," said Milton. "We ate a little better than that."

Doris—fond of steamed crabs, raw oysters and all-you-can-eat buffets—was a two-time cancer survivor who raised two sons by herself not far from where Milton grew up on South Paca Street.

If you were a relative or neighbor and came down with a bad cold or something worse, Doris was there with chicken noodle soup or a homemade cake. Sometimes both. She knew everybody's favorite dessert and raffled off many a strawberry shortcake at the VFW No. 3217 on Washington Boulevard where she belonged to the Ladies' Auxiliary and played a mean shuffleboard.

If you were the person who delivered the mail or the

crew that picked up the trash, Doris was there with a cold drink on a hot day.

And she paid for more than one family funeral—including her mother's—when no one else stepped up, doling out money from a strong box in which Wop Jenkins used to keep his gambling receipts.

Longtime neighbor David Gale, 61 and a native of New York State, learned the essence of Baltimore through Doris, her kindness and her emblematic patois.

[While other folks might vacuum the rug, Doris put her elbow grease into "val-culming" it. "Wooder" ran from a "spick-it" into the "zinc."]

"She was a character, a treasure. Not much education but really knew people," said Gale whose home security system was the eyes and ears of Doris Geng.

"She would start out easy-going when she met someone but she was savvy too," said Gale. "Some people—sometimes family members—might get over on her because her heart was bigger than her tough image. No one got over on her twice."

Milton's was a scrappy childhood; a hand-to-mouth struggle not unlike the one Babe Ruth had a generation before him on the same streets off the corner of Light and Pratt, a time when just about every bar had an upright piano against the wall.

"It was a big thing to walk through the Cross Street Market and look at all the things you couldn't have," he said.

The delicacies he craved included fresh sauerkraut, limburger cheese and dark rye.

"Sometimes we might have some," he said. "If you could get the limburger past your nose you were all right."

Once he made a quarter for telling a man on Hamburg Street where to find the neighborhood speakeasy. Another time, he watched foreign sailors make turtle soup at a German bar in Pigtown.

"I never seen a turtle so big," he marveled.

He dropped out of grade school to help his mother, the former Sadie Connelly, who more-or-less raised Milton and his siblings—Walter and Jack—with little help from their a-rabber father.

"I sometimes felt ashamed that I didn't have an education," he said. "It makes you feel funny, but what can you do?"

Doris had a public school education that stopped short of a high school diploma. Her learning involved needle and thread, street smarts and a waitress apron. She learned to sew as a girl and made her own curtains and table cloths along with outfits for her grandchildren—some from old curtains—and Halloween costumes.

One of her first waitress jobs was at Jenkins Café. She waited tables from the World War II era of the 1940s on through the hippie years of the '60s. After that, she managed a bakery, where she met Carl A. Geng.

Carl would come in for coffee before going to work and—kibitzing over the doughnuts, flirting a bit—they got to know each other, marrying in December of 1966.

Though fiercely independent—the kind of woman who got along just fine without a man (Carl was her second husband)—things got easier for Doris. She enjoyed sitting on the front porch of her house at 2802 Carroll near Washington Boulevard, shooting the breeze with friends and neighbor or finding a bargain at Value Village.

Nothing made her happier than a can of cold domestic beer and a pile of steamed crabs on a newspaper-covered table. The talk might turn to gossip but it wouldn't be cruel, yakking with friends and family about good old days that often only looked good in hindsight.

Crabtown, USA

Days like the ones Milton Farson loved talking about when he and I would drive down Hollins Ferry Road through Lansdowne and Arbutus to his dialysis appointment. Once he pointed out a corner gin mill and said: "I haven't been in there since 1934."

1934!

"I was 27 when I started driving but looked 16," laughed Milton not long before his death, talking about his career driving street cars and a rookie's 60 cents an hour pay. "I stopped on this corner to pick up passengers and a woman backed away from the door.

"She said, 'Are you old enough to drive this thing?'"

Milton Farson's life spanned the American Century and there was little of its rich pageant he didn't experience.

An early memory was going with a neighbor who used a small rifle to hunt blackbirds in the marshes near Patapsco Avenue. The old-timer bagged enough birds for a pie.

I had thought such things were mere nursery rhymes— *"four and 20 blackbirds, baked in a pie"*—but not so. Milton had been there, had sung a song of sixpence.

Milton served in the Navy during World War II. His long career as a schedule driven transit driver in Baltimore—six minutes to the next stop, eight minutes to the one after that, no margin for tardiness with bone-tired working people who depended on him—explained his need to be on time no matter what the destination—and enjoyed a long marriage and fatherhood in Morrell Park through the prosperity of the 1950s and 1960s.

By the 1970s, the grandchildren started to come along and a man whose smile came naturally began to grin a little wider.

On our weekly drives from Linthicum to Arbutus for

dialysis [the family asks that donations be made to the National Kidney Foundation], Milton would look out the window at places that were gone. It was like he was staring at an old map.

"How come I've lived so long and everyone else I grew up with or worked with is dead?"

Milton knew the question had no answer but for some reason he enjoyed asking it.

I bet he knows now.

Understands why people were privileged to know him from the pre-Depression age of Silent Cal to the post-recession days of the first African-American president of the United States.

Milton knows because he's hanging out with Doris— the cousin who was like a sister—and all the other good people he outlived.

In the last year of her life, Doris suffered with Alzheimer's and struggled to remember people she had known for years. The folks she left behind aren't having such problems.

Said David Gale: "We think of Doris every day . . ."

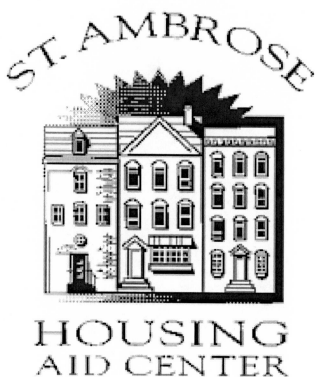

ST. AMBROSE

HOUSING
AID CENTER

Wear the world like a loose garment.

VINNIE QUAYLE

When the nation's mortgage crisis boiled over in 2008, Vinnie Quayle, nearing the end of a long career of fighting the good fight, was tired.

Quayle is the face and soul of the St. Ambrose Housing Aid Center, which he founded in Baltimore in 1968 with a Jesuit mentor and the Msgr. Edward Miller, now pastor of St. Bernadine parish.

A longtime parishioner at St. Francis of Assisi in Mayfield, Quayle helped thousands of low-and-middle income families buy homes.

Named for the Northwest Baltimore parish where Miller was assigned in 1968, St. Ambrose is the city's oldest non-profit housing provider. It has served more than 100,000 families since it began. Each year, some 3,000 new families get assistance.

As people began losing their homes because they should never have been given mortgages in the first place—instead of traditional pitfalls like illness, divorce or unemployment—Quayle knew a disturbing shift had taken place.

"Something different was going on," said Quayle. "But by then we had mellowed. Back in the old days we'd have been out picketing banks and raising hell."

At the end of 2011, the 72-year-old Quayle decided to retire after 43 years in the fair housing game, a smart and brave run in which only a handful of families helped by St. Ambrose lost their homes before the current crisis.

Quayle, who oversaw the development of the Marian House in Waverly for women recovering from drug abuse and their children, says he is going to take it easy now.

A student of the Indian Jesuit and mystic Anthony De Mello [1931 to 1987], Quayle said he will now choose, perhaps in the spirit of the prayer of St. Teresa of Avila, to let nothing disturb him.

"I refuse to get angry," he said, driving to Timonium to be fitted for a tuxedo in advance of being named 2012 "Hibernian of the Year" by the Baltimore chapter of the Irish-American society. "I'm going to do everything slowly."

Perhaps that's because the former priest—taught in high school by the Rev. Daniel Berrigan at Brooklyn Jesuit Prep in the 1950s—gave everything he had to his lay vocation.

"There's no more noble deed than helping people find homes and Vinnie fought his rear-end off to do it," said Church of the *Immaculate Conception* parishioner and Hibernian Society of Baltimore president Daniel P. Cahill.

Married to the former Patricia Connolly—a School Sister of Notre Dame when the couple opted for secular life—the Quayles reared three boys off of Walther Boulevard in the Beverly Hills section of Northeast Baltimore. Their sons, Thomas, Matthew and Paul, are all practicing Catholics.

"I thought we'd solve all of the city's housing problems, that we could really help people own their homes," said Quayle, looking back on 1968, a year of miracles and nightmares. "We were believers."

In the '60s, he said, there was plenty of federal money, people with their hearts in the right places and religious willing to work beyond the parish. Unemployment hovered around 3 percent.

"But there were larger forces—drugs and the breakdown of the family and loss of jobs," said a humbled Quayle. "It was all bigger than us and we didn't realize it."

Pamuk told me there'd be days like this.

SNOW STORY

I t had everything: a beautiful girl making dinner in her pajamas, refugees from war in Europe, a fight against the elements to wish my daughter a happy birthday and nearly two feet of snow on the streets of Baltimore.

From the earliest monster snows I can remember [January 1963, when Cardinal Shehan told Catholics they could skip Sunday Mass] to the last one, the blizzard of 1996 remains the most memorable blizzard of my life.

Between January 7th—my daughter Sofia's 11th birthday—and January 13th, 22 inches of snow fell on Maryland.

[Accumulation in the Free State in 1996 was measured at 62.5 inches, smashing the previous annual record of 51 inches when "the Great Arctic Outbreak" hit on Valentine's Day of 1899.]

The 1996 storm was a nor'easter and parts of the Atlantic seaboard were buried under four feet of wind-whipped drifts.

The threat—not idle, but imminent—began the afternoon of Saturday the 6th. I was at the Patuxent River Naval Air Station in St. Mary's County, covering something forgettable for *The Baltimore Sun,* where I wrote hundreds of weather stories over years.

[Note to would-be reporters in the post-newspaper

age: it is much easier to cover heat than cold. Quotable clichés spill freely from men working jackhammers and women squirting down the sidewalk and your fingers don't freeze when you're trying to take notes.

But snow, which changes the way the world looks, allows more dramatic prose.]

As the snow began, a young woman held dinner for me in an apartment near Johns Hopkins University. Our paths had crossed through Chaim Potok [1929 to 2002] when the writer was teaching at Homewood. Let's call her Minna.

Snow was coming—lots of it—and all I wanted to do was get back to Baltimore.

At the time, I was sponsoring Bosnian refugees at my house in Highlandtown, including a young man named Eldin Cengic, who arrived via Lutheran Social Services craving peanut butter, Nutella and a Volkswagen to call his own.

The first thing Eldin saw when he walked in from the airport were pepper plants growing from a pair of beat-up pair of Converse high-tops filled with dirt. Before long, he and I were going on double-dates with Minna and one of her friends from the Hopkins Schools of Advanced International Studies.

The fish Minna had baked was cold by the time I made it back to Charles and 33rd but the apartment was warm (the Depression-era building had radiators that rattled and hissed, making it so hot we cracked the windows even though a blizzard raged outside) and we made do.

The next morning—the 7th, Sofia's birthday, a day before the King's—we were snowed in and I was determined to make it the 3.1 miles from Charles Village to Mayfield on the other side of Lake Montebello to see her.

Crabtown, USA

My 1989 Subaru wagon, which a few years before had taken the kids and me to Stovall Plantation in Mississippi, was parked on St. Paul Street near 33rd. Minna and I shoveled out the tires, someone gave us a push and off we went down 33rd toward Waverly and the majesty of Memorial Stadium in the snow.

[Inclemency could not dim the glory of their deeds. For that it took extraordinary civic bone-headedness. The ballyard was razed in 2002.]

Trudging east, there was a lot of slipping and sliding (*she's a solid sender, you know you better surrender*) but no real problems, even on the oval of Montebello Terrace.

The snow kept coming in swirls and gusts and it was great fun; an hour of weird motoring freedom—a little recklessness combined with the silent wonder of a big snowstorm.

All was well until we hit Harford Road for the drive down to 2231 Kentucky Avenue, where my kids lived. Turning down the hill where Kentucky runs toward Pelham Avenue, someone was stuck in front of us.

I ditched the Subaru and with the help of the Sunderland family, good friends and old neighbors, pushed the stalled car to the side.

Though our time together ended not long after the Blizzard of '96—somehow it fell apart during an Al Greene concert in Washington—an indelible memory is Minna in a knit cap, her breath visible before her round Middle Eastern face, flakes of snow melting across the freckles on her nose.

I told her to stand by and ran the rest of the way to sing happy birthday to Sofia, no present but my presence.

[The birthday girl didn't seem too impressed by my heroics, but I was able to take off my coat, give her a big squeeze and promise that when the snow cleared, we'd go out and do something fun.]

Rafael Alvarez

More snow soon followed and reporters started living in the newsroom at 501 North Calvert Street.

As I write this, a week before Christmas, snow is said to be arriving by the weekend.

Don't forget the milk and toilet paper.

Rewrite, get me Sweetheart . . .

AGING NEWSPAPERMEN

We are a group of men and women who remember when the Sunday paper was fat; the newsroom was noisy, crowded, cantankerous and irreverent; and reporters got paid a living wage to wander the streets of Crabtown in search of stories.

We are the Aging Newspapermen of Baltimore and Ladies' Auxiliary and for the past several years have met in Highlandtown every Friday for lunch and cross currents of hot air.

Around the long tables at Roman's—a South Decker Avenue corner saloon known in my father's day as Hess's, famous when McKeldin was mayor for sour beef and dumplings—is enough talent to run any city desk in America.

[Or could if they stayed up past 10 o'clock at night to make the second edition. The "aging" description, though nettlesome to some, is well earned. Some of the scribes once labored at the *The News-American*, the afternoon paper of Baltimore's working class and dead since 1986.]

The line-up includes David Michael Ettlin, a 40-year veteran who manned the *Sun* rewrite desk for much of that time; Antero Pietila, a one-time Moscow and Johannesburg correspondent whose major work is *Not In My Neighborhood* [2010, Ivan R. Dee publisher]; and, when he can stand to be around his former colleagues for

more than an hour, Michael Olesker, the sage of all that is
gone.

The satirist D.R. Belz always gets the turkey club and
Jim Burger and Edwin Remsberg—who both toiled on
Calvert Street when photography was still the realm of
chemists—represent the Weegee brigade.

But the deans of the final edition– like the South
Baltimore gourmand James S. Keat, a former *Sun*
assistant managing editor who covered India for the Sun
in the 1960s and retired religion editor Frank P.L.
Somerville—are only part of the story.

There is new, pixilated life percolating across from the
dusty by-lines of yesteryear.

A young crowd joins the Aging Ones or codfish cakes
and lima bean soup (tellingly, almost no one orders beer);
20-something journalists who have never written for print
media, up-and-comers of cyberspace sitting next to men
with bad knees and faulty memories to hear stories of
Mister Diz, Paul Blair and Spiro Agnew.

The new talent arrived at Roman's via Stacy
Spaulding, a journalism professor at Towson State
University and reigning chair of the Ladies' Auxiliary.
Spaulding, a Maryland transplant who has embraced East
Baltimore as her own, is a historian of Crabtown
journalism.

To her classroom, Spaulding has brought Olesker and
the fabled Tom Nugent, the mad-man of out-sized prose
who almost single-handedly led *The Sun's* late 1970's
transition from the "Women's Pages" to a modern features
section.

Many of the young reporters and editors work for
patch.com, a nationwide series of AOL-owned websites
that specialize in extremely local news, bread and butter
beats like crime and school lunch menus. Bruce Goldfarb,

founding editor of welcometobaltimorehon dot com is also a regular.

It's a good mix. Old-timers get to tell war stories (like the time Mike Bowler of the *The Evening Sun* published an editorial about a downtown building that deserved to be saved from the wrecking ball a day after it had been torn down.)

The new generation gets pointers about how to leverage a politician into telling at least part of the truth and bar owner Roman Kuzmiw—the biggest Oriole fan in Baltimore, even in these dark times for the orange and black—does good business on Friday afternoon.

Often there's an empty chair and I imagine my last night editor Norm Wilson, who spent some 30 years with the *Sunpapers*—sitting in it.

Norm had the greatest smile in the world, called everybody *podna* as though the City Desk was a campfire on the dusty trail and did his best to protect his reporters from the big boys in the corner office.

Few were better at weeding 20 paragraphs of dreck from some poor rookie in over their head or an old gray mare put out to pasture—and then turning that crap into a crisp brief to fill a hole next to the weather table—than Norm.

Norman was orphaned as a boy and was raised by his maternal grandmother. As an 11-year-old playing in a city park, Norm saw a woman drop her pocketbook. He picked up what had scattered and ran it over to the woman, who happened to be accompanied by a friend on the staff of the *New York Times*.

The die was cast: The *Times* reporter took a shine to the young do-gooder and paid his tuition to a Catholic high school and St. Francis College in Brooklyn Heights, N.Y., where Norm earned a bachelor's degree in English and applied his love to books to newspaper work.

Rafael Alvarez

Said Ernie Imhoff, an *Evening Sun* assistant managing editor: "He loved to rip a story out of his typewriter after two paragraphs and yell to the copyboy, `This page has a train and plane to catch, so move it, son.'"

I once heard him say when a male reporter received flowers in the newsroom: "Give me a fifth of whiskey, boy. Send me flowers when I'm dead . . ."

Norman T. Wilson died in August of 2001 while mowing the lawn at his Brooklyn Park home in preparation for his daughter's 10th birthday. A heart attack got him, just like Norm always said it would when we'd eat Royal Farms fried chicken on the City Desk at 10 p.m.

I often think of how much Norm would enjoy talking the news game with the apprentices who show up each week for the Aging luncheon off the corner of East Baltimore Street and Decker Avenue. These are kids with the courage to enter journalism in the 21st century, a time when reporters have been reduced to content providers with pocket-sized video cameras.

Norm could have told them what it was like to be the first African-American editorial writer in Baltimore, although he'd never have brought it up on his own.

I wonder: will they make the time to find the people—the kind who live up in Joseph Mitchell's old hotel—that no one else thinks is important?

Will they look at the hole in the block where a rowhouse used to be and find out who lived there and why they don't live there anymore?

Will they try to stand up for the little man?

The guy who winds up getting a free private education in exchange for a good deed done simply because it was the right thing to do?

Una bella anima

MRS. ZANNINO

Much is made of the last words the dying speak before passing to the next world. The writer William Saroyan, whose stories celebrate living life to the fullest, phoned his exit line into the Associated Press shortly before his death at age 72 in 1981.

"Everybody has got to die, but I have always believed an exception would be made in my case. Now what?"

Rarely do you hear about a last laugh. Who goes out with a chuckle?

Immacolata "Tina" Mastellone has the honor of giving Maria Santa Zannino a comforting moment of mirth before her beloved aunt died at age 80 on August 24 just outside of Baltimore.

They were in Mrs. Zannino's room at the Gilchrist Hospice, talking about the good old days, the early 1970s when Maria and her husband Joseph would pack up their eight kids along with friends and relatives and head to Ocean City for a much-needed vacation from the family funeral business in Highlandtown.

"It was the summer of 1974 and my aunt called it the summer of the white bikini," said Mastellone, who wore her black hair almost to her hips, a teenager sporting the white two-piece against a bronze Italian tan.

Aunt Maria, a former model long admired for her own beauty, enjoyed telling young Tina how "exquisite" she looked.

"I went to see her about two days before she died," recalled Mastellone. "I told her I almost wore the white bikini but I didn't have the body for it anymore. She laughed and my cousins told me it was the last time she laughed like that."

Born at St. Joseph Hospital in Baltimore (she was a lifetime city resident), the former Maria Santa Glorioso grew up on Keyworth Avenue in northwest Baltimore and graduated from St. Ambrose parochial school on Park Heights Avenue.

She took piano at the Peabody Conservatory for four years and in 1951 graduated from Seton High School on North Charles Street. The following year completed studies at the Walters Academy of Baltimore, a former modeling and charm school, also on Charles Street.

Her brief modeling career included many pageants, including, her children said, a run at the Miss Maryland title.

"Some agency wanted Mom to go to New York to model lingerie and she said NO," laughed her daughter Rosemarie "MiMi" Zannino, a poet. "She was very modest."

After high school, she worked as executive secretary to the controller/treasurer of Johns Hopkins Hospital. In 1957, she married Joseph N. Zannino, Jr. 84, who survives her along with eight children and many grandchildren.

In 1958, Mr. Zannino founded the business that bears the family name and in 1965, Mrs. Zannino joined him as a funeral director. The funeral home stands at 263 South Conkling Street, just north of Eastern Avenue and south of East Pratt Street. The area is also home to Our Lady of Pompei Church and DiPasquale Grocery and was once known as Baltimore's second Little Italy.

Street smart, book smart and highly observant, Mrs.

Crabtown, USA

Zannino served her customers with genuine empathy, not by-the-book etiquette. When my Spanish grandfather Rafael Alvarez [1904 to 1990] died, he was taken from an Eastern Shore nursing home to the rowhouse parlor at the corner of Conkling and Gough.

When the body arrived, Mrs. Zannino called my parents and said, "Dad is with us now." My folks never forgot the kindness.

Once, when a recently divorced young man was leaving a party at her home (above the funeral parlor), Mrs. Zannino commented to one of her daughters, "That's the saddest boy I've ever seen. Look at how he walks."

Her own funeral was handled by her son Charles, who earned his state funeral director's license in 1983.

On through the end, she was involved in just about all aspects of "Zannino's," and was reviewing bank statements (usually finding discrepancies) and spreadsheets almost to the day she entered Gilchrist.

Mrs. Zannino loved rooting for the home teams—the baseball Orioles and the football Ravens and the team that will never die, the *Baltimore* Colts—and just last week was asking her children how the Birds were doing in the American League East.

[The answer depended on which day she asked.]

"To me, she was all about beauty," said Tina, who was chosen to give one of the eulogies. "At first glance, she was movie star beautiful but Aunt Maria's beauty was transcendent: an appreciation of beautiful things . . . the beauty of the heart.

"When you had a conversation with her she made you feel like you were the only person in the world."

Hey Danny, remember Miss Vilma?

PINEY POINT

Summer meant vacation, a fun combo of cousins and the kids of men my father worked with on the Fells Point tugboats. We always spent a week down the ocean and often a week here in the historical holy land of Southern Maryland.

We'd pack up the car and go down to Piney Point.

Named for the tall, lonesome trees that dot the sandy soil, Piney Point is a small town of about 1,000 near St. George Island on the Potomac River. The town name is also shorthand for the Paul Hall Center for Maritime Training and Education, a 60-acre expanse that was once a Navy testing area for torpedoes.

In 1966, the campus was purchased by the Seafarers International Union, to which my marine engineer father has belonged for a half-century.

The SIU negotiated the 1960's labor contracts that put my family in an expanding middle-class. The union's pension and retirement benefits—along with Social Security, thrift and prudence—have allowed Mom and Dad to remain in a shrinking middle class.

In 1967, the Harry Lundeberg School of Seamanship opened in Piney Point and in a few years we were vacationing there for a song with other Baltimore tugboat families.

In the summer of 1972, just before I entered high

school, Al Green was singing "Let's Stay Together" on AM radio, Earl and the Birds were in regular contention for the pennant and the last thing my father—who left home at 17 to sail on Venezuela-bound ore ships out of Sparrows Point—wanted was for me to become a seaman.

Around us kids were cadres of young people apprenticing for work in one of the three departments on ships: deck, engine and steward.

We swam, rode bicycles and played basketball and saw free movies—including *The Strawberry Statement*, which was quite intoxicating for a 13-year-old at the height of the Vietnam War. I was smitten with Joyce Ann, the daughter of my father's Dundalk deckhand buddy Bobby Machlinski and the last thing on my mind was going to sea.

There didn't seem much chance of that: I was a bookish kid obsessed with the Beatles and knew from a very young age that school was easier than work. My father often said he didn't want his boys following him "down to the boats."

Four years later—a bookish kid obsessed with Frank Zappa—found me working on a container ship to pay for an education intended to save me from a life of working on ships. My father's union connections allowed me to by-pass training at Piney Point.

At first he refused to pull those strings. Then I started getting into a little bit of rock and roll trouble and the old man changed his mind. One day I was getting my Mt. St. Joseph High School diploma at the Cathedral of Mary Our Queen. The next I was heaving hawser lines, pretending I knew what I was doing.

The experience convinced me more than college ever did that—for richer or poorer—I would be a writer.

The Class of 77 Prepares to Leave the City ● Pimlico Plays the Favorites
Backstage with Southside Johnny and Ronnie ● News and Reviews

City Squeeze

VOL. 1, NO. 1   FREE   BALTIMORE   FREE   MAY 27, 1977

RIC PFEFFER
TENURE CONTROVERSY SEE PAGE 3

Loose Shoes at Marble Bar

Not a snowball's chance in Highlandtown

BEYOND BELIEF

Back in 1977, if I'd told my father that one day there'd be a bronze statue of Frank Zappa at the corner of Eastern Avenue and Conkling Street, he'd have said, "Better stop smoking that shit, Ace."

That same year—four decades ago, Jimmy in the White House and the Sex Pistols pissing on the Queen— Russ Smith (editor) and Alan Hirsch (businessman) launched a smart, smug and impudent tabloid called the *City Squeeze*.

And if someone had told Smith that the *Sunpapers* of Baltimore would eventually adopt his bitching baby, Russell would have told them to pass the shit his way and get their head out of their ass.

It's not that he wouldn't have sold the paper to *The Sun* if the price was right. A decade after the first issue hit Crabtown, Smith and Hirsch unloaded *City Paper* on Times-Shamrock Communications of Scranton, Pa. for a ballpark figure estimated at some $8 million.

It's simply that the idea was beyond absurd; like thinking that Baltimoreans are going to start scrubbing their marble steps again on Saturday mornings.

In January of 1978, a revamped *Squeeze* debuted as the *City Paper* and it often seemed like it existed solely to unnerve *The Sun*. Russ Smith loved throwing rocks at the Goliath on Calvert Street, where he once worked in the library and relished having filched a file photo of Billy the Kid.

Largely through the RUMP, a juicy gossip feature, Smith so tortured former *Sun* columnist Michael Olesker that Olesker responded with an article painting the *City Paper* as a schoolyard bully desperate for attention. Which, of course, tickled Smith greatly.

The once-mighty *Sun*, owned by the Tribune Company of Chicago since 2000, has long been a shell of its former, glorious and global self.

[Its editorial board single-handedly put Harry Hughes in the governor's mansion in 1978. The paper once operated eight foreign bureaus—from Mexico City to mainland China—and boasted in house ads that "The Sun Never Sets on the World."]

Today, you'd think the only daily in town was a house organ of the Baltimore Ravens.

And now, for a sum surely less than the $8 million Times-Shamrock reportedly paid for it in 1987, *The Baltimore Sun* has purchased a one-time weakling fat with ads that would make longtime state censor Mary Avara choke on her Polack Johnny's.

"It would have been absolutely unthinkable for this to happen when we started," said Ken Sokolow, 58, a Hopkins alumnus who wrote "First Degree Burns," a long-ago *CP* political column. "The management of the *City Paper* and [management at] *The Sun* practiced mutual detestation."

Today?

"It's like the owner of the *Titanic* sitting in a lifeboat," said Sokolow. "As the great ship sinks he turns to an underling and says, 'I'm going to buy the *Lusitania.*'"

Crabtown, USA

What do they say about living long enough?

You'll see it all, Hon.

I was 19-years-old in the fall of 1977, just off a summer as an ordinary seaman on a Puerto Rican container ship and a sophomore at what was then Loyola College. One day, a stack of papers that was decidedly not the Loyola *Greyhound* appeared in the cafeteria. It was the *City Squeeze* and the masthead listed a phone number.

I called and said I was a writer, which was not exactly true but it also wasn't a lie.

[I had kept journals since the 10th grade; rewrote the lyrics to Robin Trower songs and called it poetry; spent time on the curb in front of my grandfather's rowhouse in Highlandtown using words to sketch the homes across the street.]

I'm pretty sure I was the first non-Hopkins kid to work for the *Squeeze*, which Smith and Hirsch—along with classmates Eric Garland, Jennifer Bishop, Craig Hankin, Joachim Blunck and others—first published under the noses of the deans from the campus *News-Letter* office.

I pitched a story about a longshoreman's strike that had shut down the port of Baltimore, used my father's waterfront connections to scoop *The Sun* and was welcomed into the fold.

Soon, Russell and I were piling bundle upon bundle of each week's issue into the trunk of my brand new, 1978 Ford Granada, dumping papers around town until the springs began to give way on the car my folks had bought to get back and forth to Loyola.

My parents were happy that I was doing what I had always wanted and invited Russell and his future and now ex-wife Katie Gunther (a writer) to their Linthicum home for a big dinner to celebrate my 20th birthday with my future and now ex-wife Deborah Rudacille (a writer).

[Russell liked a cold beer and a good story and my old man liked cold beer and a good story. After dinner, Pop broke out the Anis del Mono and Cuarenta y Tres for a Spanish *digestif* known as "sol y sombra" and Smith liked that even more.]

For a solid three years, I was under Russ Smith's formidable spell: smoking reefer at the editor's desk while discussing assignments (Muddy Waters at the Marble Bar, the decline of National Bohemian beer, riding a garbage truck for a day) and rock and roll (he worshiped Dylan, I remained possessed by Quadrophenia).

At home, I have a photocopy of the first check, signed by Alan Hirsch, I ever received for my writing. It came after a year of working for the thrill of a by-line. The pay back then, some 36 years ago, was $25 for 1,000 words. That's $25 more than most websites pay today.

Through it all, I had a night job dispatching delivery trucks in *The Sun* circulation department. There, I used a secretary's IBM Selectric to write *City Paper* stories on the sly while keeping an eye out for a job—any job—in the newsroom on the fifth floor.

Though Smith never let up in his disdain for the morning paper, he wrote a beautiful letter of recommendation for me when I took my *City Paper* longshoreman's story to Dick Bosaco in *The Sun* personnel department and asked to be a clerk in the sports department.

I got that job, was soon promoted to the City Desk and for the next 20 years filed stories there on everything from Orthodox Jews to Ostrowki's Polish sausage. But I'll never forget that the *City Paper* was the first place to give me a chance.

Smith and Hirsch (Russell irascible, Alan lovable) were fun, irreverent and, when it came to the product, no-nonsense.

Crabtown, USA

Early on, I used a close friend to photograph a story and Russell was not pleased with the results. When I argued that my buddy would surely get better over time, he snapped: "We're not here to teach people how to do their job."

The message was clear. This was not an experiment by wannabes attempting to publish a newspaper. It *was* a newspaper.

Whether it will remain one is the only question the Calvert Street brain trust should be asking themselves today.

I have been reading Borges for thirty years
and I still don't know what he is talking about.

GOSPEL TRUTH

"In my Father's house, there are many mansions . . ."
—the Book of John

The Wire & the Cable Ship

In 2002, I began writing for the HBO crime drama *The Wire,* the much-lauded story of American left-behinds filmed in my own backyard.

I'd made it all the way to Hollywood without having to leave East Baltimore!

It was never my intention to leave the Holy Land of my childhood, the narrow, concrete back yards of trashcans and rosebushes, retired shipyard workers listening to the ballgame on the radio. The only other destination I truly desired was the shelves of bookstores and libraries around the world.

But once I accepted an invitation to the dance, the Tinseltown cha-cha began having its way with me.

The initial come-on came in 1996 from David Simon, who sat next to me in the newsroom of the Baltimore Sun when we were kid reporters on the City Desk. Simon's book *Homicide: A Year on the Killing Streets*, had been developed into a dramatic series for NBC by Baltimore native Barry Levinson and was a cult favorite.

"I can help if you wanna give it a try," said Simon, who'd risen through the ranks of the show's writing staff after leaving the paper. "It's easier than reporting and pays a lot better."

I didn't own a television, having gotten rid of it when the kids were little in favor of Chinese checkers, crayons and copy paper brought home from work. My children were not pleased: "Dad," they whined, "kids need TV!"

As though it were air.

Simon gave me a pile of *Homicide* scripts and videos of the show. I bought a TV and a cheap VCR player in a Tom Waits suburb of Baltimore called Glen Burnie and sat down to read the scripts while screening the accompanying episode, looking up now and then to see how the words translated into image.

And then I sat down to abuse the tab key on an old IBM personal computer—one of those "towers" from the mid-1990s—to build a script like a set of monkey bars in which a lot of the pieces don't fit and others are missing. I'd never done it before, had never wanted to.

When I give readings, people often ask me to explain the difference between writing fiction and writing for television. First, there is the Rubik's Cube constrict of a one-hour episodic script, especially a network teleplay in which the drama must be manipulated to hover at the edge of each commercial and do so compellingly that it often feels false.

The biggest way the genres vary, and the part that disappoints me most, is how useless the camera renders description, how moot the precision and rhythm of language I'd worked on for so long: the way sunlight looks on the side of a building and how different that light strikes the same building at 10 a.m. versus 4 p.m. Screenwriting sums it all up in a single direction, one that no one has better sustained throughout an entire film than Terence Malick in *Days of Heaven.*

Magic Hour.

Scribbling quotes in a reporter's notebook for so many years, however—listening for lyricism instead of looking for it—proved to be sound preparation for screenwriting. When my characters speak, no matter what ridiculous situation they might be in on a cartoon-ish show like the Black Donnellys they tend to sound like real people. Or at least what passes for real in Baltimore.

With no small amount of cynicism, it comes down to this for me: spend a half a lifetime in letters and you're lucky you win a hundred readers who can discern your work stripped of your by-line. But go and get that same name attached to the credits of something that airs on television a half dozen times and you get invited to write essays like this.

[Which, by the way, falls into the category of writing that pays the least.]

———

I knew very little of this when I sat down in the fall of 1996 to write my "spec" script—a try out, an audition, if you can bounce, then bounce high—for *Homicide.*

My idea was to tell a story about the kinds of killings that don't get much attention in the ballistic age: someone using their bare hands in intimate slaughter, preferably between best friends.

I named one of the homicidal, glue-sniffing goofs Butchie. I can't remember who Butchie beat to death, but he did it by the railroad tracks at the end of Foster Avenue, around the corner from my grandfather's Macon Street rowhouse, the place where I heard my first stories at the kitchen table: Spain and it's Civil War, sailing ships and the men who went ashore in Baltimore and sometimes made their way to that same table with stories of their own.

With Simon's support and fine-tuning [from him I learned that dialogue, however clever, can not twist the actor's tongue], the script was good enough to freelance an episode for *Homicide's* fifth season. The idea was assigned by producer Jimmy Yoshimura, who wanted a murder pivoting on AIDS and an urban legend which held that drinking bleach could cleanse the victim of the virus.

The episode, "All is Bright," aired on Dec. 12, 1997 and actually retained some of the scenes and dialogue I had written. I was especially pleased that my suggestion for music to accompany a key scene—Suzanne Vega's "Blood Makes Noise"—was used.

Simon's bosses, however, didn't think the work quite good enough and it was back to the City Desk for me.

Five years later, I had left the newspaper to go to sea. For $7.80 an hour plus health insurance, I washed dishes and mopped decks on the *Global Link*, a Tyco cable layer that docked near the Port Covington printing plant of *The Baltimore Sun*. In port—stretched out in my rack reading *Half a Life* by V.S. Naipaul—I'd look out the porthole and see the giant logo of the paper where I'd learned to write 20 years earlier. And did not miss it a bit.

At the same time, Simon had sold *The Wire* pilot to HBO and was preparing for the show's inaugural season. I was invited to write a script that first year—"One Arrest"—which aired July 14, 2002 as I tossed bags of garbage into an incinerator aboard a British cable ship, the Atlantic Guardian, off the coast of the Virgin Islands.

"Sure you wrote a TV show," my shipmate on the incinerator detail laughed. "How about you throw me another bag of garbage."

Crabtown, USA

The next year, *The Wire* moved to those same docks where the cable ships tied up, its plot anchored deep in the long, slow death of a well-paid working class protected by organized labor. I joined the staff full time.

At the same time I scrambled to complete a book manuscript much larger and more difficult than anticipated when, broke and waiting for a ship, I accepted the job over the summer of 2001: a history of the Archdiocese of Baltimore commissioned by Cardinal William H. Keeler.

Overbooked as usual—like the small-time home improvement guy who promises to renovate a half-dozen kitchens and as many bathrooms just so he can make ends meet with the down payments—I began taking my lime, clamshell Mac i-Book to the set of *The Wire*.

I'd sit in a canvas Hollywood deck chair behind whatever director was working that episode and bang out boilerplate on parish after parish, hammering 400 years of Catholic history on both sides of the Chesapeake Bay into a manageable text. My goal was to leaven the history, well documented by scholars, with first person remembrances of as many everyday Baltimore Catholics as possible.

Every now and then I'd look up and make sure the actors were saying their lines as written, my primary chore as staff writer on set. One day, Simon asked that I not take the laptop to filming. He claimed to not care, but Nina Noble, his fellow producer and the show's wrist-slapper-in-chief, did not like my attention so flagrantly divided.

[Sort of like a short order cook scanning the sports page while flipping eggs. The mug who owns the joint knows the quality of the food isn't suffering, he just doesn't like it.]

So I began printing out pages of the Archdiocese

manuscript, shoving them in my pocket and taking them to the set, editing as many paragraphs as possible while making sure that the British-born Dominic West didn't lapse from Balti-moron cockney into Limey cockney in his portrayal of Detective Jimmy McNulty.

On both of the Global Link and the Atlantic Guardian, I'd welded together a few Catholic chapters and between ships and scripts took the archdiocese manuscript to ballgames, holidays by the sea and out-of-town assignations that would serve as first drafts for short fictions.

In the end, my experience on *The Wire*, working alongside the 150 or so people it takes to get an American television show on the air, informed my Catholic history as my knowledge of Catholic Baltimore would inform *The Wire*.

As a manager, Simon plays to people's strengths and early on I was assigned to write the Catholic scenes. The first task was to create a pastor for St. Casimir, the southeast Baltimore church where my parents were married in 1953 and the place where waterfront union leader Frank Sobotka went fishing for political favors upon which season two would pivot.

Virginia-based actor Tel Monks won the role of the Rev. Jerome Lewandowski and wanted to know why I'd created a priest from Poland, which was the accent he'd been working on.

"Not a Polish priest from Poland," I laughed, channeling the spirit of my Polish grandmother, Anna Potter Jones. "A Polack from East Bawlmer."

As this was something not to be found in the Olivier repertoire, we hopped in my car and headed to the far reaches of East Baltimore, over the county line into Dundalk where my ex-wife had been raised among Polish and Italian and Southern steelworkers both white and black; down Route 40 to a stainless steel diner owned by a Greek who'd launched himself in America with a hot dog cart.

I scanned the joint, found my mark and led Monks to a booth behind a middle-aged woman who looked like Divine except that she wasn't a man and this wasn't a movie. It was just a heavy-set woman on her lunch break, legs spread to get as close to the plate as possible.

I sat Monks with his back to the woman, plopped down across from him and gave direction: "Just listen to what she says and how she says it. Somewhere between bites of that open-faced turkey sandwich she's destroying is the voice of your Polish priest."

[This is what passes for a day of work in TV land.]

Monks nodded, intrigued that I'd so quickly navigated a route to the soul of his character. I've known people like this my entire life; was related to them, carried them inside of me. But Monks's time in Baltimore was brief, his task of nailing the *echt* of the locals and how they spoke nothing a day player could prepare for. His performance bore this out.

A few weeks later, *The Wire* filmed on board the *S.S. John W. Brown*, one of two Liberty Ships still operational out of 2,710 built in Baltimore and other port cities around the country to ferry military freight in World War II.

In this episode, Detectives Bunk Moreland and Lester Freamon board the *Brown*, re-christened the *Atlantic Light* for the small screen, to interview seamen about the deaths of 14 Eastern European women found asphyxiated in a shipping container on the piers.

As we filmed, volunteers who keep the Brown afloat sat in the galley, taking it all in. Hanging with them between shots, I mentioned that my father's old tugboat buddy, the souse-making and cabin cruiser building Chester Rakowski had done some welding on the *Brown*.

The men just nodded; but. when I mentioned the Catholic history project a quiet man in the corner spoke up. He said his name was Jay Tinker, a volunteer deckhand on the Brown and a devout Catholic. Soon, Tinker was sitting for a portrait in the ship's chapel and telling of his devotion to the rosary, the Eucharist—from the Greek, meaning Thanksgiving—and his work with the Knights of Columbus.

What was the result of so much research seemingly at odds with itself?

"A People's History of the Archdiocese of Baltimore," published in 2006 by Editions du Signe of Strasbourg, France.

And the preservation of a way of life all but lost. The stevedoring season of The Wire not only captured the culture of labor along an urban waterfront for the small number of folks who'd lived it, many of whom made cameos and were interviewed at length before the first camera rolled.

The artifice of television made it real for millions who'd never seen anything like it.

II.
Crimson Hexagons & the Meandering Mississippi

How vast the universe of storytelling when glimpsed through the prism of a library!

How boundless when that library is harnessed to television!

Crabtown, USA

Imagine that the fabled sorcerer Jorge Luis Borges—author of *The Library of Babel*—was head honcho of his own network, able to fling moving pictures through all the cathode tubes of Earth for our enjoyment.

"I, who imagined paradise as a kind of library . . ." declares Borges on the Argentinean postage stamp honoring him upon his death in 1986.

A curious paradise marked by a crimson hexagon wherein there is a book holding the truths of all other books; the librarian who is capable of divining its contents on a par with the Divine.

[Borges, of course, would "broadcast" in the original sense of the word, the farm term for sowing seed over a wide area, scattering by hand. Not always in a row, for the best narratives, like time itself, are not linear.]

In the golden age of television (how strange the honorific golden applied to a genre's infancy), literature was the primary source for small screen drama, back before Hollywood was being run by the fourth generation of kids raised on the medium.

Way, way, way back . . .

Back when young people still dreamed of writing the Great American Novel.

Consider an extraordinary episode of *The Outer Limits* from 1963 called "The Man Who Was Never Born."

Directed by Leonard Horn and wrapped in the soft lighting of Conrad Hall, the episode was written by Anthony Lawrence, who—in the potluck so peculiar to Hollywood—would go on to write a TV movie about Liberace.

In the story, a very young and earnest Martin Landau gives a time traveling astronaut from Earth a short tour of the future, a 2148 A.D. glimpse of what remains of the once-vaunted human civilization.

415

"Come," says Landau, human and monstrously deformed, his face a bloom of boils and blisters created by the same corrupted microbe that destroyed the race. "I will show you all that's left of moments, men and places . . ."

And takes the astronaut to a deserted library where the architecture is futuristic and spare, the books old, leather bound. Had the show been filmed in Technicolor you might see a crimson hexagon shimmering beyond the stacks.

"Here lies the protected history of man," says Landau, acting out the essence of each immortal tome. "The cherished words and pictures of all he has known and loved. The noble Hamlet; Anna Karenina putting on her gloves on a snowy evening; Gatsby in white flannels. Moby Dick and Mark Twain's whole meandering Mississippi."

Stung, the astronaut grabs Melville from a shelf and reads a random passage aloud: "Hope proves a man deathless . . ."

"There is no hope here," says the mutant Landau.

"There has to be."

"There is no future. Only a safe and dear host of memories."

Holy host, as my old editor Cardinal Keeler might say; host from the Latin *hostia* for victim. And memories like ghosts who sacrificed their lives to create them.

Whether writer or waitress (and so very often both at once), we pay for our stories with our lives.

To this day I can see Gilbert Lukowski, a long dead stevedore from a long gone Baltimore, standing in front of the waterfront saloon where he grew up, just across the cobblestones from the pier used by NBC to film *Homicide*.

Lukowski, a tough guy with a strong sense of himself, the brother of my father's best friend from the tugboats, called me up on the City Desk one day to say he wanted to read his obituary before he died.

To that end, to see the memories for which he'd traded his life in nine point type across the local page, Gilbert gave me a time machine tour of the once rough and now gilded neighborhood of his Great Depression youth.

With tears in his eyes, a man who'd never backed down from anything staring at his mother's house at 1718 Thames Street and spoke as though talking to himself.

"Nobody remembers," he said, "but I think about it every day . . ."

From Borges to Hollywood science fiction to tears in a longshoreman's jaded eyes, every permutation of narrative: high, low and vast.

III.
Books on Film

My writing career has followed two, parallel and simultaneous paths: the stuff I do for money, which can be just about anything, although I once drew the line at dialogue for a particularly violent video game; and the prose over which I labor because I am moved to bring it into the world.

The writing I care least about—television—pays the most, enough to dream the kind of dreams not every writer dares: to be left alone to write as one pleases whether anyone cares or not.

The work dearest to my heart, fiction about life on the un-tethered planet of Baltimore, pays the least; less even, than the odd piece of journalism I bang out when the subject demands, like an essay on the warrior nuns in the worst parts of Baltimore giving kids a private education for free.

On season two of *The Wire*, all of the important things—money, subject matter and a cumulative importance greater than the subject itself—came together in a way I've yet to experience again.

Like me, I don't believe David Simon ever dreamed about telling stories on television. I've heard him say he envisioned a long career not just in newspapers but specifically at the *Baltimore Sun*, one big enough to include leaves of absence to write books he believed in. And then, always, a faithful return to the paper.

For generations, this privilege was granted ambitious writers at the *Washington Post* and the *New York Times* but was not looked upon kindly by newsroom management on Calvert Street in Baltimore in the mid-1990s.

At *The Sun*, founded in 1837 by A.S. Abell and controlled by his descendents the next 150 years, corporate buy-outs began after Times Mirror corporation bought the paper for $600 million in 1986. The pace of early retirement picked up when the Tribune Company swallowed Times Mirror whole in 2000 for $8.3 billion.

Simon exited in 1995, leaving a job he might admit to loving more than any before or since; his departure part of a hemorrhage of talent that claimed dozens of *Sun* reporters who might have stayed had the culture been more sympathetic to the quirks of the individual, once a hallmark of the best newsrooms, however parochial.

Finding a new home at HBO after his second adapted-for-TV book—*The Corner*—won the cable network a pair of Emmys in 2000, Simon began using screenplays to write the books he would have tackled as a journalist.

Thus, the five seasons of *The Wire*, an open-ended

The Incomparable.

narrative as vast as the history of North America from the time the first slave ship landed, break down along these stated themes:

The failed war on drugs.
The death of the working class.
The hollow promise of reform.
The failure of public education in the American city.
The media complicit in all of the above.

I wrote one episode in each of the first three years—"One Arrest," "Backwash," and "Homecoming"—before moving to Los Angeles to find work during *The Wire's* nearly two-year hiatus between seasons three and four.

Each episode was integral to the one before and after it just as each season built upon and advanced those on either side. Simon's sociological arguments provided a sweeping outline, driven always by the crime story percolating beneath it, for even HBO, after all, is television. More so than on any other show I have yet to work for, I was permitted to draw between those lines with freedom.

The colors I chose came from the Crabtown quarry I've mined since selling my first story to the weekly *City Squeeze*—precursor to the Baltimore *City Paper*—in 1977—an overview of an International Longshoremen's Association strike not unlike the labor strife covered by *The Wire* nearly 30 years later.

When it was my turn to bring a script full of dockworkers to life in "Backwash," I conjured the Italian knife grinders who once roamed the alleys of Baltimore to sharpen kitchen utensils, repairing everything from loose handles on stew pots to umbrellas. Their stories had come my way through a family of local knife grinders named

Crabtown, USA

Vidi via an anecdote from the incomparable composer and Baltimore native Frank Zappa.

In a key scene from Episode No. 20, dock chief Frank Sobotka—deluded by his quixotic "all's well that ends well" scheme to bring more work to the port—is getting bad news from a lobbyist (hired with money from stolen cargo) about the state's reluctance to dredge the harbor.

When Frank rails about robots taking jobs that should be the birthright of many generations of Sobotkas to come, the lobbyist argues that education—and not nepotistic craft guilds—are the only way to survive in the United States.

The Italian lobbyist, played by Keith Flippen, says how his grandfather pushed a stone grinding wheel up and down the alleys and demanded that his son graduate high school. And that man demanded that his son go to any college that would take him. And *that* guy—the lobbyist whose grandfather pushed the grinding wheel—raised a boy who went to Princeton.

All because when I got the chance to interview one of my adolescent heroes—the guitar hero Zappa who'd been born right down the street from *The Baltimore Sun* at Mercy Hospital—he told me that one of his earliest memories before the family moved to California was watching the knife grinder man come down the alley.

The cherry on top was the last shot in the scene, something so parochial and so brief that perhaps only a dozen people caught it the first time around.

When the lobbyist leaves Sobotka's shack on the pier, the angry union boss hurls a dart at a board on the wall. In the center of that board, a photo of Robert Irsay, the man who moved Baltimore's Colts to Indianapolis in 1984, a crime that continued to cause civic nausea as late as 2007 when the blue horseshoes won Super Bowl XLI.

This is the nature of a real Baltimore story, as infinite as love lost, as faithful as grudges held: Nothing goes to waste.

IV.
The Card Catalog as
Schindler's List

I have knelt by the side of the bed and prayed for my characters; that they might choose to do what they were fated and not coerced into what I think is best.

I wish for them what the sages who constructed the *kabbalah* maintain: the universe in its entirety—*olam mullay*—spinning within each and every one of us.

Thus, the most poetic of wisdoms: He who saves a single life has saved the world.

But what of the Samaritan who rescues that beaten high school copy of *A Tree Grows in Brooklyn* from the nickel and dime bin at a suburban yard sale?

I would argue that if the cosmos exists in each of us, then an infinite library lies between the lines of each story told: by mouth, in the hieroglyphics of ink on paper and the rivers of light pushing pictures across silver screens.

A library to dwarf the lost palace of papyrus of ancient Alexandria; bigger by four score than the one Jefferson launched; stacks upon stacks of shelves beyond anything in the hexagonal rooms of Borges's "Library of Babel."

Once, when teaching fiction workshops with George Minot at an East Baltimore gin mill known as Miss Bonnie's Elvis Bar (where the students included the short story writer Jen Grow), George declared: "Only two things last: love and stories . . ."

Crabtown, USA

Radiation has a half-life, but turn your back on narrative for five minutes—particularly if let in the hands of a confidante—and it starts to rise and twist like pizza dough in a monster movie.

Writers may tear off a piece to bake a cupcake here, a loaf of raisin bread there, temporarily containing it with shape and heat, but the dough keeps growing.

As does my on-going soap opera of the luckless lovers Orlo and Leini in which the couple's ritualistic assignations paint a history of 20th century Baltimore.

[As for the power of soaps, my Italian-American, legally blind grandmother loved her "stories" and would put on her thick eyeglasses from the Wilmer Clinic at Hopkins and sit an inch or two away from the screen to follow *As the World Turns*.

At the typewriter, I summon her voice, hear her tell a lady friend at the huckster's produce truck in the alley that she was going inside: It was time for her stories.]

We lost Grandmom over the summer of 1976, not long after I graduated high school and went to sea for the first time, not to learn how to splice line but how to braid sentences.

Thirty years later, I have placed her—Frances Prato Alvarez and the life she carried with grace and humility for 70 years—at Leini's side, the Greek beauty's best friend.

A key motivation for the Orlo and Leini stories is the altar they provide to display all of not just who my grandmother was but what she meant to me: the blindness, the siblings who didn't care quite as much as they could have, the hard-headed husband who came from the West Virginia of Spain to make a home with her in the East Baltimore house where I live today, a sanctuary to which she allowed Leini invite Orlo when no one was home.

423

And while the Baltimore of my stories will always be the Baltimore laid out in street maps and the morning paper, I have set my grandmother—known in the tales as Francesca Bombacci Boulossa—upon a broad stage she would not have recognized.

Think of non-fiction, the facts and anecdotes of my grandmother's temporal life, as a gallon of clear water. Think of fiction, the long summer nights Francesca sat with Leini as clouds sailed past half-a-moon above the Patapsco—as a single drop of blood.

In the diffusion, see scarlet pass to vermillion to pink to mauve to wisps too subtle to name as Leini gives Francesca the dignity of being able to write her name at a church carnival on the other side of town.

I did not dream up the scene in which Leini teaches Francesca how to escape the humiliation of making an X in place of her signature. It arrived one afternoon as my then-teenage daughter Amelia conducted an oral history with my father. There was something she'd wanted, money for something, and I told her I'd give it to her if she talked to my father about his life as I took notes.

I'd interviewed my dad many times—he was always cooperative and as thorough as possible—but somehow the story of how he'd taught his mother to sign her name when he was 15 never came up.

"We traced it over and over," he said.

"Like learning a dance step," said Amelia.

And I had a new Orlo and Leini story, yet one more in a sweep of narrative that I have come to see as a mural.

The Orlo and Leini tales were written out of order, beginning with Orlo's death in 1988 before jumping around between 1922—when the 13-year-old Leini discovered she'd been traded to a barren couple in

424

America for 14 sewing machines—on through Leini' own passing in the early 1990s.

Each story is grounded in a different part of Baltimore, each new panel invigorating the ones around it. Sometimes a newly imagined Orlo and Leini tale will fit tongue in groove with those already in place; other times they claim a path of forest not yet cleared.

As I concentrate smaller amounts of information into each telling, reducing a relationship of some 60 years down to the sharing of an orange on a city bench, the panorama becomes exponentially larger, each tile amplifying not only what has come before it but what's been left unsaid.

A few years ago, the metaphor became literal (interpretation the impregnation through which literature procreates) when artist Minas Konsolas was asked to contribute an image for a wall of Greek themes behind St. Nicholas Orthodox Church a couple blocks from my house.

On the wall that faces Oldham Street, Minas chose to portray Leini in the prime of her beauty, the apex of her suffering. She now broods over passersby just a few blocks from the rowhouse on Ponca Street where she lived all of her adult life, across from the public transit bus yard and a few blocks from her friend Francesca.

For years, Leini took those municipal buses to meet Orlo with a basket of food on her lap. Though she never ventured far beyond the city, the stories documenting her journeys have traveled the globe. Each year, out of my own pocket [again, the writing I care most about remains the least rewarded], I get together with a friend who works in design and my artist son Jake to produce 1,000 copies of whatever story is keeping me up at night.

And then I throw them to the wind, giving away copies

at readings and coffee shops and gas stations on cross country trips; to friends willing to slip a couple copies in their luggage when they travel overseas.

In this way, tales of Orlo and Leini's heroic adultery have been left for wayfarers to find in Budapest, Borges's Buenos Aires and Beijing, where copies were left in crevices of the Great Wall.

Perhaps the stories aren't any more accessible than Leini's inscrutable gaze is to those who see her face as they walk along Oldham Street. I like to imagine people—old men and little kids, folks who don't speak English—happening upon the 10-foot visage and imagining her story anew.

Leini alive!

"Very alive," said Konsolas, who immigrated to Baltimore from Greece as a young man. "Her story stirred up things inside of me, things I went through myself. As I read her story, I found myself putting in my own conversations."

It's hard to imagine that the street drunks with their Mad Dog and junkies scoring methadone from the Johns Hopkins Bayview campus up the road give a shit about the woman on the wall.

But perhaps, in the proper narcotized haze, pupils rolling back as their heads find the curb, the lost soul's eyes meet Leini's for the only exchange that matters in this world: "I know how you feel . . ."

A mural no frame can hold.

It sparkled with a light I'd never seen in any museum in Europe.

SALOON SCHOOL

"Painting is just another way of keeping a diary."
—Picasso

I can't agree on this one with the Spaniard, the man who told Gertrude Stein that you cannot apply cubism to prose. [Not that Stein listened or cared.]

When I read a diary, I don't want to guess—is that a bird or a fish?—I want to know.

In the basement of a corner rowhouse near the Stadium Lounge in Waverly, the art collector Mary Bond has amorous correspondence from former boxer and racetrack handicapper Clem Florio along with diaries from her 1960s and 1970s bohemian life in Crabtown.

"I was never one of the producing artists," she says. "I supported them."

The artwork—of the Baltimore barroom school, with pieces by John Kefover, Glenn Walker and Charlie Newton—is on display for any visitor to her East 34th Street home to see.

The diaries and correspondence are tucked away and, though I have asked many times to see them—just a peek—not to be shared.

It's an understandable policy, not everyone cares to run their secrets naked down the alley while they're still alive. But if Bond's policy is carried to its inevitable conclusion and the people left to assess her treasures are unaware of what molders beneath old coats and galoshes, Baltimore will be the poorer.

I think I'll ask her again.

There's no way to delay that trouble coming
every day.

CRABTOWN AFLAME

When things turned very ugly in Baltimore on the day they laid Freddie Gray to rest [04.27.15]—widespread looting, massive property destruction, arson and assaults on police, motorists and pedestrians—I called a friend to see if she was okay.

Riots sparked by teenagers—a social media organized "purge" targeting police—began when school let out about 3 p.m., overshadowing peaceful protests against the April 19th death of Gray, 25, whose spinal cord was crushed while in police custody.

My call was to Sister Peggy Juskelis, a School Sister of Notre Dame and lifelong Baltimorean who serves as president of Mother Seton Academy, a tuition-free Catholic school in a neighborhood that took a beating in the riots that followed the assassination of the Rev. Martin Luther King in 1968.

Sister Peggy works in a vulnerable neighborhood on the eastside and lives in one just as tenuous on the Westside. Her life's work has been to ask for money for the education of poor kids, to give some of the tens of thousands of have-nots in Baltimore a chance to move up and out of poverty or stay behind to help the next generation.

Juskelis said she'd made it home without problem but kept repeating, "This is not my city, this is not my city . . .

433

Rafael Alvarez

"This is not my city."

As a good Catholic boy—taught that the highest law is one's conscience—I respectfully disagreed.

"I'm sorry Sister," I said, "but this is your city."

As it is mine.

My beloved Crabtown—some 620,000 mostly good and often strange people (think of John Waters' movies as documentaries)—is where the National Guard was activated during a state of emergency in the worst pandemonium since the King riots of a half-century ago.

Baltimore is a historic port city (my father worked the harbor tugs for decades, his father arrived from Spain as a seaman) with a history of atrocity and violence going back to its colonial beginnings.

[In a 1773 letter-to-the-editor, an alarmed resident called for more streetlamps to deter gatherings of hardened criminals. The population at the time was a mere 5,000.]

The first casualties in the Civil War took place not on a battlefield but the streets of Baltimore, already known as Mobtown. In 1861—on a long-ago April 19th—pro-Confederate civilians attacked a militia of southbound Union soldiers with bricks and pistols. Four soldiers and a dozen rioters were killed.

More than a 150 years later, Baltimore maintains deep reservoirs of racism—originally white against black, though the resentment has been pretty evenly distributed for some time—and the Freddie Gray riot was manna for the haters.

My parents' longtime next-door neighbor in the suburbs south the city, a man who has never lived outside the county line, spotted me in my folks' driveway yesterday.

An angry, Obama-hating white man (you can tell when

he's really pissed off by how aggressively he rakes the lawn), he knows I have long lived in the City, knows that I love and am well left-of-center.

From his yard he shouted, in a mock black accent: "CHARM CITY—HA!"

Yeah, Charm City—birthplace of the Star Spangled Banner—where you can have a plate of the greatest seafood in the world, be killed on the sidewalk before the meal's been digested and have the person who took your life murdered by the police on the way to jail.

But 99 times out of 100, only if you're African-American.

Or, like me—not privileged via wealth but the good fortune of education, pigment and vocation—you can live a long and productive life without becoming a victim of crime. Which held true yesterday, perhaps because the riots kept me from getting back into the city from my parents' home.

Back in 1968, the riots were much larger and widespread with shots fired at firemen trying to put out burning buildings. The chaos swiftly brought martial law and federal troops to the city.

Then Maryland-governor Spiro Agnew's caustic stance against rioting African-Americans made headlines and his career, bringing him to the attention of Richard Nixon and his Southern strategy (luring white Democrats by pitting them against blacks) for winning the White House.

Yesterday, Baltimore Mayor Stephanie Rawlings-Blake was widely seen as tentative (the trouble began Saturday night, paused for a day and erupted in full yesterday) and it likely damaged her political ambitions.

I was 10 the last time Baltimore burned. As a tugboat man, my father was considered part of essential city services—keeping the port open to trade—and crossed police lines on his way to the docks.

Between shifts, he'd come home and tell stories of what he'd seen. Yesterday, I got caught at that same house near the airport and was unable to get back into the city to be with my bride of two weeks, whose North Baltimore neighborhood was untouched.

Again, mere inconvenience compared to what happened in poor black neighborhoods that still haven't recovered from the '68 riots.

Some 20 years ago this summer—in July of 1995—I rode a bus through Baltimore with a group of mayors from Israel who wanted an up-close look at a city working hard to keep its head above water.

We stopped near Sandtown-Winchester, the Westside neighborhood where Freddie Gray lived until his arrest for the crime of running away from police. Looking around at the entrenched blight, Arik Raz, the mayor of a region near Galilee, asked a local minister, "Who is responsible?"

A church elder named Clyde Harris explained: "Before segregation, all black people were in the ghetto together, the rich and the intellectuals along with the poor. After integration, they left the poor behind.

"We were full up with hatred when Martin Luther King [was murdered] and that was the spark that ignited, and we just burned everything. He was our light, and when they took that away we just didn't care anymore and we destroyed everything."

Absolutely anything is possible in Baltimore, from medical miracles at Johns Hopkins Hospital to those random acts of clichéd kindness to cruelties the Islamic State would admire.

But, like the line of ministers who marched arm-in-

Crabtown, USA

arm through the streets yesterday for calm (led by a man in a wheelchair, some of the clerics kneeling along the way in prayer) most Baltimoreans share a love and a hope for this fucked-up city that borders on the delusional.

Faith in things unseen.

A belief in better days.

437

crabtown usa

Anything is possible in Baltimore—on any
street corner, on any day.

DEAR CRABTOWN

I could live anywhere in the world—in storybook capitals or pastoral hamlets greatly desired—but, God help me, I choose to cohabitate with you.

You are, by far, the longest relationship of my life; nearly six decades save for a brief fling in Hollywood.

[It was just money, baby—didn't mean a thing.]

To abide you—a salty old broad with harsh edges and ridiculous hair-dos; the way your progeny throws trash from moving cars and believes the best way to cross the street is to walk (in fuzzy slippers and pajama bottoms) directly into traffic . . .

To put up with all of your bullshit I pass our assignations inside a sanctuary sculpted from more comforting material.

The evening sun setting over the Patapsco River— where Francis Scott Key wrote the Star Spangled Banner 200 years ago—fires pink and orange a thousand shattered panes of the shuttered bottle cap factory at the end of my block.

But in the morning, as I lay supine before the city of my fancy, it warms stained glass brilliant with all the good things.

People willing to lend a hand when their own cupboards are bare; aging, lion-hearted stevedores holding the door to the coin-laundry for young women comforting their children in Spanish; tugboats churning past the 120-foot by 70-foot Domino Sugars sign while saints sweep the sidewalk in front of the St. Jude Shrine—you are *not* hopeless, Lovey, no matter what the TV says—just a venial sin or two away from Lexington Market.

On land donated by Revolutionary War hero John Eager Howard, the market dates to 1782: a bazaar of grilled kielbasa, fresh roasted peanuts and true crab cakes, delicacies as big around as a softball, deep fried or broiled to a golden brown, the lump back fin of *callinectes sapidus*—beautiful swimmers of Chesapeake lore—bound with the merest dusting of breadcrumbs.

I write to you all hopped up on love and mercy for despite the frequent atrocities (east to west, some staged outside those same market doors) everybody does the best they can.

Don't they?

Love for your hard-headed belief that hard work (both underground and legit) will carry the day even though your bounty of plentiful jobs—good pay, good benefits—is long diminished. And mercy for those who missed every boat that passed your way.

Four miles east of Lexington Market, I pour my heart into an old reporter's notebook over a plate of French fries and gravy at G&A Coney Island Hot Dogs, just around the corner from a library marked by a bust of native son Frank Vincent Zappa [1940-1993] on a stainless steel pillar.

This is the Holy Land of my imagination where my family—Polish on Mom's side, Dad's parents from Spain and a part of Italy called Western Pennsylvania—has lived since the 1920s; where my grandmothers bought me baby clothes near a popcorn store that made its own caramel and a blind man sold pencils while drumming his fingernails against a meatloaf pan, the syncopation he made becoming deeper as the tray filled with change.

Love for rebirth: a Peruvian restaurant specializing in rotisserie chicken now sends the smell of fire-roasted fowls onto Eastern Avenue where the popcorn store once filled the air with hot caramel.

Mercy for the left-behinds: the blind man has been replaced ten-fold by beggars, all of whom can see.

Yet passion can be a many splintered thing and, dear Crabtown—*del mio cuore* as they say at the century old DiPasquale's market two streets away from the hot dog diner—let me be clear.

Though many tens of thousands of my fellow Baltimoreans are hostage to your often lethal charms, I am not. They do not have the luxury of storing up treasures of amber narrative with which to build a cathedral. Or the middle-class option to leave it behind if reality intrudes on make-believe one too many times.

I have been lucky in love—unharmed for many a year while cruising every corner of your 92 square miles—but I don't underestimate you.

I know that anywhere, at any moment I may be kissing your cheek for the last time.

Photo Credits:

South Broadway / Leo Ryan, Jr.

Narrow Alley / Cheryl Fair

Footlong Franks / Macon Street Books

Kitchen Obscura / Jennifer Bishop

Divorce Decree / Jennifer Bishop

Hot Dogs / Macon Street Books

First Grade / Alvarez Family Archives

Gospel Truth No. 1 / Illustration by M. Jacob Alvarez

Wooden Steps / Macon Street Books

David Maulsby / Jennifer Bishop

Catholic Boy / Ryan Family Archives

Bosnian Coffee / Macon Street Books

Deviled Eggs / William "Billy D" Driscoll

Sip & Bite / Vasiliades Family Archives

Charm City / Chris "Gombus" Connell

Aging Newspapermen / Jennifer Bishop

Crabtown Aflame / Mike Oswald

Dear Crabtown / Chris "Gombus" Connell

If you enjoyed
Crabtown, USA don t
pass up on these
other titles from
Perpetual Motion
Machine . . .

TALES FROM THE HOLY LAND
BY RAFAEL ALVAREZ
ISBN: 978-0-9860594-0-7
Page count: 226
$12.95

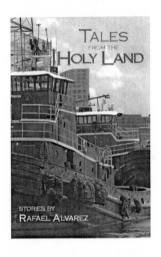

Tales from the Holy Land is the third collection of short fiction from the Baltimore author and screenwriter. The stories take place along the narrow streets and alleys of Alvarez's heartbreaking hometown, charting secret histories of the last 100 years through the difficult and hopeful lives of tugboat men, junk collectors, beautiful women, short order cooks and an artist who captures it all in house paint on the sides of abandoned buildings.

DEAD MEN
LIBROS DE INFERNO: BOOK 1
BY JOHN C. FOSTER
ISBN: 978-0-9860594-7-6
Page count: 372
$14.95

Roaring south in a black Cadillac, John Smith is on the road trip from Hell through a nightmarish version of Americana, a place of rotting hollows and dusty crossroads, slaughterhouses and haunted trains. He doesn't know how he woke up after sitting down in the electric chair, where he got the black suit with the slit up the back or even the cigarettes in his pocket. All he knows is that there is a woman guarding a great secret and he's supposed to kill her.

"Frankly, I haven't been this impressed with an authorial debut since Clive Barker's Books of Blood. And no, that isn't hyperbole. John C. Foster really is that good."—Joe McKinney, Bram Stoker Award Winning Author of Dead City

TRUTH OR DARE
EDITED BY MAX BOOTH III

ISBN: 978-0-9860594-5-2
Page count: 240
$14.95

Halloween night. The freaks are out and having the time of their lives. The kids of Greene Point High School have organized a massive bonfire out in the woods. One drunken teen suggests playing a game, a game called Truth or Dare. That's always a fun game. Always good for a laugh. By the end of this night, nobody will be laughing. Alcohol, sex, deadly secrets, and oceans of blood await them. Do you dare to play? Truth or Dare is a shared-world horror anthology featuring the morbid writings of many prominent authors in the field today, as well as quite a few new kids on the block you're gonna want to keep an eye on.

The Perpetual Motion Machine Catalog

Bleed | Various Authors | Anthology
    Page count: 286 | Paperback: $16.95
    ISBN: 978-0-9887488-8-0

Cruel | Eli Wilde | Novel
    Page count: 192 | Paperback: $9.95
    ISBN: 978-0-9887488-0-4

Dead Men | John C. Foster | Novel
    Page Count: 360 | Paperback: $14.95
    ISBN: 978-0-9860594-7-6

Four Days | Eli Wilde & 'Anna DeVine | Novel
    Page count: 198 | Paperback: $9.95
    ISBN: 978-0-9887488-5-9

Gory Hole | Craig Wallwork | Story Collection (Full-Color Illustrations)
    Page count: 48 | Paperback: $12.95
    ISBN: 978-0-9860594-3-8

The Green Kangaroos | Jessica McHugh | Novel
    Page count: 184 | Paperback $12.95
    ISBN: 978-0-9860594-6-9

Last Dance in Phoenix | Kurt Reichenbaugh | Novel
    Page count: 268 | Paperback: $12.95 |
    ISBN: 978-0-9860594-9-0

Long Distance Drunks: a Tribute to Charles Bukowski
    Various Authors | Anthology
    Page count: 182 | Paperback: $12.95
    ISBN: 978-0-9860594-4-5

The Perpetual Motion Club | Sue Lange | Novel
  Page count: 208 | Paperback $14.95
  ISBN: 978-0-9887488-6-6

The Ritalin Orgy | Matthew Dexter | Novel
  Page count: 206 | Paperback $12.95
  ISBN: 978-0-9887488-1-1

Sirens | Kurt Reichenbaugh | Novel
  Page count: 286 | Paperback: $14.95
  ISBN: 978-0-9887488-3-5

So it Goes: a Tribute to Kurt Vonnegut | Various Authors
  Anthology
  Page count: 282 | Paperback $14.95
  ISBN: 978-0-9887488-2-8

Stealing Propeller Hats from the Dead | David James Keaton
  Story Collection
  Page count: 256 | Paperback $12.95
  ISBN: 978-1-943720-00-2

Tales from the Holy Land | Rafael Alvarez | Story Collection
  Page count: 226 | Paperback $14.95
  ISBN: 978-0-9860594-0-7

The Tears of Isis | James Dorr | Story Collection
  Page count: 206 | Paperback: $12.95
  ISBN: 978-0-9887488-4-2

Time Eaters | Jay Wilburn | Novel
  Page count: 218 | Paperback: $12.95
  ISBN: 978-0-9887488-7-3

Vampire Strippers from Saturn | Vincenzo Bilof | Novel
  Page count: 210 | Paperback: $12.95
  ISBN: 978-0-9860594-8-3

Forthcoming Titles:

2016

Dark Moon Digest #22

The Violators
    Vincenzo Bilof

Live On No Evil
    Jeremiah Israel

Dark Moon Digest #23

The Train Derails in Boston
    Jessica McHugh

The Ruin Season
    Kris Triana

Lost Signals: Anthology

Dark Moon Digest #24

Mojo Rising
    Bob Pastorella

Quizzleboon
    John Oliver Hodges

Gods on the Lam
    Christopher David Rosales

Caliban
    Ed Kurtz

Dark Moon Digest #25

Speculations
    Joe McKinney

Night Roads
    John Foster

Website:
www.PerpetualPublishing.com

Facebook:
www.facebook.com/PerpetualPublishing

Twitter:
@PMMPublishing

Instagram:
www.instagram.com/PMMPublishing/

Newsletter:
www.PMMPNews.com

Email Us:
Contact@PerpetualPublishing.com

CPSIA information can be obtained at www.ICGtesting.com
Printed in the USA
LVOW10s1914160116

470957LV00008B/611/P